RV

ELECTRICAL SYSTEMS

*A Basic Guide to Troubleshooting,
Repair, and Improvement*

Bill and Jan Moeller

R·M·P

Ragged Mountain Press
Camden, Maine

McGraw Hill

Published by Ragged Mountain Press

20 19 18 17 16 15 14 13 12

Library of Congress Cataloging-in-Publication Data
Moeller, Bill, 1930–
     RV electrical systems : a basic guide to troubleshooting, repair,
and improvement / Bill and Jan Moeller.
          p.   cm.
     Includes index.

     1. Recreational vehicles — Electric equipment.   I. Moeller, Jan,
1930–   . II. Title.
TL272.M53   1994
629.25'4 – dc20   94-30072
                                                                                              CIP

Questions regarding the content of this book should be addressed to:
Ragged Mountain Press
P.O. Box 220
Camden, ME 04843

Questions regarding the ordering of this book should be addressed to:
The McGraw-Hill Companies Customer Service Department
P.O. Box 547
Blacklick, OH   43004
Retail customers: 1-800-262-4729
Bookstores: 1-800-722-4726

A portion of the profits from the sale of each Ragged Mountain Press book is
donated to an environmental cause.

ISBN 978-0-07-183792-7

Photographs and drawings are by the authors, unless otherwise credited.

Design by Dan Kirchoff
Production by Dan Kirchoff
Edited by Jonathan Eaton and Constance Burt

CONTENTS

Preface

Electricity in residences is taken for granted because it is always there, except for the rare power outage, and accessing it requires nothing more than flicking a switch or plugging in an electrical appliance. In an RV, however, electricity is not quite so straightforward. RVers themselves are responsible for bringing electrical power to the RV, which they do when they plug into a campground's electrical hookup. Additionally, there are two electrical systems to deal with: the familiar, 120-volt alternating current (AC), the type supplied to residences; and the often not so familiar 12-volt direct current (DC) supplied by the RV's batteries.

How these systems operate and interact is a mystery to many RVers; it is for them that this book is written. It provides a better understanding of what electricity is and what it does. It contains information that helps solve electrical problems that sometimes occur: why interior lights dim or burn out too rapidly, why batteries won't charge properly after a night without an electrical hookup, why there is no power, why batteries die sooner than expected, why there isn't adequate voltage at a campsite. The book explains how to make repairs to both systems, what tools and equipment are needed, and how to improve and upgrade RV electrical systems.

It will be obvious to those with a knowledge of electricity that the more esoteric aspects of the subject—columbs, joules, inductive and capacitive reactance, to name a few—are omitted, and that we do not delve too deeply or at all into certain theorems and laws. Anything left out, however, in our opinion, is not necessary to a basic understanding of RV electrical systems. The book also does not discuss automotive electrical systems unless such systems directly relate to the RV's electrical functions. Ignition systems are not discussed because their function is relevant only to the vehicle's engine operation; alternators are discussed because they are relevant to charging the RV batteries.

Our aim has been to keep this book as simple as possible while still enabling readers to thoroughly understand what constitutes RV electrical systems, how they work, and what to do when they don't. We have arranged the material so that, once read, the book can be used as a reference.

Acknowledgments

S o many people have given of their time and knowledge to help us in the preparation of this book; we couldn't have done the job without them.

We deeply appreciate the assistance of David Smead of Ample Power Company, and David Diamond of Country Coach, Inc., and we apologize for the numerous occasions we interrupted the work of these two busy gentlemen with our queries.

Noel Kirkby of RV Solar Electric, Neil Fridley of Cruising Equipment Company (CECO), and Keith Mann of MagneTek offered invaluable constructive criticism after reading sizable portions of the text.

To clarify a wealth of fine points about matters electrical, we sought and gratefully received advice from the following people (listed in alphabetical order by the companies they work for): Doug Mosen of Ample Power Company; Gary Davis of Balmar Power Systems; Rick Proctor of CECO; Larry Kish of Delco-Remy; Warren Stokes, Patty Crangle, and Ernie Sharer of Heart Interface Corporation; Ray Savell of Lestek Manufacturing, Inc.; John Lerch of Power Alarm; Jack Verden of Schauer Manufacturing Corporation; Boone Chommary of Schumacher Electric Corporation; Lawrence Neill of Statpower Technologies Corporation; Sam Vanderhoof of Trace Engineering; and Ron Jones of Wrangler Power Products.

This book would not be nearly so interesting if we hadn't been able to include numerous illustrations. Our thanks to the many manufacturers that provided photographs and drawings.

And we certainly don't want to overlook the helpful staff at Ragged Mountain Press who worked closely with us to make this book, which deals with a complex subject, as good as it possibly could be: Jonathan Eaton, Pamela Benner, and Dan Kirchoff. Special thanks to Hyman Rudoff, technical editor, and Constance Burt, copyeditor.

Because we are full-time RVers who travel the year round, we need someone dependable, who doesn't roam as we do, to entrust the collecting and forwarding of our mail and the taking of our telephone messages. The person who does the job in a topnotch manner is Bonnie Jensen. We would not be able to do our work without her able assistance. Many, many thanks again, Bonnie.

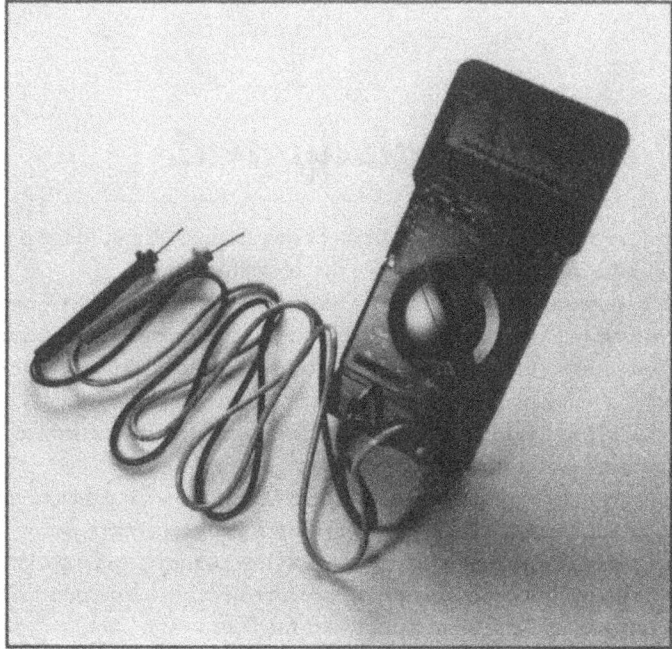

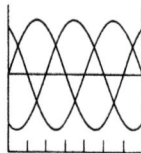

ONE

Electricity Explained—Simply

Once upon a time, we stopped at a campground in a city in Montana. It was an older campground with electrical outlet boxes that were in poor condition, inadequately wired, and equipped with household, screw-type fuses instead of circuit breakers. As is common in many older campgrounds, each outlet provided only 15 amperes of current instead of the 30 or 50 amperes found at newer parks. The day we were there, the already low voltage was further lowered because it was hot and many people were using their air conditioners.

While we were setting up, a new, large, Class A motorhome pulled into the site next to us. After much fussing to situate the motorhome just so in the site, the owner pulled out his 50-ampere shore-power cable only to find he could not plug it into the 15-ampere outlet without the proper adapters. After rooting around in a compartment for the necessary adapters, he plugged in the shore-power cable and disappeared inside the motorhome to turn on both his air conditioners. In a little while, he came over to our trailer and asked if we had any screw-type fuses. We did. Once in a while we stop at campgrounds with fused outlets, so we normally carry a supply of spare fuses in assorted ampere sizes in case a fuse blows and the campground manager can't be located to provide a replacement.

We gave our neighbor a 20-ampere fuse and, as diplomatically as possible, suggested that only one of his air conditioners should be operated when using a 15-ampere outlet. He said, rather impatiently, "I don't want to know anything about electricity." He went on to tell us that when he plugged in, he expected the electricity to "work," and if it didn't, the campground manager (or maybe helpful neighbors?) should take care of it; he didn't want to be bothered. He also told us that if anything went wrong with the electrical system in his motorhome, he would hire someone to fix it. The man continued to have problems until he left the next day, because he didn't "want to know" that he could never get more than 15 amperes from his hookup and would have to adjust his electrical usage accordingly.

1

We are all entitled to live our lives as we want, of course, but our own RVing would not be so enjoyable if we had to depend on others to solve the electrically related problems that occasionally occur. As far as we are concerned, it's just good sense to learn about the systems in our RV so that when something goes wrong, we can correct it.

Of all the systems in a recreational vehicle, RVers have the most trouble with the electrical systems (there are two), mainly because most people don't know enough about electricity. If you are one of those people, learning everything there is to know about the complex subject of electricity would take considerable study, yet just a little knowledge is all you really need. With such knowledge, you may find that many of the RV's electrical problems will cease to exist because they weren't really problems—you just thought they were. And if a real problem occurs, there's a good chance you will be able to solve it yourself or, at least, be able to assess the problem and discuss it intelligently with a professional repairperson.

Of all the systems in a recreational vehicle, RVers have the most trouble with the electrical systems.

The two types of electricity RVers have to deal with are (1) the 12-volt *direct current (DC)* system that operates, mainly, the interior lights, water pump, and furnace (and the 12-volt automotive functions of motorhomes and trailer tow vehicles); and (2) the 120-volt *alternating current (AC)* that comes from a campground's electrical hookup. While it is not necessary to know the theory of electricity to solve and fix most problems, after reading the following explanation of basic electricity, you will have a better understanding of what is actually going on in these two systems.

Atoms and Electrons

All of us have had experience with static electricity. In dry weather, our clothes stick to our bodies and we get a shock when a spark arcs between our fingers and a doorknob after we walk across a carpet. This static charge that builds up on our bodies is nothing more than the movement of electrons, and electron movement is what creates electricity.

All things on earth, and in the universe for that matter, including your body, are composed of *atoms.* Every atom is composed of *electrons, protons, and neutrons.* The *nucleus* of each atom is a cluster of protons and neutrons; electrons encircle and move around the nucleus. The electrons have a negative electrical charge; the protons, a positive electrical charge; and the neutrons, no charge. An atom in a normal state has an equal number of electrons and protons; in this state, the two electrical charges cancel each other and the atom is neutralized.

Electrons can be dislodged or knocked off an atom. This gives the atom a positive charge because it now contains more positive protons than negative electrons, and it becomes a *positive ion*. The free, knocked-off electrons are able to travel through a vacuum, gases, or metal at close to the speed of light (186,000 miles per second), or they may rest quietly on the surface of an object. If a free electron lands on a normal atom, the atom then has a negative charge and is called a *negative ion*. Resting electrons give the surface of an object a *negative static electrical charge*.

Current Flow

Resting free electrons can be nudged into moving and becoming a current if placed near positive ions (i.e., atoms with missing electrons). The positive ions attract the free electrons, causing an *electron* or *current flow*. The moving, free electrons combine with the atoms with missing electrons until the atoms again become neutral.

Light, heat, friction, and chemical reactions cause electrons to be removed from the atoms on the surface of an object, making the surface positively charged. This condition is called a *positive static electrical charge*. When you walk across a carpet to open a door, the friction created by your clothes rubbing against you causes a positive static electrical charge to build up on your body, which attracts the negative electrons of the doorknob to arc to your fingers.

A basic principle of electricity is that opposite charges attract and like charges repel. This is the basis of current flow. Negatively charged electrons flow, or move, toward a positively charged source. The more positively charged atoms are present, the faster the electrons move.

The force propelling the electrons, the *potential*, is measured in *volts*. If the proper pathways exist and there is a difference in potential, current will flow; no difference, no current flow. For example, if two batteries are wired together, positive post to positive post and negative post to negative post, and one battery has a voltage of 12.8 while the other has a voltage of 12.3, current will flow between them until their voltages equalize. (Don't try this experiment. You could ruin one or two good batteries.)

The voltage potential of an electrical energy source, such as a battery, is an *electromotive force (EMF)* and is also measured in volts.

Direct current (DC) is movement of electrons that flow in one direction only. The unit of measurement for this movement is *amperes*, or *amps*. One ampere is the passage of 6,280,000,000,000,000,000 electrons over a given point in 1 second. This may sound like a tremendous amount of electron movement but, in reality, a single electron, depending on various factors, may only move a half-inch along its pathway in that second.

Electrons should not be thought of as running back and forth over great distances from point to point within a circuit. To illustrate electron movement, imagine

3

a narrow tube, which represents a wire, filled with BBs, which represent electrons. As one BB is pushed into one end of the tube, it displaces the BB next to it, and so on down the tube, until a BB is pushed out at the other end. In effect, this is what happens to electrons when they flow along a wire.

As has been shown, current flow is from negative to positive because the positive source attracts the negative electrons. In schematics and block diagrams, however, the flow is indicated as going from positive to negative, mainly because the positive end is where the energy exists. We think of the positive wire in a circuit as the "hot" wire, and the positive post, or plus terminal, on a battery as the source of power, or "hot."

Conductors, Insulators, and Semiconductors

A material that allows an electrical current to flow through it is a *conductor.* Conductors are usually metals such as copper, tin, iron, zinc, and aluminum.

All materials resist the flow of current, some more, some less. The degree to which a given material resists the flow is called its *resistance,* which is measured in *ohms.* This unit is sometimes represented by the Greek letter omega: Ω.

The lack of resistance, or the ease with which current passes through a conductor, is *conductance.* Of the metals, silver, copper, and gold offer the best conductance. Silver and gold are too costly to be practical, so copper, followed by aluminum, is the most frequently used metal for wire conductors.

Materials that do not allow current to flow through them are *insulators,* or non-conductors, and include glass, plastics, rubber, wood, and leather.

Semiconductors are materials with special properties. Under certain conditions they can function as either conductors or non-conductors. Silicon, the most common of the semiconductor materials, is found in abundance in ordinary sand, from which it is obtained.

Ohm's Law

Although some people shy away from anything mathematical, a few simple formulas should be learned. Because of their simplicity, the formulas eliminate some of the mystery surrounding electricity and help you to understand how it works.

It takes 1 volt of potential to move 1 ampere of current through 1 ohm of resistance. The mathematical relationship of voltage, amperage, and resistance is defined in Ohm's Law:

> Amperage multiplied by resistance equals voltage.
> Voltage divided by amperage equals resistance.
> Voltage divided by resistance equals amperage.

Ohm's Law expressed in equations is:

$$I = \frac{V}{R} \qquad R = \frac{V}{I} \qquad V = I \times R$$

I represents current in amperes; V, voltage in volts; and R, resistance in ohms. Any work done by electricity is called power, and it is measured in *watts* (W).

Voltage multiplied by amperage equals wattage.
Wattage divided by amperage equals voltage.
Wattage divided by voltage equals amperage.

Or, in equation form, with I and V still representing current and voltage, and with P representing power in watts:

$$I = \frac{P}{V} \qquad V = \frac{P}{I} \qquad P = V \times I$$

RVers will probably use the formulas for computing power most often. For instance, it is sometimes important to be able to figure out if an electric heater or air conditioner can be used at the same time as a microwave oven without overloading the campground's circuit. Using Ohm's Law, a simple calculation that most people can do in their head provides the needed information. For example, a 120-volt heater rated at 1,200 watts will draw 10 amperes: 1,200 divided by 120 equals 10 amperes.

Magnetism

Magnetism is the principle on which electrical equipment operates, so to understand electricity, you must understand magnetism.

Years ago, a popular toy was a pair of plastic Scottish terriers, one black and one white, each mounted on a bar magnet. When the head of the white dog was pushed toward the head of the black dog, the magnets would attract and the black dog moved toward the white dog. When the head of the white dog was pushed toward the tail of the black dog, the black dog slid away. These movements occurred because every magnet has a north pole and a south pole—the ends of the magnet—and because of a law of *magnetism:* Opposite poles attract and like poles repel (as in electricity, where opposite charges attract and like charges repel).

This attracting/repelling is caused by magnetic lines of force that extend out through the surrounding space of a magnet from the north pole to the south pole, creating a magnetic field. A *magnetic field* is a form of power, and it always flows in one direction: from the south pole of the magnet, through the magnet to its north pole, then through the space surrounding the magnet, and back toward the south pole until a closed loop is completed (Figure 1-1). Incidentally, the earth is one big magnet with magnetic north and south poles and, consequently, its own magnetic field.

Certain metals, such as iron, steel, and nickel, have properties that allow them to be magnetized when they are placed in a magnetic field; other metals, such as copper and aluminum, can't be magnetized.

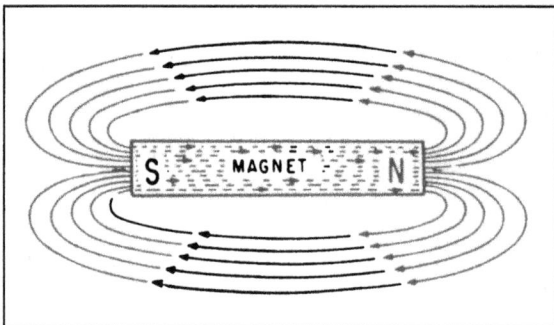

Figure 1-1. Magnetic lines of force around a bar magnet.

Electromagnetism

When electricity is used to induce magnetism, an *electromagnet* is created. If we didn't have electromagnets, we wouldn't have motors, radios, TVs, computers, or even the production of electricity itself. A simple electromagnet can be made by wrapping a few turns of insulated wire around a tenpenny nail (stuck in a board for ease of handling) and attach-

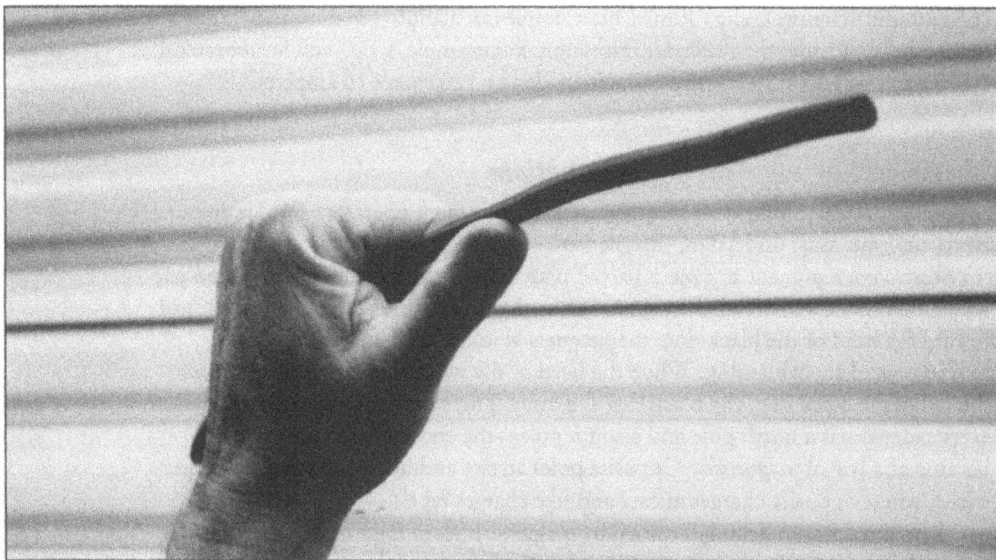

Figure 1-2. The Left-Hand Rule: With the thumb of the left hand pointing in the direction of current flow, the fingers will be curved in the direction of the magnetic lines of force.

ing the ends of the wire to a 6-volt dry-cell battery. The battery supplies an electrical current and, as it passes through the wire conductor, a magnetic field is created around the wire. Because the wire is wrapped around the nail, the nail becomes magnetized and a magnetic field is created around it. The nail can then pick up, or attract, other magnetic metal objects.

The magnetic field formed around a wire as current flows through it runs in a circular pattern and perpendicular to the wire. If you knew the direction of current flow in a wire, and you held the wire in your left hand with your thumb pointing toward that direction, your fingers would curve in the direction of the magnetic lines of force (Figure 1-2). This is known as the *left-hand rule*.

The magnetic field is very weak around a single wire, but forming the wire into a coil increases the strength of the field proportionately to the number of turns. The field around each turn of the wire affects the other turns and creates a powerful magnetic force. The coil can be formed by just a series of turns, or it can be made by wrapping the wire around a core, such as an iron bar (or a nail, as described previously). Such a coil is an *inductor,* and the magnetic field surrounding it has a property that opposes sudden changes in current flow. This property is known as *inductance* and the unit of measurement is the *henry.*

Producing Electricity Through Magnetism

With the use of magnetism, along with motion, electricity can be created, and an electrical current can be made to flow along a wire conductor. If a conductor is placed in the magnetic field of a magnet, as long as either the conductor or the magnet is in motion, a current will be induced and will flow (Figure 1-3). Cease the motion and the current will stop.

With a horseshoe magnet, the strongest lines of force of the magnetic field travel straight between the two poles of the magnet. When a conductor is passed between the poles, a current is created that flows in one

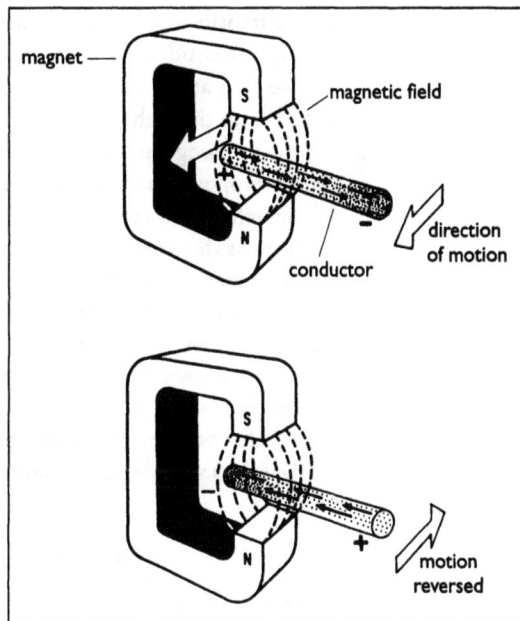

Figure 1-3. Voltage is produced when a conductor is moved through a magnetic field. Current flows in the conductor if there is a complete circuit. The direction of motion influences the direction of current flow.

Electricity Explained—Simply

direction along the conductor. When the conductor is passed between the poles in the opposite direction, the current flow along the conductor is reversed. (If the conductor is held stationary between the two poles, no current flows.) This is the basis for producing both alternating current and direct current (DC production is discussed in Chapter 2). Alternating current (AC), like direct current, is measured in amperes. Remember that DC flows in only one direction along a conductor, so it should be easy to understand why the name "alternating current" is given to current that changes, or alternates, the direction of its flow.

Transformers

Around the turn of the century, when metropolitan areas began to have electricity, DC was supplied. But there was a great loss of power between the power plant and the consumer because of the natural resistance in transmission lines. The resistance caused a considerable drop in voltage before the electricity ever reached the consumer, so transformers came into use to overcome the problem.

Since current flowing through a coil of wire creates a strong magnetic field, when two coils are placed next to one another—with an alternating current passing back and forth through one coil—a strong magnetic field is created, producing another alternating current that flows through the other coil. Current thus induced is directly proportional to the number of turns of wire in each of the two coils, which are referred to as *primary* and *secondary coils*. If the secondary coil has twice as many turns as the primary coil, the voltage produced by the current is twice as high; with half as many turns, the voltage is halved. Two coils working together in such a manner constitute a *transformer*. A *step-up transformer* increases voltage in the secondary coil; a *step-down transformer* reduces voltage in the secondary coil.

By using transformers, power companies can produce electricity with very high voltage at the plant to overcome resistance in long transmission lines; by using step-down transformers near the consumers, they can reduce voltage to a safer level. Nowadays, 120 volts AC is the standard current used in the United States and Canada.

Generating Alternating Current

The previous discussion of how current can be induced to flow along a conductor included the basic principles of induction. To take this a step further, note in Figure 1-4 the darker portion of the square shape between the magnet's jaws, which is shaped like a squared-off letter C. For purposes of illustration, consider this C to have been fashioned on the end of a rod. The rod, which represents a conductor, is placed so the C portion is upright between the jaws of a magnet. In this position,

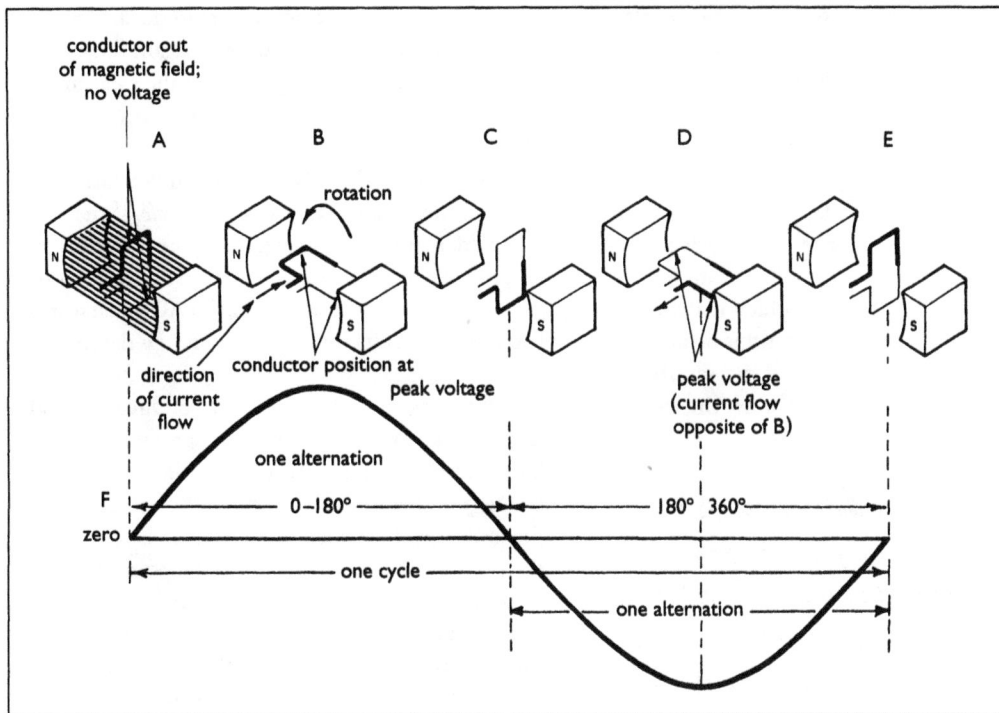

Figure 1-4. A–E: Current generated by a rotating conductor in the jaws of a magnet. During the second half of the 360-degree rotation, current flow is reversed. F: Sine wave of the current produced by the voltage generated in A–E.

the back of the C will be outside the magnetic field created by the lines of force emanating from the jaws (Figure 1-4A).

By using some kind of mechanical power, such as a hand crank, the conductor is rotated in place between the jaws. As it turns, the C begins to cut through the weaker lines of the magnetic field, current starts to flow in one direction along the rod, and voltage builds. As the C turns farther, it approaches the stronger lines of force emanating from the jaws. When the C is 90 degrees from the starting position and on the same plane as the jaws, the voltage is at peak (Figure 1-4B). As the rod continues rotating in the same direction, the C again cuts through weaker lines of force until it passes out of the magnetic field, where current flow and voltage cease (Figure 1-4C). At this point, the rod has made a 180-degree rotation.

As the rod continues to turn in the same direction to complete a 360-degree

9

rotation, it again cuts through the magnetic field—from weaker to maximum strength and back to weaker—in the opposite direction. Current again flows along the rod, but in the opposite direction from that in the first half of the rotation, until the C reaches the starting point, outside the magnetic field, where again there is no current flow or voltage (Figures 1-4D and 1-4E).

The one complete 360-degree rotation of the C, which caused the current to flow first in one direction and then in the opposite direction, is a *cycle*. If the turning rate is one cycle per second, it has a frequency of 1 *hertz (Hz)*. If the rod spins fast enough to turn 60 times in 1 second, the frequency is 60 cycles per second, or 60 Hz, which matches the frequency of 120-volt household AC. An AC generator operates on this principle. The portion of the conductor that cuts through the magnetic fields is the *armature*.

To use the current produced in the cycles, the shape of the conductor would have to be different than the C. If it were not, the current, once produced, would

Only fundamental electrical terminology and phenomena are described in this chapter; however, what has been omitted is not needed to fully understand an RV's electrical systems.

have no place to go; it must have a circuit. To make a circuit, another C, represented by the lighter C-shaped line in Figure 1-4, is joined to the first C so that both ends of the conductor (i.e., the rods) point in the same direction. The rods are then connected to other conductors that carry the current to where it is to be used. Figure 1-4F is a *sine wave*, a graphic representation of a cycle—in this case, the cycle shown above it. Note the sine wave's relationship to the conductor's movement.

The sine wave, which represents the voltage, starts at the zero-degree time line of the cycle (corresponding to the starting point of the C), travels upward as current flows in the first direction until the voltage reaches peak, and then curves downward toward the zero line again. This represents a 180-degree rotation of the rod: one half-cycle, or *alternation*. Next, the line curves downward as current flows in the reverse direction, until the voltage again builds to peak, when the line begins to curve upward toward the zero line, completing the second alternation, as well as one 360-degree rotation.

Not all peak voltage produced in a half-cycle is useful for doing work. The term *root mean square* (rms) designates the useful voltage, and is the value usually referred to when AC voltage is discussed. Common household current, 120 volts, is rms voltage. Rms voltage multiplied by a factor of 1.41 equals peak voltage; peak voltage multiplied by 0.707 equals the rms, or effective, voltage (see Figure 3-4, pg. 40).

Only fundamental electrical terminology and phenomena are described in this chapter; however, what has been omitted is not needed to fully understand an RV's electrical systems.

THE 12-VOLT

DC

DIRECT CURRENT

SYSTEM

TWO

The Battery

A good way to illustrate the complicated subject of batteries is to use lightning as an example; the ionization that causes lightning is similar to the ionization that occurs in a battery.

Lightning forms when cumulonimbus clouds become electrically charged and a chain reaction occurs: As negatively charged particles in the base of a cloud are attracted toward positive charges on the ground, the positive charges move upward, and a lightning stroke occurs. The heat of the stroke causes more ionization, establishing a pathway so more strokes can occur along this route as the negative electrons flow to the positive ground surface.

Thunder is the noise of the explosion caused by an electrical charge superheating the air as it passes through. The air can be heated to more than 60,000°F, and lightning can develop as many as 100 million volts in a single stroke.

When the lightning completes the path between the ground and the clouds, a circuit is established that allows current to flow to the positively charged field of the ground from the negatively charged field of the cloud until the charges are neutralized. This is a form of direct current, the ground and the clouds being a source of electrical energy. A similar but less violent source of electrical power—a battery— provides the direct current used in an RV.

Battery Theory

Electricity can be generated in a variety of ways: chemically, magnetically, and thermally, to name just a few. Chemical generation is at work in the battery.

A crude battery can be made by using a glass jar with a piece of wood covering its top. Two strips of different metals are inserted through drilled holes or slots in the wood to hang down into the jar. A chemical reaction occurs when an *electrolyte,* which is any solution that allows an electrical current to flow through it, is placed in the jar. It may be an acid, basic, or salt solution, in either liquid or wet-paste form.

When the two metals are immersed in the electrolyte, ionization takes place, and the metal strips become *electrodes,* or *terminals.* The positive ions migrate toward one strip, the negative ions toward the other. The strip attracting the positive ions becomes the positive electrode; the other, which attracts the negative ions, becomes the negative electrode.

If one metal strip is copper and the other is zinc, and they are in a salt solution, there would be a potential between them of 1.10 volts. Other pairs of metals in different electrolytes would show different potentials. Table 2-1 lists the Electromotive Series of Elements in the order in which they become ions, and the potential each creates.

Table 2-1.

	Electromotive Series of Elements	
	Elements	**Potential in Volts**
Most Noble—Cathodic	Gold	−1.40
	Platinum	−1.20
	Mercury	−0.85
	Silver	−0.80
	Copper	−0.34
	Hydrogen	+0.00
	Lead	+0.12
	Tin	+0.13
	Nickel	+0.25
	Cadmium	+0.41
	Iron	+0.44
	Chromium	+0.74
	Zinc	+0.76
	Aluminum	+1.66
	Magnesium	+2.37
	Sodium	+2.71
Least Noble—Anodic	Calcium	+2.87
	Lithium	+3.04

NOTE:
Elements are arranged in ascending order by their tendency to become ions. Elements with plus voltages have the tendency to lose electrons and those with minus voltages tend to gain electrons. When two different elements are used as electrodes in a salt solution, it is possible to determine the voltage potential between the two elements by adding or subtracting the voltage differences.

If a metal conductor outside the jar connects the two metal strips, a current will flow through the wire as electron movement, and through the electrolyte as ion movement, thus completing a circuit. This type of chemical generator, or battery, is a *voltaic cell*—a device that converts chemical energy into electrical energy.

If the electrolyte is in liquid form, it is a *wet cell*. A battery with a paste electrolyte, or with the solution soaked into paper, is a *dry cell*.

Zinc-carbon (not alkaline) flashlight batteries—the least expensive type of the common AA, C, and D cells—are dry cells that have a carbon (graphite) positive electrode in a paste (with manganese dioxide as the active ingredient) in the center of the battery surrounded by a paper separator containing an electrolyte of ammonium chloride. The battery case, made of zinc, is the negative electrode.

Effects of Chemical Reactions

For two centuries, it has been known that a current flows between two different metals when they are placed in an electrolytic solution, and that some metals readily dissolve and combine chemically with the elements in the solution and some do not. Metals that are *inert*—that is, do not dissolve easily in solution—are said to be more *noble* than other metals. Gold, platinum, and silver are among the most noble metals; zinc and magnesium are among the least noble. With two dissimilar metals in solution, current flow occurs when electrons leave the least noble metal as it dissolves and flow to the more noble metal.

In a zinc-carbon flashlight battery, because the negative electrode (i.e., the case) is zinc, the case will dissolve as electricity is produced. When the battery is dead (no longer producing electricity), the zinc, greatly reduced in thickness, may allow the electrolyte to leak out of the case, perhaps ruining the flashlight. This is why manufacturers recommend removing batteries from battery-operated items when not in use.

While a flashlight battery is a dry cell, it is also a *primary cell* because once its energy is dissipated it is useless. A *secondary cell* is a wet-cell battery. The electrodes and the electrolyte are altered during the current flow; however, the battery can be restored to its original condition by forcing a charging electrical current to flow in the direction opposite to the discharge-current flow. RV batteries are secondary-cell batteries and thus can be recharged.

Most batteries for both motorhomes and trailers, and those for cars and trucks, are 12-volt batteries, so designated because each battery is composed of six cells, each with a potential of 2.105 volts: 6 multiplied by 2.105 equals 12.63, the voltage of a completely charged 12-volt battery. The batteries have plates of two different metals, which are suspended in the solution. The plates are perforated with a grille-like pattern to allow maximum surface contact with the electrolyte. To prevent the different-metal plates from touching one another, which would short out the cell, an insulat-

14

ing separator is placed between them. The separator may be in a leaf form or each plate may fit into its own envelope, which supports the plate and protects it from damage.

The positive plates of a cell are all connected by a conductor, as are the negative plates. The positive and negative plates are interleaved with the separators between, thus forming the elements of a cell. Each cell has a positive and a negative post, which are joined with the opposite posts of the other cells (positive post to negative post) to make the complete battery (Figure 2-1).

In RV and automotive batteries, the basic plates are simply lead grids. The positive plates carry in their grids a paste of lead dioxide, a compound of lead and oxy-

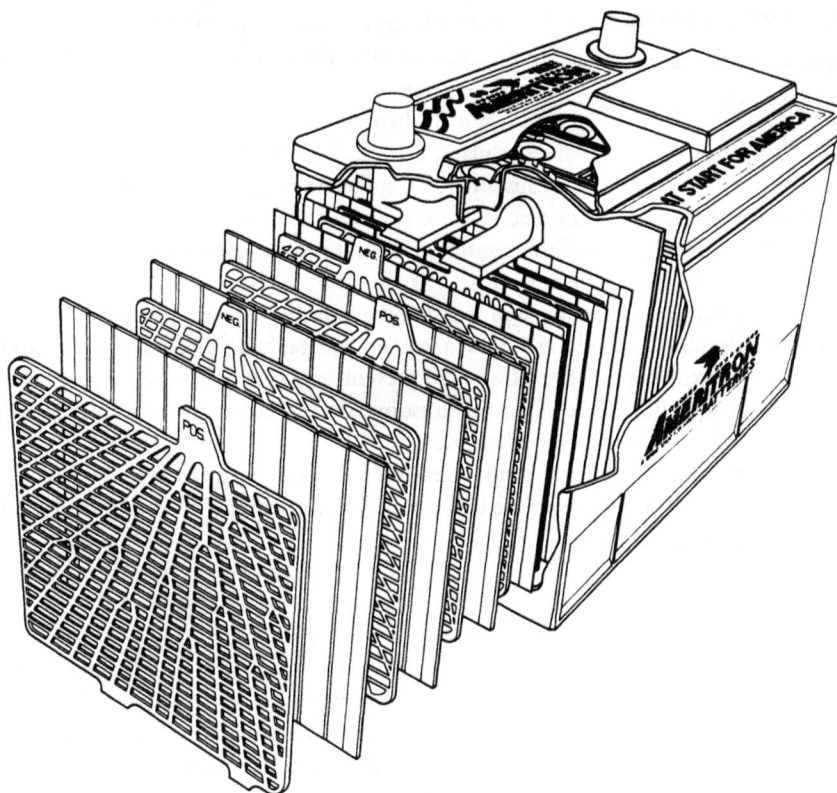

Figure 2-1. Cutaway view of battery plates. Separators are between each positive and negative plate. (Illustration courtesy of Interstate Batteries)

gen; the negative plates are pure lead. The plates are submerged in an electrolyte that is a 25-percent solution of sulfuric acid (hydrogen sulfate) and water. A lead-acid battery is the result.

As the battery discharges, chemical changes take place. The acid reacts with the lead of the plates, causing the molecules of the acid to break down into hydrogen and sulfate, which releases both positive (hydrogen) and negative (sulfate) ions. The lead combines with the sulfate ions, creating lead sulfate, which collects on the plates. The oxygen in the lead dioxide combines with the hydrogen ions to make water. As more of the sulfate and lead combine, and as more of the hydrogen and oxygen make water, the voltage potential decreases. Eventually the electrolyte becomes highly diluted with water, which gives it a lower specific gravity reading (see the following section). The battery is then discharged and the chemical reactions cease.

To prevent an excessive gas build-up, vents in the battery caps allow some of the gas to escape. Battery compartments must be well ventilated so the vented gas can dissipate.

When a battery is recharged, a reverse process takes place. Current flows in the opposite direction and causes the lead sulfate to recombine with the hydrogen in the water to make sulfuric acid. The oxygen released from the breaking down of water reacts with the lead of the positive plates, forming lead dioxide, while lead is deposited on the negative plates.

As the battery is charging, a process known as *gassing* occurs: Hydrogen gas forms and bubbles around the positive plate; oxygen gas bubbles around the negative plate. This mixture is highly explosive. To prevent an excessive gas build-up, vents in the battery caps allow some of the gas to escape. Battery compartments must be well ventilated so the vented gas can dissipate.

A fully charged battery at rest—when it is being neither discharged nor charged—self-discharges over time because of the small current generated by the dissimilar metals of the plates.

Specific Gravity

A *hydrometer* is used to determine the state of charge in a battery and the condition of cells by measuring the *specific gravity* of the electrolyte. *Specific gravity* is the measure of how heavy a liquid is, compared with water. Water has a specific gravity of 1. At 77°F (25.0°C), the specific gravity of the sulfuric-acid electrolyte of a fully charged battery cell is 1.265, which means the sulfuric-acid solution weighs 1.265 times as much as water. At the same temperature, a specific gravity reading of 1.131 indicates a discharged battery. Because ambient temperature affects this reading, a

Table 2-2.

Conversion of Specific Gravity to Voltage in a 12-Volt Battery

Specific gravity (average of all cells, fully charged)	1.265
Constant	+ 0.840
Voltage per cell	2.105
Number of cells in 12-volt battery	x 6
Battery state of charge in volts	12.630

Table 2-3.

Battery Capacity by Specific Gravity and Voltage

Remaining Capacity (Percent)	Percent of Discharge	Specific Gravity at 77°F	Volts per Cell	12-Volt Nominal Battery Voltage	24-Volt Nominal Battery Voltage
100	0	1.265	2.106	12.63*	25.27
90	10	1.251	2.091	12.54	25.09
80	20	1.236	2.076	12.45	24.91
70	30	1.221	2.061	12.36	24.73
60	40	1.206	2.046	12.27	24.55
50	50	1.191	2.031	12.18	24.37
40	60	1.176	2.016	12.09	24.19
30	70	1.161	2.001	12.00	24.01
20	80	1.146	1.986	11.91	23.83
0	100	1.131	1.971	11.82	23.65

NOTE:
*Other tables that give the voltage of a fully charged battery as 12.7 or 12.8 volts were compiled using temperatures other than 77°F. (Data courtesy of Photocom, Inc.)

standard of 77°F was established; readings taken at other temperatures must be adjusted up or down to be accurate. An adjustment scale is on the hydrometer.

To convert the hydrometer's specific gravity readings to voltage: Average the readings of the individual cells, add a constant of 0.84 to this average, then multiply by the number of cells in the battery. The product represents volts and is the *state of charge* in the battery (Table 2-2). Table 2-3 compares the specific gravity and the voltage of a battery in different stages of discharge. (Hydrometers are discussed further in Chapter 11.)

Wet-Cell Batteries

RVers use two types of batteries. One is the *automotive battery*, which in a motorhome or tow vehicle (or automobile, for that matter) is for starting the engine and providing power for other electrical loads related to automotive functions. This type is also called a *starting/lighting/ignition (SLI)*, *cranking*, or *chassis battery*. The other type is the *deep-cycle battery*, the *"house"* or *coach battery* used for operating the interior and exterior lights, water pump, furnace, stereo, and other house equipment. Both types are usually 12-volt batteries; however, in some cases, two 6-volt batteries combined in one *bank* (two or more batteries constitute a bank) are used for a house battery. A suitable deep-cycle house battery should be labeled "For marine/RV use." This indicates the battery has the heavy-duty components and construction needed for deep-cycle use.

The standard 12-volt battery in an automobile is usually lightly constructed. Each cell's many thin, porous plates allow a fast chemical reaction between the electrolyte and the plates. Such a battery can handle the initial heavy discharge required for the few moments it takes to start the engine, and then can be recharged quickly to have power available for other automotive functions. This 12-volt battery is not designed to be deeply discharged for long periods; if it were done regularly, the battery would soon be ruined.

Although some SLI batteries for motorhomes and trucks are more heavy-duty than ordinary automotive batteries and can stand more abuse, they are not necessarily intended to be discharged to a high percentage of their capacity.

Deep-cycle batteries have fewer, but heavier and thicker, plates per cell than their lightweight counterparts, so they can be more deeply discharged without any ill effects. Although a deep-cycle battery can withstand an occasional discharge as high as 80 percent of its capacity, its life will be prolonged considerably if it is not allowed to become discharged to below 50 percent.

Recently an inexpensive hybrid battery has been introduced. It is purported to be a deep-cycle battery with the capabilities of an engine-starting battery. In our judgment, such a battery would suffice as an engine-starting battery, but we doubt it would be practical for long-term deep-cycle use.

Sealed Batteries

The batteries discussed previously are conventional wet-cell batteries that require a certain amount of maintenance. Water must be added occasionally to bring the elec-

Figure 2-2. Various sizes of Prevailer gelled-cell batteries.
(Photo courtesy of GR Battery Systems, Inc.)

trolyte back up to the proper level and the state of charge should be checked periodically with a hydrometer. If you don't want to bother taking care of a battery, a *sealed,* or *no-maintenance, battery* may be your best choice.

The technical but cumbersome name for a sealed battery is an *immobilized-electrolyte battery,* and sealed batteries fall into two classes: *absorbed electrolyte* and *gelled electrolyte.*

The absorbed-electrolyte type uses spongelike separators between the plates to hold the electrolyte in close contact with the plates. The separators are usually made of microporous fiberglass or felt. Such a battery has some liquid solution to keep the separators moist, but does not have the large reservoirs of liquid that a wet-cell battery has. It is sealed permanently with a positive pressure to minimize gassing. The outer case is made of a tough material that resists cracking and damage.

When the electrolyte is in a gel rather than a liquid form, the battery is the gelled-electrolyte type (Figure 2-2). Gelled batteries, which are completely sealed, are excellent deep-cycle batteries because they accept deeper discharging and have a faster rate of recharging than any other type of battery. They are long lasting; some even have a 10-year warranty. A gelled battery may have a lower *ampere-hour (Ah)* rating than a comparable wet-cell battery. For example, a gelled battery of a given size might have an 86-ampere-hour rating, whereas a wet-cell battery of the same size might have a rating of 95 to 105 ampere-hours. (See the discussion of battery ratings in the following section.)

Because there is no liquid acid to contend with, sealed batteries are much safer to handle. No servicing is required; no water ever need be added and, because of the absence of acid, there is no terminal corrosion. Gassing does not occur except in the case of overcharging; even then it is minimal. Special pressure-relief valves take care of venting, if needed, before gases build up to a dangerous level; once venting is done, the valves reseal themselves.

Sealed batteries may cost more than other types of batteries. Gelled batteries are the most expensive, sometimes costing twice as much as wet-cell batteries. It is not possible to use a hydrometer to check the state of charge in any sealed battery; a *voltmeter* must be used (see Chapter 11 for voltmeter applications).

It is probable that in the future almost all batteries will be sealed because of the no-maintenance and safety features.

Battery Ratings

When shopping for a battery, the buyer is faced with many different ratings, most of which are confusing and some of which have no relationship to the type of battery needed. In years past, the only battery rating was in units of ampere-hours. This is a true measure of a battery's capacity—*capacity* being the amount of energy a battery can store—and is the rating RVers need to know before purchasing deep-cycle batteries. In many cases, however, the ampere-hour rating has been eliminated; it is not suitable for SLI batteries, so other ratings have been developed.

Cold cranking amperes (CCA) is essentially what the name implies: the number of amperes available to start, or crank, an engine when the ambient temperature is cold. Established by the Battery Council International (BCI), the basis for this rating is the number of amperes a battery can deliver for 30 seconds at a temperature of 0°F (–17.8°C) while maintaining a voltage of at least 1.2 volts per cell. CCA ratings of batteries in a bank are additive: Two batteries, each with a CCA rating of 900, have a CCA rating of 1,800 when connected in parallel (see the last section of this chapter).

Marine cranking amperes (MCA) is a new rating that applies to batteries for marine and RV use. It is not an official rating of the BCI. The MCA rating also measures cranking amperes, but it is based on a higher temperature than the CCA rating. It was developed because RVs and boats aren't generally used in zero-degree weather. For most MCA-rated batteries, the rating is based on a temperature of 60°F

(15.5°C), although some manufacturers use 32°F (0°C). MCA ratings can be calculated from CCA ratings by the following formulas: For a 60°F basis, the MCA rating is the CCA rating multiplied by 1.486; for a 32°F basis, multiply the CCA rating by 1.224. In the future, MCA ratings probably will be included in the technical data on all marine and RV batteries.

Another rating, *reserve capacity*, often called *reserve minutes*, is based on the number of minutes a battery sustains a 25-ampere load at a temperature of 80°F (26.6°C), before the voltage drops to 10.5 volts. This rating is useless for determining the ampere-hour capacity of a deep-cycle battery because the ampere load of an RV operating on battery power is rarely, if ever, more than 10 amperes. Even if high-ampere equipment is used, its operation is usually intermittent in nature and would not appreciably add to the hourly total. A reserve-capacity rating based on a 25-ampere load can be roughly converted to ampere-hours by multiplying by 0.65.

Before all these ratings came into use, batteries were rated by the ampere load required to discharge a battery to 10.5 volts in a 20-hour period. This so-called 20-hour rate was used to arrive at a battery's ampere-hour capacity: Assuming a load of 5 amperes, 5 (amperes) multiplied by 20 (hours) equals 100 (ampere-hours). The rating of the battery was stated in ampere-hours. Nowadays, in many instances, the ampere-hour rating has been replaced with a rating measured in hours. Some manufacturers use 5, 6, 8, 18, or 100 hours instead of 20 hours. The 20-hour rate is more applicable to the discharge rate of most RV batteries, so, for an RVer's needs, it is the most suitable rating.

An hour rating is based on the fact that a battery's ampere-hour capacity varies according to the rate at which energy is withdrawn from the battery. For example, a 100-ampere-hour–capacity battery provides 1 ampere for 100 hours. It might be assumed that the same battery would supply 50 amperes for 2 hours; however, this is not the case because battery capacity varies according to the rate of discharge (Table 2-4, pg. 22). A battery's capacity is neither exact nor fixed, so a slow rate of discharge results in a higher capacity; conversely, a fast rate of discharge results in a lower capacity.

When buying a deep-cycle battery, look for one that gives you either a true ampere-hour rating or a rating based on a discharge of 20 hours or longer.

What this all boils down to is: When buying a deep-cycle battery, look for one that gives you either a true ampere-hour rating or a rating based on a discharge of 20 hours or longer.

A warranty-period rating is becoming more common on batteries sold by mass merchandisers. It is absolutely worthless as a rating because it provides no information other than the number of months for which the warranty is good; often no CCA, MCA, or reserve-capacity ratings are given. The purchaser may be led to

Table 2-4.

Reserve Capacity at Various Amperage Rates				
	Group 24		Group 27	
Load (Amps)	Time (Hours)	Capacity (Ah)	Time (Hours)	Capacity (Ah)
5	16.0	80	20.0	100
10	6.9	69	9.0	90
15	4.2	63	5.0	75
20	2.7	54	3.4	68
25	2.0	50	2.7	67.5

NOTE:
Differing loads affect the ampere-hour rating of a battery. In normal use, loads vary in both amperage and the length of time they are applied, so these figures should be considered a guide rather than an accurate representation. Ampere-hour ratings vary depending on the size of battery, the manufacturer, and method used to calculate the rating.
Ah = ampere-hour

believe that a battery with a longer warranty is better, but this is not necessarily true.

Rating information (such as it is) is found on the battery case or in the manufacturer's literature where the batteries are displayed.

Battery Classification

In addition to the type of battery needed, other considerations must be the physical size, the capacity, and sometimes even the style. Most batteries carry a BCI group classification number that usually—not always—identifies the voltage, physical size, and terminal arrangement.

Some manufacturers have their own classification numbers and letter codes to designate, among other things, whether the battery posts are on the top or the side, and whether they are the tapered, marine type with a wingnut on top, or the flag type with a flat, upright post with a hole in the center. Other letter codes denote further information about the product. In most cases, the BCI group number appears in the coding, but a conversion chart must be consulted to make a true comparison of similar batteries from different manufacturers.

SLI, deep-cycle, and hybrid batteries may have a Group 27 classification. Group 27 deep-cycle batteries are very popular for RV house batteries, and are readily available from a variety of sources. A Group 24 hasn't enough ampere-hour capacity to be practical for use in any but the smallest RVs.

Six-volt golf-cart batteries are often used in a bank of two for house batteries,

Table 2-5.

Battery Sizes and Ratings Used in RV Applications

BCI Group	Volts	CCA Range at 0°F	MCA Range at 30°F	Reserve-Capacity Range	Ah Rating Range
4D*	12	775–1314	1240–1645	250–285	150–190
8D*	12	920–1050	1595	350–430	221
24*	12	370–950	490–788	75–120	50–85
27*	12	550–600	615–800	110–160	80–105
29	12	675	845	—	110–117
30H	12	405–575	—	135–160	93
31	12	550–900	—	130–180	115
58*	12	430–540	—	70–75	SLI
64	12	610	—	120	SLI
65*	12	850	—	160	SLI
78*	12	600–770	—	115–125	SLI
4	6	775	—	310	165
5D	6	835–920	—	325	182
7D	6	900–920	—	380–430	221
GC-2*	6	575–1150	1450–1668	345–350	208–225

Trojan Batteries**

BCI Group	Volts	CCA Range at 0°F	MCA Range at 30°F	Reserve-Capacity Range	Ah Rating Range
T-105	6	deep-cycle	deep-cycle	419	217
T-125	6	deep-cycle	deep-cycle	477	235
T-145	6	deep-cycle	deep-cycle	530	244

NOTES:

*In this group, sealed batteries are also available.

**Trojan does not use BCI group sizes for its batteries, so they are listed separately. Some cross-reference charts list the GC-2 batteries of other manufacturers as an equivalent to the T-105 and T-125 batteries. Trojan batteries are included because the company's golf-cart batteries are popular for RV use.

This listing was compiled using information from various manufacturers who all seem to use different methods and factors to calculate ratings; this accounts for the wide range of ratings for particular battery types.

The most popular battery sizes may be available in both SLI and deep-cycle versions. Some of the bigger truck batteries, such as the 8D and 31, are often expected to function as both an SLI and a deep-cycle battery.

Ah = ampere-hour, BCI = Battery Council International, CCA = cold cranking amps, MCA = marine cranking amps, SLI = starting-lighting-ignition although they are found more often in motorhomes than in trailers because most trailers don't have room for these large, tall batteries. Golf-cart batteries have a high ampere-hour capacity, can be deeply discharged without damage, and recharge quickly. Table 2-5 (pg. 23) lists battery groups that might be used in RV applications.

Ampere-Hour Ratings

When ampere-hour ratings are known, they can be used to determine how many and what size batteries you need for your RV. The habits of the RV's occupants and

Table 2-6.

Amperage Draw of 12-Volt RV Equipment	
Equipment	**Amps**
Incandescent light, single socket, type 1141 bulb	1.5
Incandescent light, double socket, type 1141 bulb	2.5
Incandescent light, single socket, type 1003 bulb	0.9
Incandescent light, double socket, type 1003 bulb	1.8
Fluorescent light, single tube, 8-watt	0.7
Fluorescent light, single tube, 15-watt	1.2
Fluorescent light, double tube, 30-watt	2.0
Water pump	4.0–8.0
Forced-air furnace	5.0–8.0
Evaporative cooler, 12-volt	5.0–6.0
Roof vent fan, 3-speed (depending on brand and speed)	1.8–7.3
Wall-mounted fan (depending on brand)	1.2–5.0
Bathroom vent fan	2.0
Range hood fan	2.0
Refrigerator, 12-volt DC, compressor-type	6.0
Refrigerator, 3-way (AES), on 12-volt setting	15.0–35.0
TV, AC/DC, 9-inch, color, on DC	3.0–4.0
TV, AC/DC, 5-inch, black-and-white, on DC	1.0–1.5
Stereo/cassette player, automotive-type	1.7–6.0
Equalizer/amplifier on stereo/cassette player	1.0–2.0
CB radio, receive-only mode	0.5
Video cassette player, 12-volt	1.5

NOTE:
AES = automatic energy-selecting

how the RV is used also should be considered when determining the number and size of house batteries needed.

Those who prefer to stay in campgrounds with full hookups have different requirements than RVers who enjoy primitive camping without hookups. If you like a variety of camping, as we do, the batteries should be selected accordingly.

RVers who never boondock and always stay in places with electrical hookups can probably get by with one good-quality, deep-cycle battery (in addition to any SLI battery); most likely, it can handle all their needs. Those RVers who sometimes or regularly depend on battery power for their house systems need to do some calculating in order to have enough batteries of the proper size to meet their requirements.

Those who prefer to stay in campgrounds with full hookups have different requirements than RVers who enjoy primitive camping without hookups.

The first step is to figure a typical day's ampere-hour consumption. It's easy to do: Simply multiply the amperage draw of each item of equipment in the RV by the number of hours it will be used each day. Amperage draw is found on equipment labels, stamped into the casings, or in the instruction booklets. The RV owner's manual may list the amperages of some equipment. On some equipment, watts may be given instead of amperage. Watts can be converted to amperage by using Ohm's Law: Wattage divided by voltage—in this case, 12 volts—equals amperage. If amperage draw or wattage cannot be found, it can be obtained from the manufacturer. Typical amperage draws of common RV equipment are listed in Table 2-6; how these are used to calculate daily consumption is shown in Table 2-7.

The total daily consumption of 31.75 ampere-hours shown in Table 2-7 may not seem like much, but, in relation to battery capacity, it can be considerable. If the RV has only one Group 24 battery with a capacity of 75 ampere-hours, using 31.75

Table 2-7.

Daily Ampere-Hour Consumption for a Typical RV	
Three lights for 4 hours (4 hours x 4.5 amps)	18.00 Ah
Water pump for 45 minutes; includes two showers (0.75 hour x 5 amps)	3.75 Ah
TV, color for 2 hours (2 hours x 4 amps)	8.00 Ah
Miscellaneous (clock, LED pilot lights, etc.)	+ 2.00 Ah
Total ampere-hours used in 24-hour period	31.75 Ah

NOTE:
All figures are approximate and based on typical ampere-hour usage. Ah = ampere-hour.

ampere-hours would deplete 42 percent of the battery's capacity. As stated previously, to prolong battery life, a battery should not be discharged below 50 percent of its capacity. The 42-percent depletion is close to 50 percent; therefore, a battery with a 75-ampere-hour capacity is not really suitable for this amount of usage. If the RV were equipped with a bank of two 75-ampere-hour batteries, this same usage would discharge the bank by 21 percent—which is acceptable—but an even better installation would be a bank of two Group 27, 105-ampere-hour batteries, for a total of 210 ampere hours. With this bank, a 31.75-ampere-hour discharge would amount to only 15 percent of capacity.

A water pump or furnace imposes an intermittent draw, so the full amperage draw of either should not be used in a daily-consumption calculation; instead, how many amperes such equipment will consume in an hour must be estimated. The water pump operates for only a few seconds at a time except when used for showers, when the pump might run continuously for several minutes. A thermostat-controlled furnace might cycle for 5 minutes on and 10 minutes off, which would amount to a consumption rate equal to just one-third of its ampere-hour rating.

Phantom Loads

The miscellaneous amount listed in Table 2-7 represents several *phantom loads* (i.e., current consumption RVers may not be aware of). Nearly every recently manufactured RV has some equipment with phantom loads, yet older RVs may have none.

Our refrigerator is the common electric/propane type. The automatic ignition system of the propane mode operates on 12-volt DC power and draws 0.5 ampere. The refrigerator also has a switch for normal and high-humidity situations. When the switch is set for high humidity, another 0.2 ampere of 12-volt power is used hourly. The 0.7 ampere of the two combined loads amounts to 16.8 ampere-hours per day.

Other common RV phantom loads include the stereo, which constantly consumes a small amount of 12-volt power to run the clock and maintain station memories; propane-leak detectors that operate on 12-volt power; security systems; automatic-ignition water heaters; and any switches with a pilot light. On many RVs, the water pump switch has a pilot light, as may other switches. These switches are usually illuminated by a *light-emitting diode (LED)*. The amount of current an LED consumes usually is measured in *milliamps*—a small amount individually, but several items consuming milliamp loads each day can add up to a considerable amount. A phantom load of 500 milliamps equals half an ampere, and that can result in a daily consumption of 12 ampere-hours.

Certain phantom loads can be eliminated. We installed a switch on our stereo that shuts off the clock and memory, but we cannot get rid of the automatic-ignition load on the refrigerator. When we are in a dry climate, however, the high-humidity setting is not necessary.

When calculating the daily amperage draw for a recently built RV, some allowance for phantom loads must be included. If the phantom load amperage is not listed in the manufacturer's literature or cannot be measured (see Chapter 10), an estimate will have to suffice. It is wise to estimate on the high side.

If our refrigerator's amperage draw (on the high-humidity setting) were added to the miscellaneous category in Table 2-7, the amount of daily amperage consumption would increase from 31.75 to 48.55 ampere-hours, resulting in a single 75-ampere-hour battery being drained to 64 percent of its capacity, two 75-ampere-hour batteries to 32 percent of their combined 150-ampere-hour capacity, and 23 percent of a 210-ampere-hour–capacity battery bank. Phantom loads do add up and, when combined with the amperage draw of other equipment, contribute to a significant battery drain.

In motorhomes, some equipment with phantom loads may be connected to the SLI battery. If the SLI battery is dead after a long period when the motorhome hasn't been used, phantom loads may be the cause.

In motorhomes, some equipment with phantom loads may be connected to the SLI battery. If the SLI battery is dead after a long period when the motorhome hasn't been used, phantom loads may be the cause.

Battery Considerations When Shopping for an RV

When a new RV is purchased, if it is a motorhome, it will probably come from the manufacturer equipped with house batteries (along with an SLI battery, of course). Trailers are often sold without batteries, so the battery compartment should be checked out to see if it is large enough to hold the size and number of batteries you need. If it is not, determine whether space is available for additional batteries. It is possible to buy a battery box with venting tubes attached, but sometimes it's difficult to engineer a proper and safe installation for such a box.

The box in the battery compartment on our fifth-wheel trailer was designed to hold two Group 24 batteries, but we were able to enlarge it to accommodate the two Group 27 batteries we wanted. In our opinion, any midsize or large RV should have space for a minimum of two Group 27 batteries, but many manufacturers persist in installing boxes sized for only one Group 24 or Group 27 battery.

Most conventional trailers have a frame on the tongue for accommodating one, or a maximum of two, Group 24 (rarely Group 27) batteries. Tongue-mounted batteries should be kept in a box to protect them and keep them clean. Boxes are available that hold both Group 24 and Group 27 sizes. Batteries should be accessible for easy maintenance.

Along with the size of the battery compartment, location is important. Some RV manufacturers don't seem to give much thought to the placement of battery compartments. Batteries should be as close to the motorhome or tow-vehicle engine as possible. For trailers, they should be located in the front. If batteries are located at the rear of a trailer or far away from a motorhome's engine, recharging them adequately will be a problem because of the long wire run to the engine alternator (see Chapter 4).

When shopping for an RV, people often ignore the batteries and the accommodation for them, but it will prove a great convenience if you can carry the number of batteries you need for your RVing lifestyle, and have them located for easy recharging and maintenance.

Types of Battery Chargers

RV batteries may be charged by the engine alternator of the motorhome or tow vehicle; a converter/charger in the RV; a portable generator; a portable battery charger; solar panels; the built-in battery charger of an inverter; or a genset, which is the name given to a built-in, or nonportable, generator. Each type of charger is discussed in detail in later chapters.

The Battery Charging Process

Chemical Changes

A discharging battery undergoes certain chemical changes as its power is used, and a reverse reaction occurs when the battery is charged: The electrical current flowing into the battery converts the electrolyte, which is now mostly water, back into sulfuric acid as the lead sulfate deposits dissolve. As the battery discharges and recharges over and over again, some of the lead sulfate clumps on the plates during the discharges and becomes a little slower to redissolve on each charge cycle. These clumps eventually reduce the effectiveness of the plates in interacting with the acid; this process continues until the cell loses most of its voltage.

Each discharge/recharge cycle diminishes a battery's life. A wet-cell battery that has never been discharged to more than 50 percent of its rated ampere-hour capacity should be good for up to 1,000 cycles, but batteries that occasionally have been deeply discharged to 80 percent of capacity may have only 200 to 600 charge cycles. Batteries regularly discharged to only 10 percent of capacity might have a life of 20,000 cycles. Sealed, immobilized-electrolyte batteries have an even greater number of cycles.

Temperature Effects

Temperature and heat are important factors affecting battery recharging and, ultimately, effective life. Most calculations concerning recharging are based on a temperature of 77°F (25°C). The ampere-hour capacity of a battery is based on this temperature: A battery with a 75-ampere-hour capacity can deliver its rated 75 ampere-hours only at 77°F; lower temperatures reduce its capacity. For every degree below 77°, the ampere-hour capacity drops by 0.7 percent. Temperatures above 77°F increase a battery's capacity, but not significantly.

Heat is a by-product of the charging process and, if the temperature of the electrolyte rises above 120°F (50°C), the battery can be ruined. If an unregulated charger is used to charge a battery and the voltage is allowed to rise high enough to create violent gassing, heat is produced, the temperature rises, and eventually the plates buckle as the electrolyte boils away. In a worst-case situation, the battery can explode. Allowing a battery to overcharge repeatedly, even slightly, also damages it severely. Amperage should taper off as the battery reaches 50 percent of its charge to prevent excessive gassing and heating. High ambient temperatures can cause more gassing during the recharging process.

Recharging Rates

The best and safest way to recharge a battery is to charge it at a rate of 3 to 10 amperes until the battery voltage reaches 14.2 to 14.4 volts. This is the point where vigorous gassing begins and where a further voltage increase could lead to overcharging and overheating. Charging in this manner allows the battery to accept the charge at its own pace; however, it takes many hours for the battery to become fully charged because, as the charging progresses, amperage tapers to an ever-reducing flow. In fact, if a battery is discharged to a specific gravity of 1.120, it takes 14 hours to recharge at a 10-ampere initial rate; even after this many hours, the battery will not be charged to its fullest capacity.

During the charging process, the battery reaches a false-high, surface-voltage reading, which is not the same as the reading obtained after the battery has rested.

A fully charged battery at rest, in which no recharging or discharging has occurred for 24 hours, has a voltage of 12.63 volts; a completely discharged battery has a voltage of 11.82 volts, a span of slightly less than 1 volt. During the charging process, the battery reaches a false-high, surface-voltage reading, which is not the same as the reading obtained after the battery has rested.

For charging, a voltage source that has a higher voltage than that of the discharged battery is connected to the battery. The higher voltage causes current to flow into the battery. Current will not flow unless two differing voltages are present; it is the voltage differential that causes the battery to charge—not the amperage of the charger. *Amperage,* as far as the battery is concerned, is the rate, or speed, at which the charge is accepted by the battery. A battery charger's amperage rating denotes the maximum current that the charger can produce at a constant voltage; this is why chargers are rated by amperage and not voltage. The amperage rating is usually based on an intermittent, not constant, output because many chargers can produce amperage continuously at only half their rated output. Furthermore, the battery controls the rate of amperage it can absorb. A battery discharged to about 50 percent of capacity can absorb a high-amperage charge for a long period before it begins to slow its acceptance rate and refuses a higher charge.

As chemical action occurs in the recharging battery, the voltage rises, but the chemical action eventually lags behind the voltage rise because of the slow diffusion of the acid in the electrolyte; the two actions do not take place at the same time.

Anyone who has tried to start a car on a cold morning has experienced the battery's inability to turn over the engine after a short interval of cranking. Allowing the battery to rest for a short time usually revives it enough to start the engine. Why? The electrical demands of starting are swiftly met by the battery during the initial cranking, which causes the battery's voltage to drop; however, the chemical reaction in the battery is slow and can't keep up with the dropping voltage. The acid in contact with the plates breaks down into water, and it takes time for fresh acid to diffuse through the electrolyte to again come in contact with the plates. After a time, the necessary reaction has taken place, providing the battery with a higher voltage and more power.

The same process happens in reverse during recharging: The voltage rises faster than the chemical action (the hydrogen and sulfate forming acid in the solution, and the lead of the positive plates combining with oxygen to make lead dioxide) can take place. As the voltages of the charging source and the battery approach each other, the charging, or amperage, rate naturally slows down because the battery simply cannot accept it fast enough. Here again, diffusion plays a part: The voltage periodically rises faster than the acid can form in the electrolyte, so the charging process slows. The process is completely self-regulating.

A warm battery accepts a charge more readily than a cold battery because heat speeds up the chemical reaction; therefore, heating a battery, or keeping it warm in the first place, aids in starting a car in cold weather.

Battery manufacturers recommend that charging be done at a constant 13.8 volts, with an initial rate of 10 to 15 amperes tapered down by the charger to 3 to 5 amperes until the battery is charged. This way, the charging is done slowly without damage to the plates. The reason for the recommendation is that manufacturers are interested in having the battery last only until its warranty expires. With the recommended procedure, however, the battery will never reach its full capacity. By charging to a higher

14.4 volts, the gassing point, the battery can reach beyond the rated capacity.

For every ampere of current removed from a battery during discharge, theoretically, 1.2 amperes has to be replaced during recharging. This is called the *charge-efficiency factor*. A 105-ampere-hour battery that is 50 percent discharged would require 6.3 hours of charging at a rate of 10 amperes to bring the battery to full capacity.

For the best performance, a battery should be allowed to rest for 24 hours after recharging. Cycles of discharging and recharging shorten a battery's life; uninterrupted cycles shorten it further. A rest dissipates the excess surface-charge voltage, giving the remaining voltage a chance to equalize between the cells.

Multistage Charging

One of the problems with most charging methods is that the end result is either an undercharged or overcharged battery. In recent years, sophisticated equipment has evolved that does the job quickly without damage to the battery. Depending on the manufacturer, the system is known as *performance charging*, *smart charging*, or an *advanced regulation system (ARS)*. A few manufacturers call it what it actually is: *multistage charging*, and that's how we will refer to it henceforth.

One of the problems with most charging methods is that the end result is either an undercharged or overcharged battery.

Multistage charging uses regulation that controls voltage and current flow during the charging process. Much of the regulation is automatic, but users can adjust the output of some of the stages to match the needs of their batteries and equipment. Multistage charging can be used in conjunction with alternators, portable generators, and other battery chargers.

Steps of Multistage Charging

Multistage charging is designed mainly for recharging deep-cycle batteries; these batteries can handle the fast charges that occur during some of the charge cycles. A normally discharged SLI battery can be successfully recharged by this method; however, because of the higher voltage to which the battery is subjected, it tends to become slightly overcharged.

There are four stages in the multistage charging system: the first two are charging stages; the latter two are maintenance stages (Figure 2-3, pg. 32).

Bulk or Initial Charge Stage

The multistage regulator senses how deeply the battery is discharged and initially provides a high-amperage charge rate, which should be about 25 percent of the battery's ampere-hour capacity. A 105-ampere-hour battery should receive about a 25-

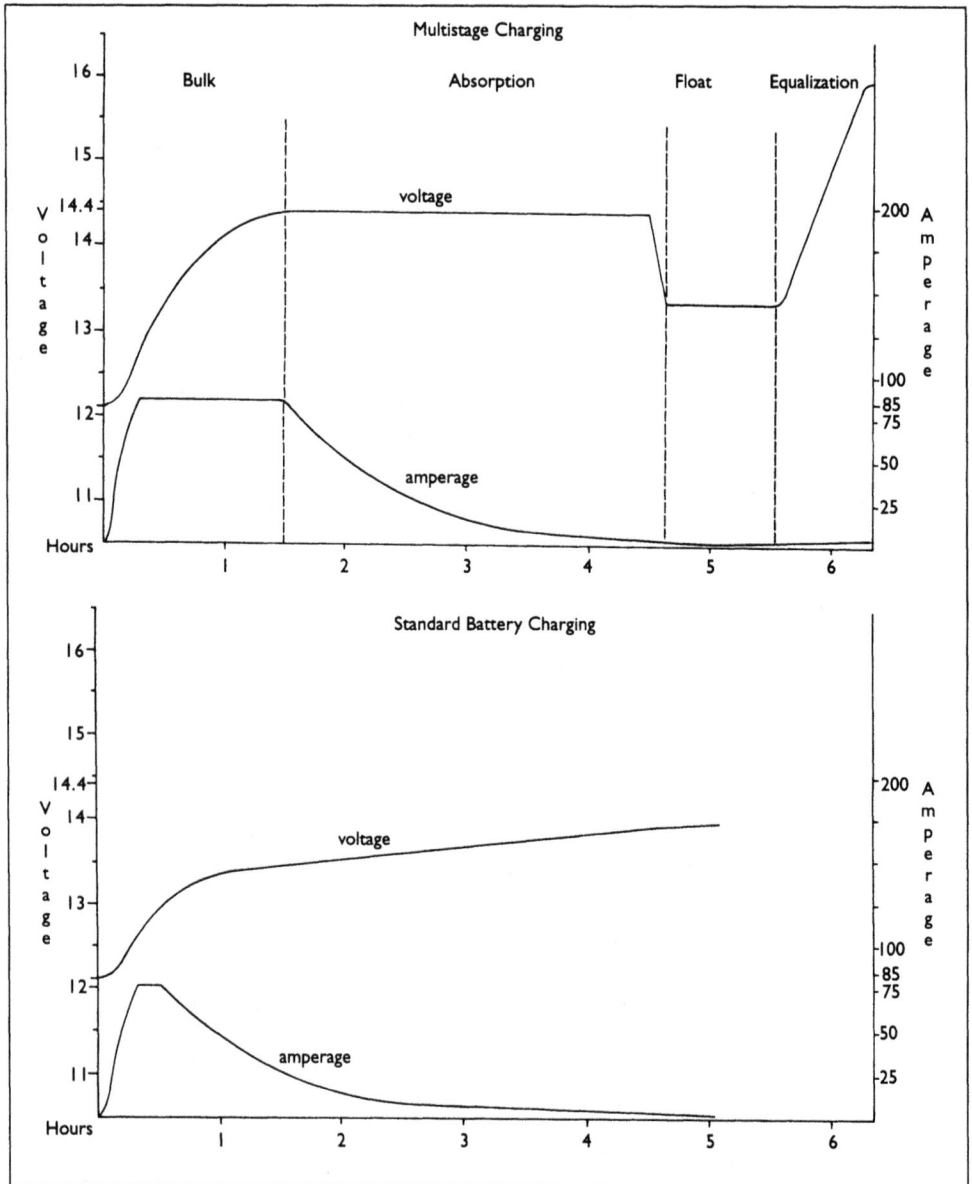

Figure 2-3. The two graphs compare multistage and standard battery charging methods using a 105-ampere alternator operating at 80-percent efficiency.

ampere charge at the beginning. If the batteries are in banks, the total ampere-hour rating for the bank would apply, so two 105-ampere-hour batteries should receive a 50-ampere charge during the bulk stage. The *bulk charge stage* continues until the voltage reaches 14.4 volts, where vigorous gassing occurs.

If the battery is discharged to below 50 percent of capacity, a higher charging rate of up to 40 percent of the ampere-hour capacity can be applied. This high rate continues until the battery reaches 50 percent of capacity, or until the voltage builds to 13.5 volts, where mild gassing begins. The charging rate is then reduced to 25 percent of capacity to minimize gassing and heat build-up, and charging continues as before until the voltage builds to 14.4 volts.

Multistage regulation is not effective unless the charging equipment it is paired with can produce the higher amperage needed with this system.

Because sealed batteries can accept a higher bulk charge (i.e., 40 percent of the ampere-hour rating of battery) than wet-cell batteries, and because they need to have minimum gassing, the bulk voltage should be no higher than 14.2, rather than 14.4 used for wet-cell batteries.

Absorption or Acceptance Stage

At 14.4 volts, the battery has been recharged to only about 70 percent of capacity. In the *absorption stage,* the voltage is held at this level to let the battery absorb the current at its own diffusion rate. The 14.4-volt level is the point where active gassing occurs, but this can be controlled by maintaining a constant voltage no higher than 14.4 volts. The amperage charge rate has been reduced at this point, thus preventing excessive heat build-up.

The constant voltage with decreasing charge rate is continued until the natural battery acceptance of the amperage flow has dropped to 1 or 2 percent of the battery's ampere-hour capacity, at which point the battery is considered fully charged. A battery charged to 5 percent of ampere-hour capacity, however, is close enough to a full charge to be satisfactory. Because of the battery's slow acceptance rate to reach full charge, several more hours of charging might be necessary to reduce the charge rate from 5 percent to 1 to 2 percent of capacity.

Other charging equipment, not having the regulation necessary for an absorption stage, charges until the 14.4-volt level is reached; however, by that time the rate of charge is diminished to where it is ineffective and the battery cannot reach its full-charge capacity.

The temperature of the battery is critical during the absorption stage because the voltage/gassing point varies with the battery temperature (Table 2-8, pg. 34). With multistage regulation, the temperature is monitored, and the timing of the charge cycle is controlled to compensate for temperature variations.

Table 2-8.

Temperature Effects on Battery Gassing and Voltage				
Temperature °F/C	50% Discharge Voltage	Float Voltage	Gas Point Voltage	Equalizing Voltage
37/3	12.29	13.59	14.49	16.29
47/8	12.26	13.57	14.47	16.27
57/14	12.24	13.54	14.44	16.24
67/19	12.22	13.52	14.42	16.22
77/25*	12.20	13.50	14.40	16.20
87/30	12.18	13.48	14.38	16.18
97/36	12.16	13.46	14.36	16.16
107/42	12.14	13.44	14.33	16.14
117/48	12.11	13.41	14.31	16.11
127/53	Severe battery damage can occur.			

NOTES:
*Optimum battery-charging temperature.
Table from David Smead and Ruth Ishihara, *Living on 12 Volts with Ample Power*, Rides Publishing Co., by permission of the authors.

Float Stage

After the battery is charged, the voltage of the charger is lowered to 13.5 volts—the *float voltage*. A battery can remain at full charge indefinitely at this voltage because it is enough to replenish the natural self-discharge.

If any 12-volt equipment (e.g., lights, water pump, or furnace) is used during this stage, the float voltage should be adjusted to a higher level; otherwise, the battery discharges accordingly. Depending on the ambient temperature, the float voltage should range from 13.5 to 13.7 volts, the lower voltage being used in warm weather. Raising the float voltage allows the battery to be maintained while providing enough extra voltage to operate the 12-volt equipment.

Equalization or Conditioning Stage

Equalization of a battery is accomplished by driving the voltage above the gassing point, to about 16.2 volts, for several hours, but allowing the amperage rate to be no higher than 5 percent of the ampere-hour capacity. After such a charge, all cells will be equalized; that is, they will all have the same specific gravity. The equalization stage also breaks up clumps of sulfate that form on the cells' plates.

The equalization stage is manually controlled and should be done periodically, perhaps monthly, for no longer than 4 hours at a time. Equalization is only effective for wet-cell batteries. Some multistage regulators don't have this stage.

Series and Parallel Battery Wiring

Batteries are joined to increase either ampere-hour ratings or voltage. They are connected to other batteries in the bank by either *series* or *parallel wiring* (Figure 2-4). When they are joined in series, the positive post of one battery is connected to the negative post of the next. The remaining posts are used to connect the batteries to the RV's electrical system. Series wiring can be visualized by thinking of a line of elephants in which each elephant's trunk holds the tail of the elephant ahead.

A single 6-volt battery, such as the type used in golf carts, cannot be used in RVs because it has the wrong voltage. Two 6-volt batteries, wired in series, double the voltage, thus providing the necessary 12 volts.

Batteries are joined to increase either ampere-hour ratings or voltage.

Another use of series wiring is in 24-volt systems, which are found primarily in bus conversions where the large diesel engines use 24 volts in the starter/alternator circuits. The house-battery system is often 24 volts as well, so that both battery banks can be charged by the alternator. Usually both the SLI and house-battery banks consist of two 8D, 12-volt batteries wired in series, although sometimes four series-wired, 6-volt golf-cart batteries are used. A 24-volt system has certain advantages: A 24-volt battery bank can do the same work as a 12-volt bank but with half the amperage draw. Ohm's Law explains it: A load of 1,200 watts divided by 12 volts equals 100 amperes; the same load divided by 24 volts equals 50 amperes. Furthermore, a 24-volt system does not need as heavy-gauge wiring in the circuits because of the lower amperage. A 24-volt system is practical in RVs because more work can be accomplished with fewer amperes.

Series wiring does not increase the ampere-hour capacity of the bank; no more ampere-hours are available than

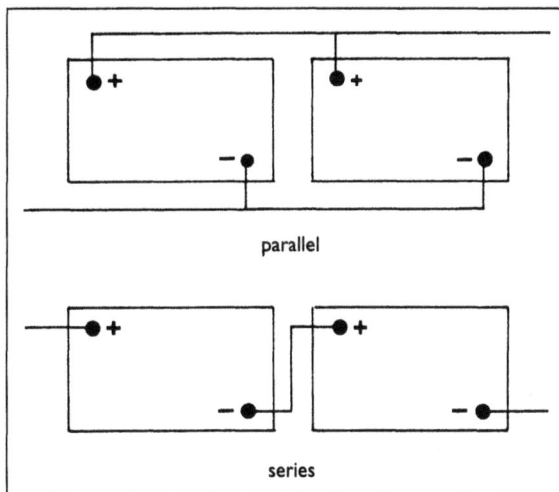

Figure 2-4. Batteries wired in parallel and in series.

that of one battery. If the batteries have different capacities, the ampere-hours available will be the same as the lowest-rated battery. With series wiring, if one battery cell goes dead, not enough voltage remains to operate any 12- or 24-volt equipment.

To use the analogy of the elephants again, parallel wiring might be likened to two elephants walking side by side with their trunks joined and their tails tied together. Their bodies represent batteries, and their trunks and tails represent the positive and negative wire connections. In parallel wiring, all positive posts are connected together and negative posts likewise. Parallel wiring is used to increase the ampere-hours of the system; the capacities of each battery are added together to get the total ampere-hour capacity of the bank. Depending on whether two, three, or four batteries are used, the total capacity will be double, triple, or quadruple that of one battery (providing all batteries have the same ampere-hour capacity).

A disadvantage to parallel wiring: Since each battery discharges at its own rate, one battery may discharge more than another; a slight current will flow as the stronger battery tries to equalize the voltage between the batteries. This can cause cell damage in both batteries. When a battery has loose or corroded connections, the problem is compounded. Such connections can create resistance, forcing the battery with the better connections to carry most of the load.

For the best service, whether the batteries are wired in series or parallel, all batteries in a bank should be the same size and age, and even manufactured by the same company.

THREE

Automotive Alternators

The battery is the heart of an RV's DC electrical system since it provides the power needed to operate the 12-volt equipment. The battery is not self-sustaining, however; the power used must be replaced by recharging, and, to many RVers, recharging presents a problem. This chapter covers the most common of the several methods of battery charging in RVs, which is with the *automotive alternator* in motorhomes and tow vehicles (Figure 3-1).

Alternators came into favor for automotive use in the 1960s after the development of the *solid-state silicon diode,* a two-element device that allows current to pass through it in one direction but not the other. An alternator is, in effect, an AC generator (see Figure 1-4), but is not to be confused with portable generators and gensets, which also produce AC.

The functions of an alternator were performed by a DC generator in years past. These heavy, large, inefficient units produced current through an armature containing several coils mounted on the shaft. How the coils were wired determined whether the current produced was AC or DC. With the advent of the solid-state silicon diode, these generators underwent a complete redesign as well as a name change,

Figure 3-1. Wrangler high-output alternator.
(Photo courtesy of Wrangler Power Products)

and became today's alternators that generate AC and convert it to DC.

An alternator converts mechanical energy into electrical energy through *electromagnetic induction*. This is accomplished by a belt that is driven by a pulley mounted on the driveshaft of the engine, which turns another pulley on the shaft of the alternator.

How Alternators Work

An alternator has a *rotor* mounted on the shaft. The rotor produces a revolving magnetic field that cuts across the *stator*—a group of conductor coils embedded in the outer case of the alternator—and induces a current flow. The spinning magnetic poles created by the turning rotor cause the rotor's magnetic fields to constantly reverse direction, which results in an alternating current in the stator coils.

The main high-amperage output of an alternator comes from the stator. Remaining stationary, it can be easily connected to the external circuit of the battery through fixed posts. Since the output circuitry is stationary, it also can be completely insulated, thus eliminating the danger of shorts.

A small amount of current is necessary to create the magnetic field of the rotor. This comes from the battery and is called the *field*, or *control, current*. It reaches the rotor by brushes that rub against two insulated *sliprings* on the shaft of the rotor. A slipring is a metal collar, made either in one continuous piece or of two semicircular pieces. One slipring is the positive contact of the rotor; the other is the negative contact.

Rectification of Alternating Current

A *rectifier* changes the alternating current of an alternator into the direct current needed by the RV's electrical system—an important function because AC cannot be used for charging a battery or operating 12-volt DC equipment, such as headlights.

With silicon diodes, it became easy to design a circuit that allows both alternations of AC to flow in the same direction, which achieves *rectification*. The circuit is designed so that it is split into two separate parallel circuits, each with a diode in it in a direction opposite from the other. Since each diode passes current in only one direction, the flow from the first alternation passes in the forward direction through the first circuit, and the second alternation's flow is blocked from passing. In the second circuit, the second alternation's flow

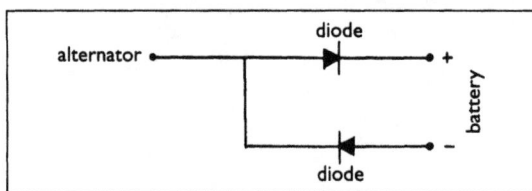

Figure 3-2. A schematic of a simple rectifier.

passes through the diode in the reverse direction, and the first alternation's flow is blocked (Figure 3-2).

Rectification is not a perfect way to convert AC to DC because it creates a pulsating, or rippling, effect on the current and is not the steady flow of pure direct current produced by the battery. The current flowing during one half-cycle, stopping before the second half-cycle begins, and then resuming flow again is responsible for the pulsating effect (Figure 3-3). If there are two alternations per cycle, for instance, and 150 cycles per second (150 Hz), there will be 300 *pulses* per second. This rhythmic pulsating is undesirable and diminishes the total power of the current. Methods of minimizing this pulsating are discussed later in this chapter.

A motor and an alternator/generator are essentially the same: A motor uses electrical energy to make mechanical energy; an alternator/generator uses mechanical energy to make electrical energy. When an engine is shut off by the ignition switch, the alternator remains connected to the battery (a power source), and it therefore must not be allowed to function as a motor. Diodes prevent this from happening.

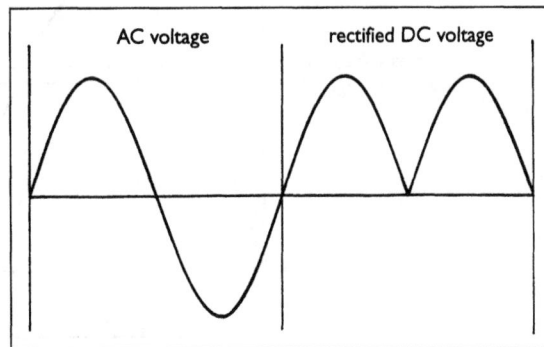

Figure 3-3. Representation of the ripple effect when AC voltage is rectified into DC voltage.

Types of Alternators

Single-Phase Alternators

Several types of alternators are in use and each induces alternating current in different ways. The simplest type is a *single-phase AC alternator*. It has four poles with coils, or *polar groups*, wired in series; these are spaced evenly around the stator. The rotor also has four poles, with alternating polarities: one a north pole, the next a south pole, and so on. As the rotor revolves, the created magnetic lines of force cut across all the coils in each polar group of the stator at the same time. This induces an AC voltage in the stator.

Since all four polar groups in the stator are wired in series, all the induced voltages are in phase, or *synchronization*, with each other, forming a pure sine wave of alternating current. Remember the elephants of Chapter 2: In series wiring, each

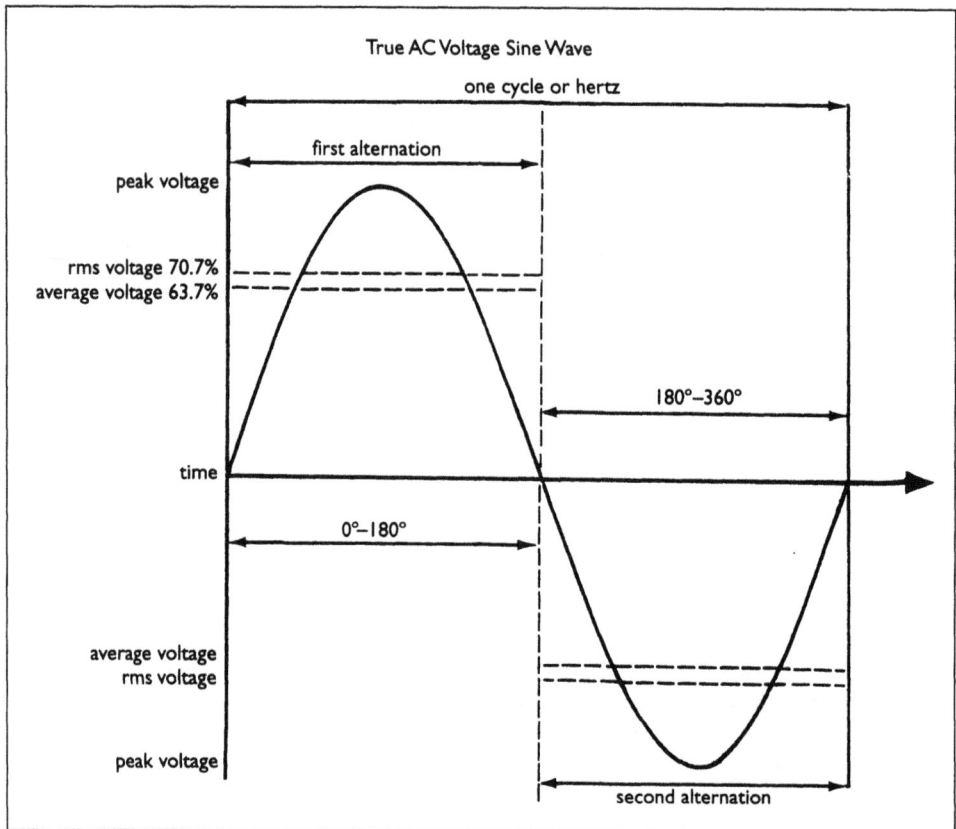

True AC Voltage Sine Wave

Figure 3-4. Voltage sine wave of one revolution of a single-phase alternator. One rotation of the rotor creates two cycles in the time required for one revolution.

element is wired to the next element (positive to negative or negative to positive), so the current passes through the first element before it passes through the second. Since there are two sets of poles, one rotation of the rotor creates two cycles of current in the time required for one revolution, creating the sine wave shown in Figure 3-4.

Three-Phase Alternators

The most popular type of alternator for automotive use is the *three-phase alternator*. It has three separate windings and three sets of poles in the stator. The windings are equally spaced around the stator frame so that when voltage is induced and a current is present, each winding creates its own sine wave, or phase of current; each of these is out of phase, or synchronization, with the others. One complete cycle of a sine wave is 360 degrees, constituting one of the three phases. Each successive phase is 120 degrees out of phase with the others. The winding of each of the three poles in the stator is joined with the others, in parallel, at a common post, thereby superimposing the three phases of the current, one over the other, in the same circuit (Figure 3-5).

Wye and Delta Wiring Connections

Two types of wiring connections are used between phases of a three-phase alternator: the *Y*, or *wye, connection* and the *delta connection* (Figure 3-6). In the Y form of winding, the start-lead end of each of the three windings is connected to a common junction, or terminal. The finish-lead end of each winding goes to a terminal that is usually connected to each rectifier diode.

In a delta connection, the finish-winding of one phase is connected to the terminal of the start-winding of the next phase. Each winding is wired similarly to series wiring, but with a terminal between each winding going to the rectifier diodes. Essentially, the end result of both Y and delta wiring is the same.

A three-phase alternator has a set of two diodes for each phase winding in the stator so that each phase coil has its own rectifier to convert the current output of that phase. This direct current output is then connected to the output of the other two phases, which provides the total current output.

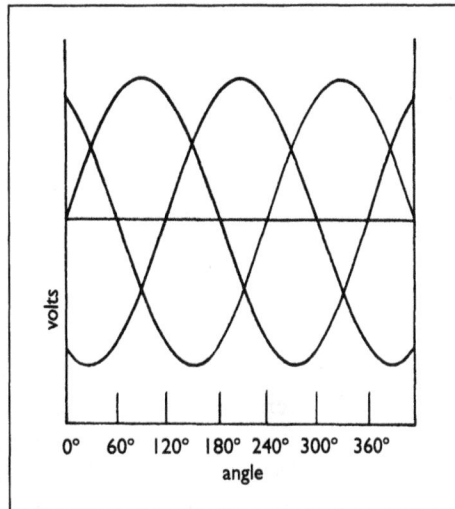

Figure 3-5. Voltage sine wave of one rotor revolution of a three-phase alternator. Each phase is 120 degrees out of phase with the other two phases and superimposed over one another.

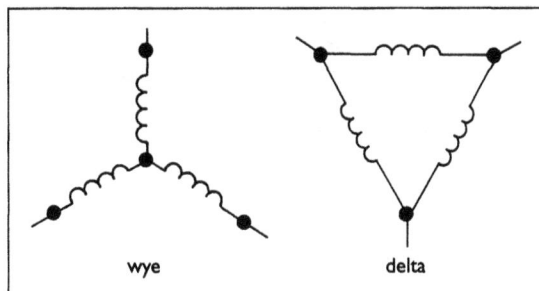

Figure 3-6. The wye and delta wiring connections between the windings of each phase of a three-phase alternator.

As explained previously, when the current is rectified in a single phase of current, the result is two alternations, or pulses, per cycle. Superimposed three-phase current has six pulses per cycle. This superimposition is one way to minimize the

41

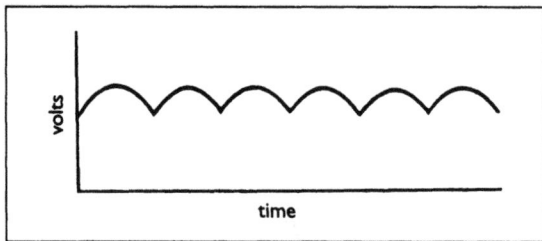

Figure 3-7. Ripple effect created by six rectified pulses in a three-phase alternator.

pulsating, or rippling, effect of direct current because the smaller pulses make for a smoother current flow (Figure 3-7).

Diode Trio

Use of a *diode trio* is one way to supply the alternator's regulator with increased power for the field current. With a diode trio, three circuits are created in addition to the three parallel rectifying circuits. Each of the trio's circuits comes from one of the three outputs of the alternator's three phases and is connected ahead of the corresponding rectifying diode. One diode is installed in each circuit. The three circuits are joined at a common terminal and fed to the field current in the alternator's regulator (discussed later in this chapter), thereby increasing the field-current flow to the rotor (Figure 3-8). The diodes in the trio carry only the small field current; therefore, diodes with a smaller amperage rating than that of the rectifying diodes

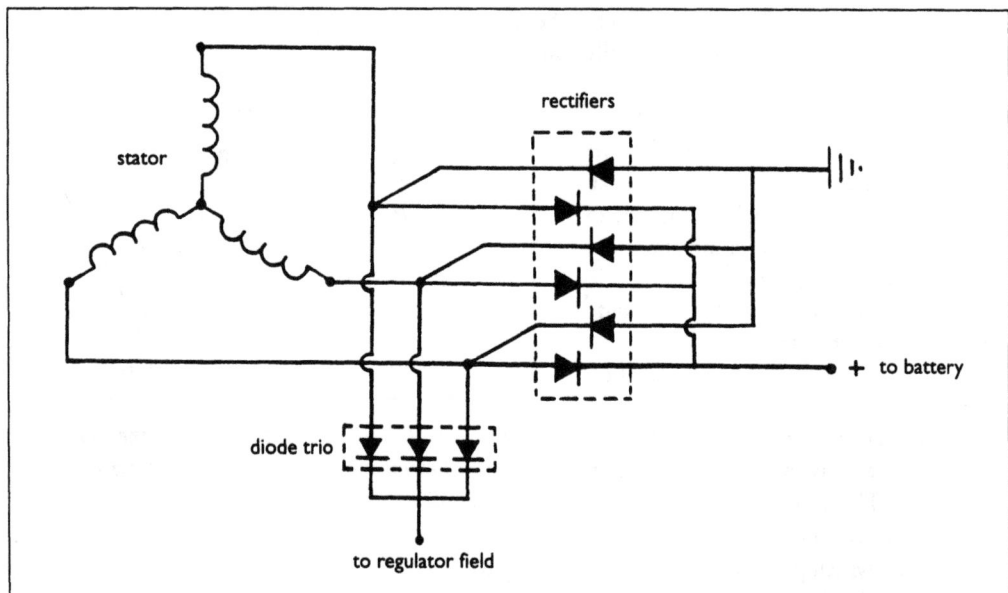

Figure 3-8. Alternator wiring with diode trio. The three circuits are joined at the common terminal connection of the regulator field.

42

are used. Diode-trio circuitry is most often found in an alternator with an internal rather than an external regulator.

N and P Types of Alternators

The difference between N (negative) and P (positive) alternators is the method employed in the wiring of the brushes that carry the field current to the rotor. In the N type, the negative field-current wire from the rotor is grounded to the regulator, so a negative excitation voltage is applied to the magnetic field. In the P type, the field-current wire to the rotor is connected at the positive side of the regulator, so a positive excitation voltage is applied to the magnetic field (Figure 3-9). You need to know what type of alternator you have if you intend to add a special regulator because certain types will not work on N-type alternators.

You need to know what type of alternator you have if you intend to add a special regulator because certain types will not work on N-type alternators.

Varying an Alternator's Output

Because an alternator is operated by a belt that runs from the pulley on the engine's driveshaft to the pulley on the alternator, the output of the alternator varies with the vehicle's engine speed during normal driving. When the engine is idling, the alternator delivers minimum current. As driving speed increases, the output increases until it reaches peak.

The speed of the alternator's rotor is also controlled by the size ratio of the belt pulley to the pulley on the engine driveshaft. The ratio ranges from 2:1 to 3.5:1, depending on the type of engine; diesel engines usually operate at lower revolutions per minute (rpm) than gasoline engines. A 2:1 ratio means that 2,500 rpm of the engine driveshaft can turn the alternator's rotor at 5,000 rpm because the alternator's pulley is the smaller of the two. Most alternators begin to produce a small amount of current at an alternator speed of about 1,500 to 2,000 rpm. Alternators usually have an extreme upper limit of about 10,000 rpm. The designed efficient operating range, where maximum amperage is developed, is usually from 4,500 to 6,500 rpm (Figure 3-10, pg. 44).

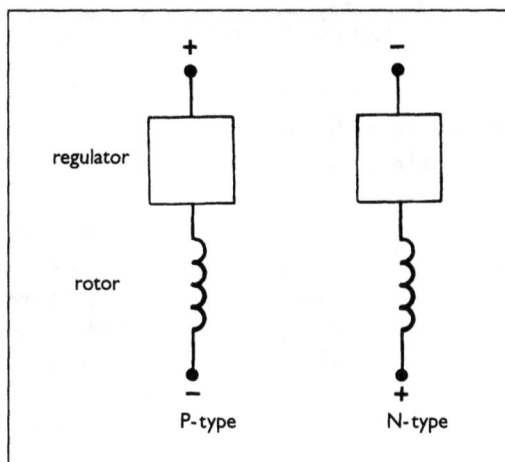

Figure 3-9. Wiring diagrams of P- and N-type alternators.

Amperage Output Curves

cold
rating

hot
rating

A
m
p
s

140—
120—
100—
80—
60—
40—
20—

1000 2000 3000 4000 5000 6000 7000
Rotor rpm

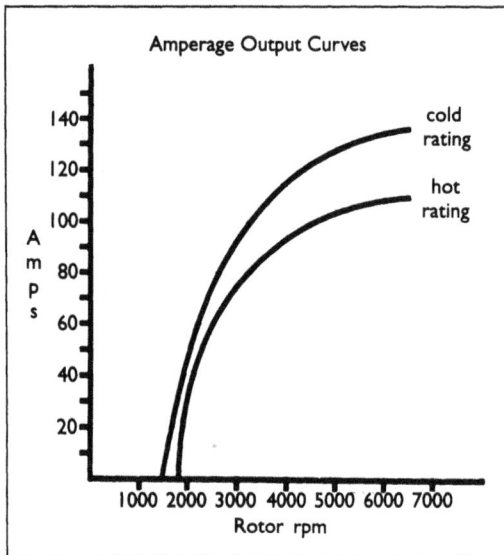

Figure 3-10. Performance of a typical 120-ampere cold-rated alternator at various rpm.

Pulley size may have to be customized to a particular motorhome or tow vehicle. Ideally, a pulley size should be selected so that the alternator produces a high rate of charge when the engine idles, but this usually can't be done because it causes the alternator to run at too high an rpm when driving at highway speeds, and the heat created could destroy the alternator. Many alternators, however, produce a decent amperage output at idle speed—below 2,000 rpm of the alternator.

Alternator Ratings

Alternators are given a so-called cold rating by the Society of Automotive Engineers (SAE) based on ampere output at an ambient temperature of 77°F (25°C). In hot weather, however, an alternator's temperature can be above 77°F even before the engine is started; therefore, some manufacturers give their products a hot rating (sometimes designated as KKK) based on the ampere output of the alternator at a temperature of 200°F (93.5°C). This rating is more realistic than the SAE's cold rating because it provides a more accurate rating of the alternator's output. Initially, the hot rating was developed for alternators used in emergency vehicles because of the large amount of 12-volt power they need.

Table 3-1 (pg. 46) compares alternator ratings from various manufacturers and includes the hot and cold ratings.

Heat

One of the by-products of alternating-current production is heat, and heat is the single most damaging factor affecting an alternator's life. As the alternator's rotor begins to turn, heat starts to build almost immediately. Heat diminishes the effectiveness of the electromagnetic process, so alternators are designed with built-in fans to push fast-moving air through the unit. The higher the turning speed of the rotor, the more current produced; however, the heat that builds with the faster rotation eventually reduces the ampere output. As the rotor spins, energy in the form of heat is produced in the wiring of its coil as current is produced in the stator. As the wiring becomes hot, resistance in the wiring increases, which, in turn, reduces alternator output. This reduced output, under normal operating conditions, is the basis for an alternator's hot rating. Heat build-up is one reason why an alternator may not deliver its cold-rated output.

Because the rectifier diodes are usually built into the alternator case, they are also subject to heat damage. In fact, the primary reason for alternator failure is diodes damaged by excessive heat. To prevent such damage, some alternator manufacturers locate the diodes of high-output alternators in a separate unit. One manufacturer, Wrangler Power Products, uses a special cooling fan to keep the diodes cool, resulting in a very high hot-rating output for its alternators.

Frequency

Another function of a spinning rotor is to control the frequency (i.e., the number of cycles per second, or Hz) of the current's ripple output. The faster the rotor turns, the higher the frequency becomes; slower turning lowers the frequency. A high frequency is desirable because it smooths out the ripples in the flow of direct current; a smooth flow is especially effective for battery charging because the charge is more readily accepted.

The number of poles in the rotor affects the output frequency. A three-phase alternator has a higher frequency than a single-phase alternator by a factor of three.

High-Capacity and Stock Alternators

The purpose of the standard stock alternator supplied with many motorhomes and most tow vehicles is usually just to supply the voltage and current needs of the vehicle—not to recharge deep-cycle batteries. The alternator supplied with large Class A motorhomes, however, being larger in amperage output, is generally better suited to handle deep-cycle battery charging than the alternator in smaller motorhomes and most tow vehicles.

In recent years, the big three automobile manufacturers have upgraded stock alternators and are equipping heavy-duty tow vehicles with higher amperage output units that are more practical for an RVer's needs. Fords, for example, currently have a 95-ampere alternator for large-size gasoline engines and a 125-ampere alternator for the diesel engine. Previously, alternator sizes were 35 to 50 amperes for gasoline engines and 60 amperes for the diesel.

After-market, high-output alternators such as the one shown in Figure 3-11 (pg. 48) provide ratings from 105 to more than 270 amperes. Small-frame alternators, those in the 105- to 135-ampere range, are the same size as stock alternators, so

Table 3-1.

Comparison of Alternator Ratings

Manufacturer	Model No.	Case Size	Dual Output	Voltage Output (Volts)	Cold Rating (Amps)	Hot Rating (Amps)	RPM
Ample Power	4023	Small	No	12	124	106	6500
Company	4024	Small	No	12	136	116	6500
	4059	Large	No	12	160	147	6500
	4060	Large	No	12	199	181	6500
	4109	Large	No	24	135	120	6500
Alternators normally supplied with the 3-Step Regulator.							
Balmar	9100	Small	Yes	12	80	N/A	3500
Products,	9110	Small	Yes	12	117	N/A	3500
Inc.	9135	Small	Yes	12	140	N/A	3500
	9124	Small	No	24	60	N/A	3500
	9235	Large	Yes	12	160	N/A	3500
	9265	Large	Yes	12	190	N/A	3500
	9200	Large	Yes	24	135	N/A	3500
	9400	Large	Yes	12	115	N/A	3500
	9612	Ex-large	Yes	12	225	N/A	N/A
	9624	Ex-large	Yes	24	150	N/A	N/A
Supplied with BRS standard regulator. Optional PB+Power feature boosts output 25% to one battery bank.							
Cruising	SB-105	Small	No	12	140	105	6000
Equipment	SB-130	Small	No	12	N/A	130	6000
Company	SB-165	Large	No	12	190	165	6000
Units sold without regulators.							
Lestek	9100	Small	No	12	119	100	4000
Manufacturing,	9135D	Small	Yes	12	135	98	5000
Inc.	9150D	Small	Yes	12	150	107	5300
	9410D	Large	Yes	12	115	88	4000
	9460D	Large	Yes	12	160	138	6000
	9490D	Large	Yes	12	190	165	5500
	Brute 210	Large	No	12	210	175	5000
	Brute 270	Large	No	12	270	248	5000
Supercharger module allows 25% boost to output.							
Computerized regulator for protection against overvoltage and spikes; adjustable voltage set point.							
Powerline	23-100	Small	No	12	100	90	4000
Division, Hehr	23-120	Small	No	12	120	100	4500
International	23-150	Small	No	12	150	115	5000

Manufacturer	Model No.	Case Size	Dual Output	Voltage Output (Volts)	Cold Rating (Amps)	Hot Rating (Amps)	RPM
Powerline	24-160	Large	No	12	160	140	6000
Division, Hehr	24-190	Large	No	12	190	160	5500
International	24-Series	Large	No	24	100	N/A	N/A
(cont.)	25-160	Large	No	12	130	N/A	3000
	25-190	Large	No	12	120	N/A	2500
	25-Series	Large	No	24	100	N/A	N/A

Large-case models with optional external rectifiers.

Manufacturer	Model No.	Case Size	Dual Output	Voltage Output (Volts)	Cold Rating (Amps)	Hot Rating (Amps)	RPM
Wrangler Power	120A	Medium	No	12	145	127	1800
Products	140A	Medium	No	12	165	148	1800
Powermate	160A	Medium	No	12	190	160	1800
	180A	Medium	No	12	215	181	1800
	140A	Large	No	12	165	148	1800
	160A	Large	No	12	190	160	1800
	180A	Large	No	12	215	181	1800
Powermate	120A	Medium	Yes	12	N/A	86	675
with	140A	Either	Yes	12	N/A	103	900
Mastercharge	160A	Either	Yes	12	N/A	105	900
	180A	Either	Yes	12	N/A	110	900
	225A	Either	Yes	12	N/A	113	900

Small-case 120-amp unit has 82-amp output at idle speed. Mastercharge version has fan-cooled external diode rectifiers allowing large-case alternator output in small-case models. These units have dual output and do not need a separate isolator. Note the low rpm needed to develop usable amperage output.

NOTE:
This table is for comparing alternator outputs at different rpm. Only the main specifications of the alternators are listed. For complete information, consult manufacturers' data sheets. For fast charging, it is desirable for an alternator to develop output at as low an rpm as possible.

switching to this type of alternator is easy because it will fit on existing brackets. Large-frame alternators hold more polar groups in the stator, which accounts for the higher output. They require large brackets that may have to be specially fabricated for certain installations.

Because high-output alternators have a higher operating amperage than most stock alternators, they usually have a higher idle rating as well. For instance, Wrangler Power Products' unit with a 120-ampere hot rating delivers an exceptional 86 amperes at idle speed—so much output at idle speed that it's enough to charge batteries with amperage to spare for other 12-volt demands. Most stock alternators deliver the highest output at highway speeds, with very low output at idle speed. Even at maximum output, these cold-rated units are only about 50 percent efficient:

47

An alternator with a cold rating of 60 amperes effectively delivers only 30 amperes at highway speeds.

Because the amperage output of an alternator is partly a function of rotor speed, which is controlled by engine speed, it is important to have an alternator with enough output to handle stop-and-go driving situations (e.g., driving a rig through cities) without losing too much amperage at idle speeds.

Those who own an older motorhome equipped with a *three-way*, or *automatic energy-selecting (AES)*, refrigerator who want to operate the refrigerator on 12-volt power while traveling should upgrade the stock alternator to a unit with a higher output. When AES refrigerators are operated on 12 volts, they can draw as much as 24 amperes. Many older stock alternators cannot handle such a load, particularly when trying to simultaneously meet the demands of the ignition system, which might be 8 amperes, and other 12-volt equipment, such as headlights. If the alternator cannot keep up with ampere demand, power has to come from some other source; that other source is the battery—until it goes dead. If you have an older motorhome, even without an AES refrigerator, it might be practical to upgrade your alternator. Most newer Class A motorhomes have adequately sized alternators with a rating of 125 amperes or higher.

Most tow vehicles built before the mid-1980s probably do not have alternators of a suitable size. Many passenger cars capable of towing, even new models, probably have undersized alternators.

Proper alternator selection depends, in part, on the style of RVing. RVers who regularly stay at campgrounds with electrical hookups may find the stock alternator satisfactory, but RVers who camp and use battery power will need an alternator capable of recharging the battery quickly and adequately.

Figure 3-11. Powerline's after-market, high-output, 120-ampere alternator. (Photo courtesy of Powerline Division, Hehr International)

Those who own an older motorhome equipped with a three-way, or automatic energy-selecting (AES), refrigerator who want to operate the refrigerator on 12-volt power while traveling should upgrade the stock alternator to a unit with a higher output.

Selecting the Proper-Size High-Output Alternator

It is not difficult to determine the right-size alternator for your RVing needs. For optimum battery charging, figure on a charging rate of about 25 amperes for a 105-ampere-hour battery, 50 amperes for a 210-ampere-hour bank, or 25 percent of the ampere-hour capacity of any battery or bank. If the battery bank is composed of gelled-cell rather than wet-cell batteries, a higher rate—50 percent of the ampere-hour rating of the bank—can be used. In addition, the amperage draw of certain other 12-volt equipment must be included. From Table 3-2, add together the amperes required for equipment normally used while driving. Add the total of 12-volt equipment amperes to the charging amperes required, and multiply this figure by 1.20 to arrive at a final total, which includes a 20-percent allowance for alternator inefficiency. The 20-percent allowance is for the so-called *80-percent rule*. An alternator should never continuously carry a load equal to its rated output. When operating for long periods, the load should not exceed 80 percent of the output rating. (This

Table 3-2.

Amperage Needs of 12-Volt Equipment During Driving

Equipment	Amperage	Wattage
Ignition system	3–6	44–87
Headlights, high-beam	12–18	245–260
Headlights, low-beam	8–14	115–200
Headlights, twin-beam	16–22	230–320
Tail/brake/side and license-plate lights	6–10	87–145
Parking lights	4–8	58–115
Roof marker lights	3–5	44–73
Driving lights or foglights	5–10	73–145
Roof off-road lights	40–70	580–1,000
Interior lights (3)	3–5	44–73
Air conditioner/heater	10–14	145–203
Refrigerator, 3-way	15–24	218–288
Stereo/cassette player	2–8	29–116
Furnace, blower	5–8	73–116
Fan, dashboard	1.2–3	18–44
CB radio, transmit mode	3	44

NOTE:
Typical amperage and wattage ranges are given. For precise calculations, use the equipment's actual amperage. For equipment rated in watts, divide the wattage by the alternator's voltage to get the amperage.

rule does not apply to all alternators, however, because some may be only 50 percent efficient.) Select an alternator hot-rated higher than the final total.

Here's a typical calculation: With a 210-ampere-hour battery bank, the deep-cycle, wet-cell batteries require an initial maximum charge of 50 amperes (about 25 percent of 210 ampere-hours). The alternator also must provide amperage for the dashboard air conditioner, 10 amperes; headlights and taillights, 24 amperes; stereo/cassette player, 2 amperes; and ignition, 4 amperes. A total of 40 amperes is required for operating the 12-volt equipment. The 50 amperes for battery charging added to the 40 amperes for the 12-volt equipment totals 90 amperes, which could conceivably be demanded of the alternator at one time. For alternator inefficiency, add 18 amperes (20 percent of 90) to 90, bringing the total to 108 amperes (Table 3-3). To properly meet these needs, an alternator with a hot rating of 100 to 125 amperes would be required; the 125-ampere rating would be best because of the extra reserve.

There might be problems with adding an after-market high-output alternator to some recent-model cars and trucks because the original-equipment alternators are controlled by the vehicle's computer system instead of a regulator. If you intend to switch alternators, consult with the alternator manufacturer for information about how such an installation should be made.

Table 3-3.

Calculating Alternator Size		
25 percent of 200-Ah battery bank		50 Amps
Air conditioner	10 Amps	
Headlights and taillights	24 Amps	
Stereo/cassette player	2 Amps	
Ignition system	4 Amps	
Total equipment amperage draw	40 Amps	40 Amps
Total amperage requirements		90 amps
Alternator inefficiency (20% of 90)		18 Amps
Total amperage required of alternator		108 Amps

NOTE:
Ah = ampere-hour

Alternator Regulation and Regulators

Years ago, one of our friends owned a sailboat powered by a big Ford diesel engine. His generator wasn't able to charge the batteries properly because of its regulator, so he rigged his own form of regulation. He installed a large-capacity *rheostat*—a variable resistor—in the field-current circuit from the batteries. The rheostat was manually adjusted to a high current-flow setting to provide maximum field current when the batteries were low, and to a lower setting when the batteries were charged. Because boat engines are generally run at a constant speed, or rpm, this system worked well—as long as he remembered to turn the rheostat down when the batteries were charged; otherwise, the batteries would be overcharged and ruined.

An advantage of this simple system was that a large bulk charge, at a high-amperage rate, could be delivered to the batteries when they were deeply discharged. The rheostat, or regulator, could then be adjusted to a lower amperage rate as the batteries became charged. Finally, a very low maintenance charge could be applied after the batteries were fully charged.

We use this anecdote to illustrate regulation in its simplest form; it should help in understanding the more complicated types. A more sophisticated form of our friend's rheostat regulator is the Weems & Plath AutoCHARGE Alternator Control (Figure 3-12).

Every alternator has a regulator, which, except for minor fluctuations, controls the alternator's output and maintains a constant, fixed voltage. In the regulator, a *transistor* acts like a switch, turning the field current on and off to hold the voltage output of the alternator as constant as needed. A regulator may also have automatic temperature compensation; a *thermistor* changes its resistance with the temperature, thereby varying the field-current flow controlling the alternator output to match temperature variations in the alternator.

The voltage control provides enough current to operate the vehicle's engine, lights, and other electrical equipment, as well as to recharge the battery when necessary. If the battery needs a charge, the regulator senses the low voltage and proportionately increases the field current to the rotor, which then increases the magnetic field. The stronger magnetic field produces more current flow, holding the voltage to the desired level to effect the charge. The regulator produces a high-charge current until the battery voltage rises to about 13 volts; the current then begins to

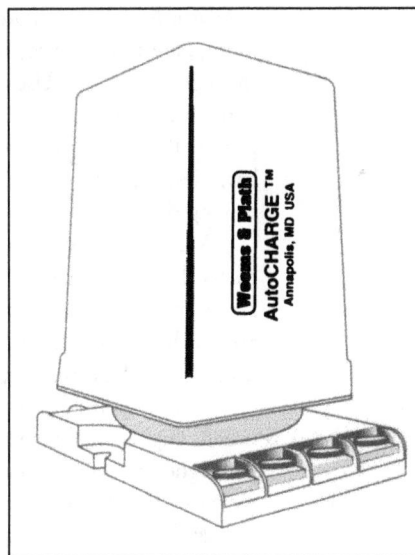

Figure 3-12. The Weems & Plath AutoCHARGE Alternator Control. This unit is a supplement to the existing alternator regulator. It allows the alternator to deliver maximum amperage until 14.8 volts is reached, then it shuts down and the existing regulator takes over.
(Illustration courtesy of Weems & Plath)

51

taper off so there is very little current flowing by the time it reaches the set voltage of the regulator.

When the battery is fully charged and there are no other electrical demands on the alternator, the regulator decreases the field current to reduce the magnetic field in the rotor, which, in turn, reduces the output just enough to hold the voltage steady. If the lights are turned on, the voltage will drop slightly, causing the regulator to again increase the field current just enough to maintain the voltage at a constant level to handle the increased load. The regulator also protects the alternator from excessive heat and voltage that could damage or burn out the unit.

Stock alternators usually have *internal,* or *built-in, regulators,* but an internal regulator has several disadvantages. The solid-state elements, along with the rectifier diodes, are subjected to the extreme temperature of the alternator, which can cause the regulator to fail. Usually an internal regulator cannot be adjusted or replaced with an external regulator. Most internal regulators are temperature-compensated to protect the alternator, but have a tendency either to undercharge or overcharge the batteries, depending on the voltage set point of the regulator and the amount of driving done.

Most stock regulators are set for an output voltage from 13.8 to 14.0 volts. A partly discharged battery with a voltage of, say, 12.4 volts, will accept a charge current until the battery voltage reaches the regulator's set voltage. As the two voltages approach equalization, the regulator holds the alternator's output at this voltage in order to handle other amperage needs of the vehicle after the battery is charged.

The set point of the regulator in most high-output, after-market alternators is usually higher than in stock alternators, ranging from 14.0 to 14.8 volts. Because of the higher voltage, an after-market alternator with the automotive type of regulator we have been discussing will be more likely over a long period of charging to overcharge the battery, boiling away the electrolyte in the process. If a high-output alternator is used to charge wet-cell batteries, the water level in the batteries should be checked frequently, particularly during hot weather.

Although a regulator's purpose is to maintain the SLI battery at full charge, along with handling the electrical demands of the vehicle, it does not perform these jobs at maximum efficiency. It would be ideal if the regulator limited the upper levels of voltage so that excessively high voltage wouldn't cause headlights, for example, which are designed to operate on 12 volts, to burn out prematurely (halogen headlights are especially susceptible), while still providing a high-enough voltage to charge the battery (usually 13.8 volts). At this normal setting, however, the regulator can't handle these demands without a compromise that primarily affects the battery: It either undercharges the battery if only a few miles are driven, or overcharges a fully charged battery during a long period of driving.

Multistage Regulators

Recharging deep-cycle batteries can be accomplished more efficiently with regulators designed for multistage charging. A *multistage regulator* functions as a constant-current regulator during the first, or bulk, charge stage. In this stage, some multistage regulators use full field current to achieve maximum alternator current; the maximum current output allowed by these units is not regulated in the truest sense, but the effect is the same. Other multistage regulators have some means of current limiting, which allows the alternator to produce only as much current as the limitation permits.

During the first, or bulk, stage, the maximum current continues until the battery voltage reaches the set point, which is typically 14.4, but can be as high as 14.6. The regulator holds this voltage constant throughout the second, or absorption, stage, but allows the current output to diminish as necessary to maintain the voltage. When the battery acceptance rate has diminished to another set point, which might correspond to 2 to 5 percent of ampere-hour capacity, the battery is considered charged; on some regulators a timer determines when this point is reached. Then, in the third, or float, stage, the voltage regulation trips to a lower float voltage, perhaps 13.5 volts, which is also held constant.

Recharging deep-cycle batteries can be accomplished more efficiently with regulators designed for multistage charging.

Other features found on some regulators are a manually set equalization stage, a switch for selecting wet- or gelled-cell batteries, and a time delay that allows 90 seconds for engine warm-up before a charge load is applied to the alternator. A monitoring panel, or panel interface, is an adjunct to some regulators, and the panel may control the regulator's operation.

The set points for 24-volt multistage charging are usually double the amount of voltage of the set points for 12-volt charging. Typically, the bulk stage set point is 28.8 volts (28.2 volts for gelled-cell batteries); the float stage, 26.4 volts (27.0 volts for gelled-cell batteries); and the equalization stage, 32.6 volts.

A high-output alternator coupled with a multistage regulator and sealed batteries, preferably gelled cells, not only increases battery capacity (yes, actually increases battery capacity), but also provides the most efficient battery charging. It's especially suitable for RVers who often camp in places without electrical hookups.

Multistage regulators and alternators are expensive compared to high-output alternators with stock automotive regulators. It is possible to install a multistage regulator on almost any alternator with an external regulator, providing the proper electrical connections can be made, but it is more practical to use an alternator for which these regulators were designed. If a multistage regulator were to

Table 3-4.

External Automotive Regulators—Special Types

Manufacturer	Model	Type	Battery Type	Adjustable Set Points	Current Limiting During Bulk Stage	Absorption Stage Limiting
Ample Power Company	3-Step Deep-Cycle Regulator	external multistage	wet or gel cell	absorption (bulk) and float voltage	no	45-minute timer
	Next Step Regulator	external multistage	wet or gel cell	absorption voltage temperature compensating	no	adjustable timer
	Smart Alternator Regulator (SAR)	external multistage	wet or gel cell	no, uses 12 voltage set points for automatic variation of charging process	switch-controlled and fully adjustable	automatic
Balmar Power Systems	ARS (Advanced Regulation System)	external two-stage	wet or gel cell	one, absorption stage	yes	none
Cruising Equipment Company (CECO)	Alpha Regulator	external multistage	wet or gel cell	absorption (bulk) and float voltage	no	adjustable timer from ½ hour to 4½ hours
	Quad-Cycle Regulator/Monitor	external multistage	wet or gel cell	none for voltage	adjustable for maximum alternator current output	controlled by charge current flow dropping to 10% of adjusted amperage limit
	Ideal Regulator	external multistage	wet or gel cell	no, fixed voltages for both absorption and float stages, selectable by battery type	yes, by rotary switch; adjustable for maximum of alternator current output	controlled by charge current flow dropping to 10% of adjusted amperage limit
Powerline Division, Hehr International	Multi-Step Marine Regulator	external multistage	wet or gel cell	absorption (bulk) and float voltages	yes	30-minute timer

This table lists only regulators with special features; no standard automotive-type regulators are included.

Warm-Up Delay	Monitoring Meter	Battery Voltage Sensing	Temperature Compensation	Comments
no	no	yes	no	regulator can be used on any P-type externally regulated alternator on either motorhomes or tow vehicles
no	no, but interfaces to Energy Monitor II panel	yes	yes	unit functions with either P- or N-type alternators, available in either 12- or 24-volt models, has voltage cutback for headlight protection, for both motorhomes and tow vehicles
yes	no, but interfaces to ESP monitor	two banks	yes	can control two alternators at same time, complete runaway voltage protection, voltage cutback to prevent headlight burnout, 24-volt model available, will fit any P-type alternators including those with internal regulators if modified, for both motorhomes and tow vehicles
yes	no	yes, three banks	no	for both motorhomes and tow vehicles
no	no	yes	no	has connecting plug compatible with most high-output alternators of other manufacturers, for both motorhomes and tow vehicles
no	yes, complete monitor control of system (see comments below)	yes, up to three banks	no, only ambient temperature of regulator	the monitoring panel is the regulator, voltage and current readings automatically control all charging functions, monitoring panel also has capability to monitor amperage consumption, AC voltage, AC current, and water and fuel tank levels, best suited for motorhome installation because of complex wiring harness needed between tow vehicle and trailer
yes	yes (see comments below)	two banks	switch selectable for hot or cold setting	regulator is an option for CECO's Amp-Hours+ and Amp-Hours+2 meters (see Table 10-1), Regulator Terminal Board connects to Monitor Terminal Board interfaced via a ribbon cable to the meter panel, best suited for motorhome installation because of complex wiring harness needed between tow vehicle and trailer
yes, 90 seconds	no	yes	yes	voltage cutback for headlight protection, can be used in conjunction with Powerline's alternators or others, for both motorhomes and tow vehicles

(continued on next page)

55

Manufacturer	Model	Type	Battery Type	Adjustable Set Points	Current Limiting During Bulk Stage	Absorption Stage Limiting
Weems & Plath	AutoCHARGE Regulator Supplement	external constant amperage control	wet or gel cell	no	no	no

This table lists only regulators with special features; no standard automotive-type regulators are included.

Figure 3-13. Ample Power Company's Next Step multi-stage regulator. (Photo courtesy of Ample Power Company)

Figure 3-14. The Alpha multistage regulator from CECO. (Photo courtesy of Cruising Equipment Co.)

be used with an existing low-amperage stock alternator, the alternator would need to have an amperage capacity to match the performance that may be required by the regulator.

The large size of some control units of multistage regulators may make installation impossible in Class C motorhomes and tow vehicles. Many of the companies that make alternators also make companion multistage regulators, which are listed in Table 3-4. Regulators from two of the manufacturers are shown in Figures 3-13 and 3-14.

Warm-Up Delay	Monitoring Meter	Battery Voltage Sensing	Temperature Compensation	Comments
no	no	no	no	This unit is not a regulator, but a supplement to the stock regulator installed in the wiring between the regulator and the alternator. It forces the alternator to deliver full amperage until voltage reaches 14.8 volts, then shuts off and the stock regulator takes over. Can be installed on many alternators, including some with internal regulators. For either motorhomes or tow vehicles.

Battery Isolators and Switches

If two batteries, or two battery-bank circuits, are joined at the alternator for charging purposes, and the engine is not running and current is drawn from the house battery, current will also flow from the SLI battery and vice versa. This creates a situation experienced by many RVers: They have been camping in a place without an electrical hookup for a short stay, or overnight, and have been operating on battery power, unaware that the SLI battery was discharging along with the house batteries. Then, when it came time to start the engine, there wasn't enough power left in the SLI battery to do so.

Those with trailers can separate the SLI battery from the house batteries simply by unplugging the trailer electrical connector cable (TECC) from the receptacle on the tow vehicle; those with motorhomes don't have this option. (This cable is called by many different names, some of which include the manufacturer's name, such as the Bargman connector; however, to avoid ambiguity, we refer to it as the TECC.) The problem can be eliminated, however, by installing either a battery selector switch or an isolator.

Battery Selector Switches

Many motorhomes are equipped with a marine-type, *three-way battery selector switch* (Figure 3-15, pg. 58). It keeps battery circuits separate and allows service to be selected from either the SLI battery or the house batteries simply by turning the switch to the desired setting. This type of switch is made by Perko, Inc.; Guest Company, Inc.; and Cole Hersee Company. The switches are explosion-proof and designed to han-

57

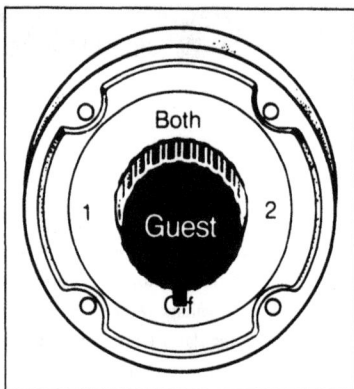

Figure 3-15. Battery selector switch.
(Illustration courtesy of Guest Company, Inc.)

dle several hundred amperes through the switch contacts.

When the battery selector switch is turned to the Battery 1 or Battery 2 setting, depending on how it is wired, current is drawn from either the SLI battery or the house batteries. The switch also can be turned to the "Both" setting for charging both banks at the same time or to provide an extra boost for engine starting by placing both banks in parallel. The usual procedure is to set the battery switch on "Both" and start the engine. After arriving at the destination, the engine is turned off and the switch is turned to the setting for the house batteries. It is important to remember to switch back to separate the banks after the engine is turned off. If the switch is turned through the "Off" position when the alternator is in operation, the output will surge from a full-power load to no load and back again, placing a huge surge of current—as high as 50 volts—on the diodes in the alternator, which can cause them to burn out. Some high-quality alternators have special circuitry built in to protect the diodes from such a surge.

Some battery selector switches have an alternator disconnect feature; the field current from the regulator to the alternator is turned off when the switch is in the "Off" position, thus protecting the diodes. Not all alternators can be connected to this type of switch, however. (Another method of protecting diodes is the Zap Stop made by Cruising Equipment Company. It is a special diode that conducts the alternator's output to ground if the voltage rises above 16 volts.)

If the switch is turned through the "Off" position when the alternator is in operation, the output will surge from a full-power load to no load and back again, placing a huge surge of current— as high as 50 volts—on the diodes in the alternator, which can cause them to burn out.

Using a battery selector switch is a simple solution to the problem created by the existence of two battery banks for different purposes.

A battery selector switch could not be used in a trailer to protect the SLI battery because the starting battery is located in the tow vehicle and is not part of the trailer's electrical system. The only reason for having such a switch in a trailer would be when two house battery banks with two or more batteries each were used. Each bank could be selected independently of the other for normal power needs; when a large ampere-hour capacity was needed to supply power for an inverter, for example, all banks could be connected together. They could also be connected together for charging, and each bank could be allowed to rest after it was charged while another bank provided the house power—a good practice for battery longevity.

There is no advantage to using a battery selector switch for just one bank of two 12-volt house batteries. It would serve no purpose, and the heavy-gauge wiring required would make such a setup cumbersome. For safety's sake, any battery or battery bank should have a switch to shut off all battery power in case of an electrical fire in the DC system. All RVs supposedly are protected by a master fuse or circuit breaker but, as far as we are concerned, we would be jeopardizing our trailer by depending on a fuse to blow in time to prevent real damage. A wiring fire broke out in a unit we once owned and the battery switch was used to immediately disconnect the batteries, avoiding serious damage.

We think RV manufacturers should be required to install a battery cut-off switch inside the RV where it can be easily reached (even an inconveniently located switch is better than none); unfortunately, no such regulation exists.

We think RV manufacturers should be required to install a battery cut-off switch inside the RV where it can be easily reached (even an inconveniently located switch is better than none); unfortunately, no such regulation exists.

Isolators

If a battery selector switch is not used, there should be some other way to prevent the batteries in one bank from being drained when another bank is being used. It is possible to install just one suitably sized diode in the SLI battery's alternator circuit, which would at least prevent the SLI battery from discharging along with the house batteries; however, it is better to use a *mechanical-relay isolator* or *solid-state diode isolator* for this purpose (Figure 3-16). It is likely that some kind of isolator is part of a motorhome's standard equipment, but those with trailers should consider installing an isolator in the tow vehicle. It's an extra safety feature that eliminates problems with untoward battery discharge.

Solid-state diode isolators achieve battery separation electronically by allowing current to flow through the diodes in only one direction from the

Figure 3-16. A 130-ampere two-battery diode isolator. An isolator separates two batteries so the discharging of one battery will not affect the state of charge of the other. *(Photo courtesy of Sure Power Industries, Inc.)*

59

alternator to each of the two batteries, or banks, but not toward each other. The battery or bank that needs the charge will receive it; the one that does not will refuse the charge.

The mechanical-relay or solenoid-type isolator is activated by the ignition switch of the motorhome or tow vehicle. When the switch is turned on, a solenoid closes an electromagnetic switch, which connects the starting battery to the alternator circuit. The battery will be charged by the alternator as long as the ignition switch is in the "On" position. When the switch is turned off, the solenoid springs back, breaking the connection, thereby protecting the starting battery from being drained as the house battery is used.

Each type of isolator has pros and cons. A disadvantage of the solid-state diode isolator is a voltage loss across the diodes that amounts to a drop of 0.6 volt or more. To overcome this loss, the alternator is forced to deliver a higher voltage than otherwise would be needed, overworking the alternator. If the isolator has a loss of 0.6 volt, the alternator has to put out 14.8 volts to deliver 14.2 volts to the battery.

Diodes can become very hot during the charging process because they carry the full ampere output of the alternator; therefore, they are usually mounted on a *heat sink*, a metal device with fins to disperse the heat into the air. A solid-state diode isolator with Schottky diodes has about half as much voltage loss as the cheaper silicon diodes found in some units. The type of diode used in an isolator should be indicated in the manufacturer's description of the product.

A mechanical-relay isolator has a direct connection by the nature of its switching and, therefore, causes no voltage loss; however, since the solenoid is spring-loaded, it is subject to wearing out and breakage. Another disadvantage is that the switch contacts carry a high amperage so the contacts can arc and burn, which would destroy the effectiveness of the isolator.

When selecting an isolator of either type, choose one that has a higher amperage rating than the alternator. For example, use a 150-ampere isolator with a 125-ampere alternator. Beware of cheap mechanical-relay isolators with a low load rating that will not carry the load of the alternator. Solid-state diode isolators can cost two to three times more than mechanical-relay isolators.

Battery Sense Lines

The purpose of a *battery sense line* is to measure voltage at the battery while it is charging; some battery sense lines also measure for temperature. Alternators with internal regulators do not have battery sense lines, and only in recent years have battery sense lines been included on some external regulators. In an alternator without a sense line, the regulator can measure only the alternator's output voltage.

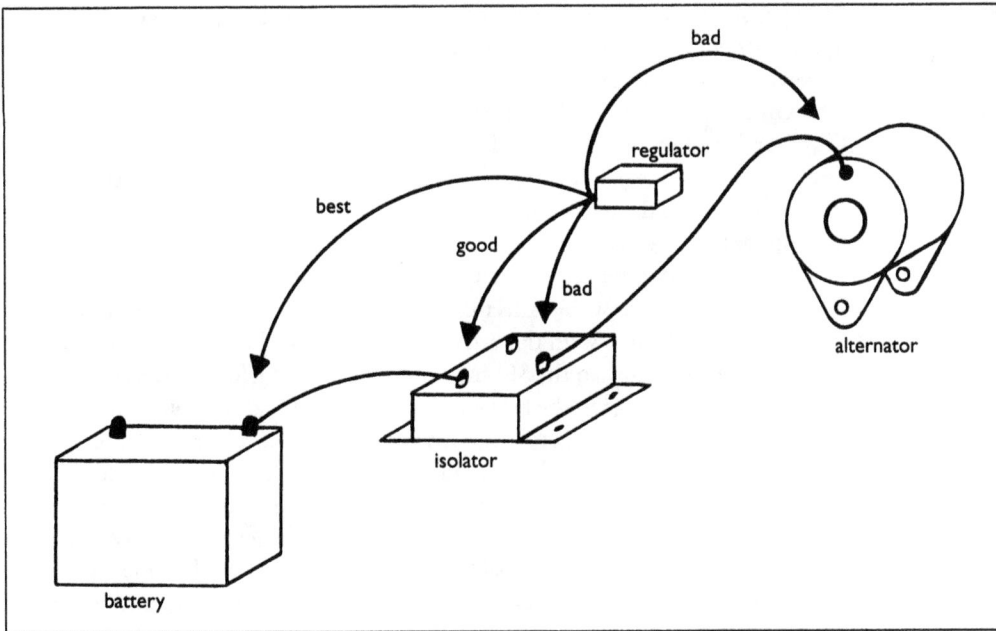

Figure 3-17. A diagram showing various ways of connecting a regulator's battery sense line.

When installing an isolator in an alternator circuit with a battery sense line, it is important to know how the sense line is connected to the battery. Trace the sense line from the regulator back toward the battery to ascertain this. A direct connection to the battery is desirable (Figure 3-17), but if the sense line is instead wired to the charging line, it must not be connected on the alternator side of the isolator. Wiring in this manner would allow the regulator to sense the alternator output voltage rather than the battery voltage, and the former is higher than the latter by the amount of the voltage drop, 0.6 volt, across the isolator diode. Thus, the regulator would reduce alternator output more than it should. If the sense line cannot be hooked up to the battery side of the isolator, a diode with the same voltage drop as the diode in the isolator, but with a lower amperage rating, can be installed in the battery sense line to the regulator. This fools the regulator into providing additional output from the alternator to compensate for the voltage drop across the isolator. A lower-amperage-rated diode can be used because it will not have to carry the high amperage output of the alternator, only the much lower amperage of the battery sense line.

These problems won't occur if the regulator has two sense lines, one of which is wired directly to each battery bank; the bank that needs the charge will get it. This

61

wiring is simple in a motorhome; however, between a trailer and a tow vehicle, two special battery sense lines have to be run: one positive and one negative, with all the necessary plug connections.

On a tow vehicle's stock alternator, the regulator usually has only one sense line, if any, and it is connected to the SLI battery. Consequently, the SLI battery is usually kept fully charged, when it is most likely the house batteries that need extensive recharging. When the sense line is connected to the SLI battery, the house batteries are constantly undercharged.

Why not connect a single battery sense line to the house battery circuit instead of the SLI battery so it would affect the regulator's field-current output? To do so would create problems. With this arrangement, the sense line would read the house battery voltage rather than the SLI battery voltage, thereby forcing the alternator to provide a greater charge to the house battery. This could be of value in motorhomes but not in tow vehicles because, when driving without the trailer, the battery sense line would not be connected to anything and the alternator would not function. Another problem with this arrangement is that the starting battery would probably be constantly overcharged by the greater output of the alternator. For these reasons, the best arrangement of a single battery sense line is to connect it to the SLI battery.

If you are having a problem with battery charging, and your regulator has a battery sense line, trace the line and make a diagram of how your system is wired.

If you are having a problem with battery charging, and your regulator has a battery sense line, trace the line and make a diagram of how your system is wired. The diagram should point out where any improper connections may have been made. Keep the wiring diagram on file; if a problem arises in the future, it will help in tracking it down and correcting it.

Circuit Breakers

A circuit breaker of a suitable amperage should be installed between the isolator and each battery bank. Suitable amperage is the next size above the alternator output amperage; for example, a 150-ampere circuit breaker for a 135-ampere alternator.

Dual-Output Alternators

A *dual-output alternator* has a built-in isolator: An extra set of diodes in the output circuit of the alternator connects to two output terminals, one for each battery bank. A disadvantage of this type of alternator is that the diodes are in the alternator case where they are subjected to the same heat build-up as units with the rectifier diodes in the case.

If you want to obtain the total amperage output of a dual-output alternator, both outputs must be measured and added together. The overall output is diminished because part of it is constantly going to a starting battery that may not need charging; therefore, that output is not available for charging the more deeply discharged house batteries.

Summary

After all this information about alternators and regulators, you may be confused about which types are best for your needs. At the risk of being criticized for turning a noun into a verb, let us "nutshell" it for you.

A stock automotive-type regulator builds charging voltage until it reaches 13.8 to 14.0 volts, where it is held constant. The battery accepts the charge at its own diffusion rate until it is charged. As the difference between the battery and charging voltages diminishes, the amperage rate declines rapidly because of the slow diffusion taking place in the battery, so it will take many hours until the charge rate drops to about 10 percent of the battery's ampere-hour rating. This "full" charge, however, is probably only about 85 percent of the battery's true capacity.

Charging with a high-output alternator and a standard regulator creates some of the same problems. A high-output alternator delivers a high-amperage rate at the beginning of the charge cycle even if its output is a low-charging voltage of 13.8 to 14.0 volts; however, many of these units have a charge voltage as high as 14.2 or 14.6 volts. This allows faster charging, but the higher voltage with its higher amperage can result in overcharging. This causes excessive heat in the battery and is the primary reason for an increased rate of electrolyte loss. Liquid has to be added to the electrolyte frequently, which increases battery maintenance.

High voltage also takes its toll on headlights and other lightbulbs by shortening their life. They are designed to operate on 12.0 volts, not 14.4 volts. If the regulator has an adjustable voltage set point, a compromise can be achieved if it is adjusted to the point where gassing of the electrolyte can be held to a minimum and bulb life prolonged. Some regulators have an automatic voltage control wired to the headlight switch. When headlights are on, the regulator limits the charge voltage to no more than 13.8 or 14.0 volts to prevent premature bulb burnout.

Multistage charging coupled with high alternator output charges batteries in the most efficient manner and is the fastest and, in our opinion, the best method for charging deep-cycle batteries.

Multistage charging coupled with high alternator output charges batteries in the

63

most efficient manner and is the fastest and, in our opinion, the best method for charging deep-cycle batteries. There is still a slight danger of overcharging the SLI battery, however, because of the higher voltages applied during the first and second stages to what may be a fully charged battery.

Multistage regulators require different voltage set points depending on whether wet-cell or sealed batteries are to be charged. Multistage regulators are more expensive than other types of regulators and, for such a highly efficient system, a more sophisticated means of monitoring voltage and amperage than just the analog ammeter or voltmeter gauges in the dashboard is needed. A digital monitoring panel, also rather expensive, should be part of the system (see Chapter 10).

The system selected should depend on the type of camping done and the RVer's particular needs. For normal use, a motorhome or tow vehicle should have at least a 90-ampere alternator. A smaller alternator cannot keep up with normal electrical consumption. The 60-ampere stock alternator in our tow vehicle provided just barely enough output to handle the load of the air conditioner and the fan at its high setting. At night, with headlights added to the load, the batteries could have become seriously depleted if we hadn't turned off the air conditioner or, at the very least, kept the fan on one of the lower settings.

Twelve-volt equipment, such as high-wattage stereos and CD players, off-road lights, fog lights, spotlights, and power winches, can require an enormous amount of amperage. Use Table 3-3 (pg. 50) to determine the size alternator you need.

Twelve-volt equipment, such as high-wattage stereos and CD players, off-road lights, fog lights, spotlights, and power winches, can require an enormous amount of amperage.

Another way of approaching this decision is to analyze your camping style. If you spend most of your time in campgrounds with electrical hookups and don't have too much high-wattage equipment that operates from the SLI battery, perhaps stock equipment will suffice. Using much high-wattage equipment, however, requires a high-output alternator. A multistage regulator with a high-output alternator is the best choice if you usually camp in places where there are no hookups and if your RV's 12-volt equipment is operated on power from the deep-cycle house batteries.

FOUR

Circuits and Wiring of the 12-Volt DC System

RV manufacturers tend to emulate houses when it comes to interior decor and furnishings, keeping pace with the latest decorating trends and designer colors. The 12-volt electrical system, however, which provides the power for the water pump, forced-air furnace, interior lights, and many other conveniences that make an RV homelike, has not been improved since the 1960s when it was first implemented in RVs. The system has not been updated for the needs of today's RVers and, what is more, in most units the way the wiring is installed makes it difficult for the RVer to upgrade or repair the system.

Wiring

Most RV wiring is installed in a manner that is convenient only for the manufacturer. No thought is given to accessing the wiring for any problems that develop. A common manufacturing practice is to string the wires for the main circuits along a subfloor, over which the main floor is then installed; the wires can't be reached unless the floor is ripped out. Main circuit wires usually come up through a hole in the floor, perhaps inside a cabinet; branch circuit wires are commonly bunched together and joined to the main circuit wires with wire nuts.

In one trailer we owned, a wire bundle was located on the floor of the cabinet under the sink. When the water pump stopped working, we found the cause: Items stored in the cabinet rubbed against the bundle when the trailer was moving, loosening the wire nut on the water pump circuit. To protect the bundle, we installed a covering that doubled as a shelf and put some of the smaller items in boxes to keep them from shifting around during travel. Another bundle was in an outside compartment, on the floor, smack in the center of the door opening, where it was bumped every time items were put in or taken out of the compartment.

Most wiring for interior and running lights is just as inaccessible because it is in the walls and end caps of the RV. If fiberglass batting is used for insulation, wiring usually runs between the insulation and the inside wall. If foam block insulation is used, the blocks are often split to provide a channel for the wire. Either way, wall panels need to be removed to reach the wires for repairs.

In units with block foam insulation, installing new electrical equipment (e.g., an extra light fixture or stereo speakers) often requires routing wires through cabinets or along the floor. We have run wiring in this manner in our present trailer; our previous trailer had fiberglass insulation and we were able to snake wires inside the wall for some installations. It would be ideal if wires could be routed loosely through conduit, PVC pipe, or a wooden channel so they could be easily reached for repairs or for installing new equipment without too much dismantling of the RV.

Wire Runs

An even more grievous problem with the electrical systems on many RVs is the illogical locations of the *converter/charger* (which converts AC voltage to DC voltage and charges the batteries), fuse panel, and batteries; their installation seems to be an afterthought. Where these items are located, especially relative to one another, is extremely important because of the wire runs involved. We have seen many newer mid-size and large RVs, both trailers and motorhomes, in which the converter/charger is located in a cabinet at the rear of the unit and the batteries are at the front. In this arrangement, connecting wires have to run the entire length of the RV. The manufacturers who locate this electrical equipment so far apart either don't know or ignore a basic tenet of electricity: The longer a length of wire, the greater the resistance to current flow; the greater the resistance, the higher the voltage drop at the other end of the wire.

We have seen many newer mid-size and large RVs, both trailers and motorhomes, in which the converter/charger is located in a cabinet at the rear of the unit and the batteries are at the front. The manufacturers who locate this electrical equipment so far apart either don't know or ignore a basic tenet of electricity.

When current flowing in a circuit exceeds the wire's *ampacity* (i.e., the capacity, in amperes, a wire can accommodate), heat builds and resistance increases, creating a larger voltage drop than normal. As the voltage drops, the equipment operating on the circuit requires more amperage to function at its proper wattage, or power, thereby building more heat and further increasing the resistance until either a fuse blows, a circuit breaker trips, or, worse, the wire insulation begins to burn.

We recently saw a 31-foot trailer with a converter/charger incorporating a fuse panel (many new RVs have this equipment) installed in a cabinet on the rear wall, with the batteries located at the front. In a straight line, they were 25 feet apart (we measured it); the actual wire run was probably about 5 feet longer due to routing up through the floor and into the cabinet and battery compartment, making a wire run of about 30 feet. Of course, a circuit cannot be completed without a positive and a negative wire, so the total distance was about 60 feet. This long wire run with its inherent problems—mainly that the batteries won't be efficiently charged—could have been avoided if the converter/charger had been located closer to the batteries.

Voltage drop can be largely overcome if the proper gauge wire is used, but, here again, many manufacturers use wire of a gauge that is not heavy-duty enough. A wire's diameter is its *gauge,* which is denoted by a number printed at intervals on the wire's covering. Preceding the number are the letters AWG, the abbreviation for American Wire Gauge. Wires rated to carry the most amperage have lower numbers. For example, 4-gauge wire is rated to carry more amperage than 10-gauge wire. Wires with low-number gauges have greater diameters than wires with higher gauges.

If the converter/charger is putting out 14 volts (a typical output), a half-volt drop means that only 13.5 volts is reaching the battery, so it will take many hours for a full charge.

It is not uncommon to find RVs with 10-gauge wire being used for a long run between the converter/charger and the batteries. As Table 4-1 (pg. 68) shows, 10-gauge wire has a resistance of 0.00102 ohm per foot. The resistance multiplied by the number of feet of wire equals the resistance in the run; for example, a 60-foot run of 10-gauge wire has a resistance of 0.0612 ohm. If the converter/charger is an 8-ampere model (as it was in the 31-foot trailer), the voltage drop amounts to 0.4896 volt (0.0612 multiplied by 8) or, rounded off, almost half a volt. If the converter/charger is putting out 14 volts (a typical output), a half-volt drop means that only 13.5 volts is reaching the battery—not enough to charge it at more than a *trickle charge,* so it will take many hours for a full charge.

The manufacturer that makes the converter/charger described previously also makes a 20-ampere unit. The same figures applied to the higher amperage converter/charger would result in a voltage drop of 1.224 volts, so only 12.78 volts would reach the battery. Since the voltage of a completely charged battery is 12.63 volts, the converter/charger with the 1.224-volt drop could not charge the battery quickly, if at all. It might take many weeks for recharging because the voltage reaching the battery is just slightly more than when the battery is fully charged. If the proper gauge wire is used, however, both the 8- and 20-ampere converter/chargers can do the job for which they were designed.

Some wiring problems are a result of the National Electric Code (NEC), which is concerned only with fire safety, not operational efficiency. Article 551, which cov-

12-Volt Circuits and Wiring

Table 4-1.

Copper Wire Specifications				
American Wire Gauge	Maximum Ampacity*	Resistance in Ohms per Foot	Diameter in Mils**	Area in Circular Mils
4/0	260	0.000050	460.0	212000
3/0	225	0.000063	410.0	168000
2/0	195	0.0000795	365.0	133000
1/0	170	0.0001	325.0	106000
1	150	0.000126	289.0	83700
2	130	0.000159	258.0	66400
4	95	0.000253	204.0	41700
6	75	0.000403	162.0	26300
8	55	0.000641	128.0	16500
10	30	0.00102	102.0	10400
12	25	0.00162	81.0	6530
14	20	0.00258	64.0	4110
16	10	0.00409	51.0	2580

NOTES:

*Rated at 86°F (30°C) for continuous use.

**A mil is 0.001 inch. A circular mil is a square mil multiplied by pi/4. The circular mil (c.m.) of a wire is the square of the mil diameter.

Some numbers are rounded off to nearest whole number.

Another method of determining voltage drop is by using the c.m. of the conductor. This method takes into consideration the footage of the wire run. The formula is:

$$V = (10.75 \times L \times I) \div C$$

Where V is the voltage drop, 10.75 is the factor, L is the length of wire run, I is the amperage of the circuit, and C is the c.m. of the conductor.

For determining the wire size for a given voltage drop, the formula is changed to:

$$C = (10.75 \times L \times I) \div V$$

Because of variations in the formula, it's best to use the next size larger wire than the formula indicates.

ers RV construction, stipulates that manufacturers must protect each circuit with a fuse or circuit breaker no greater than the ampacity of the wire used. No mention is made of the length of the wire run or the voltage drop. Manufacturers can install whatever wire size is required by the NEC for the converter/charger's rated output, but need not consider how well the converter/charger functions with that size wire.

Table 4-1 lists the figures for the ampacity of wire on a continuous basis. For example, using 10-gauge wire for a long period at a steady 30 amperes safely carries the load, although it can carry slightly more amperage on an intermittent basis. For

RV Electrical Systems

the battery to receive the proper voltage using the 20-ampere converter/charger mentioned previously and 10-gauge wire, the total run would have to be no longer than 13 feet (6½ feet each for the positive and negative wires).

Here's how this example was determined (by trial and error): Using 14 volts (the typical charging rate) for the charge voltage, and multiplying 13 feet by a per-foot resistance of 0.00102 ohm, equals a total resistance of 0.01326 ohm. The next step is another application of Ohm's Law (resistance multiplied by amperage equals voltage, or $R \times I = V$): 0.01326 ohm, multiplied by 30 amperes, results in a 0.3978-volt drop. This is slightly less than the recommended drop of 3 percent of 14 volts (0.42) for most circuits. A 3-percent drop is acceptable for some wiring applications; however, since the wire in this example is a charging circuit, the wire size should allow a drop of no greater than 1 percent for efficient charging.

Table 4-2 compares voltage drops for various voltages at 1 and 3 percent. No matter what the voltage drop, wire smaller than 14 gauge should not be used for normal DC house circuits.

Table 4-3 (pg. 70) can be used to figure voltage drops. Determine the maximum amperage the wire will carry and select the corresponding amperage chart. Find the distance of the wire run and the anticipated wire size. The figure at which these two columns intersect is the voltage drop. If the wire size allows too great a voltage drop, select a wire size that provides a smaller voltage drop. Include the combined length of the positive and negative wires in the calculation.

Table 4-2.

Voltage Drops of 1% and 3% for Different Voltages

12 Volts

1%	(14 volts x 0.01)	=	0.14 voltage drop
3%	(14 volts x 0.03)	=	0.42 voltage drop
1%	(13 volts x 0.01)	=	0.13 voltage drop
3%	(13 volts x 0.03)	=	0.39 voltage drop
1%	(12 volts x 0.01)	=	0.12 voltage drop
3%	(12 volts x 0.03)	=	0.36 voltage drop

24 Volts

1%	(28 volts x 0.01)	=	0.28 voltage drop
3%	(28 volts x 0.03)	=	0.84 voltage drop

NOTE:
The 3% drop is acceptable for all wiring except charging circuits, which should have no more than a 1% drop.

Table 4-3.

Wire Sizes & Voltage Drop at Different Amperages

Voltage Drop at 10 Amps

Distance Run in Feet

AWG	5	10	15	20	25	30	35	40	45	50	
6	.0201	.0402	.060	.080	.100	.120	.140	.161	.181	.201	1%
8	.0322	.0645	.096	.129	.161	.193	.225	.258	.290	.322	
10	.0509	.1018	.152	.203	.254	.305	.356	.407	.458	.509	3%
12	.0809	.1619	.242	.323	.404	.485	.566	.647	.728	.809	
14	.1287	.2575	.386	.515	.643	.772	.901	1.030	1.158	1.287	
16	.2470	.4940	.741	.988	1.235	1.482	1.729	1.976	2.223	2.470	
18	.3255	.6510	.976	1.302	1.627	1.953	2.278	2.604	2.929	3.255	

(1% and 3% lines on left at AWG 14 and 18)

Voltage Drop at 25 Amps

Distance Run in Feet

AWG	5	10	15	20	25	30	35	40	45	50	
4/0	.0060	.0125	.018	.024	.030	.036	.042	.048	.054	.060	
3/0	.0078	.0157	.023	.031	.039	.047	.054	.062	.070	.078	
2/0	.0099	.0198	.029	.039	.049	.059	.069	.079	.089	.099	
1/0	.0125	.0250	.037	.050	.063	.075	.088	.100	.113	.125	1%
1	.0158	.0315	.047	.063	.079	.095	.111	.126	.142	.158	
2	.0198	.0397	.059	.079	.099	.119	.139	.158	.178	.198	
4	.0316	.0632	.094	.126	.158	.189	.221	.253	.284	.316	3%
6	.0503	.1006	.151	.201	.252	.302	.352	.402	.453	.503	
8	.0801	.1602	.240	.320	.401	.481	.561	.641	.721	.801	
10	.1275	.2550	.383	.510	.637	.765	.893	1.020	1.147	1.275	
12	.2025	.4050	.607	.810	1.012	1.215	1.417	1.620	1.822	2.025	
14	.3225	.6450	.967	1.290	1.613	1.935	2.257	2.580	2.903	3.225	

(1% and 3% lines on left at AWG 10 and 14)

NOTES:

For charging circuits, use any combination of wire gauge and distance that appears above the 1% line. For all other circuits, use any wire gauge and distance combination above the 3% line.

For distances greater than 50 feet, enter the column for half the total distance and double each of the voltage drops in that column above the appropriate percentage line. Select a voltage drop that, when doubled, does not exceed the percentage drop desired. Use the wire size opposite that figure.

This table can be used for 120-volt AC calculations; however, use a 10% voltage drop for all AC wire sizes.

Voltage Drop at 50 Amps
Distance Run in Feet

AWG	5	10	15	20	25	30	35	40	45	50	
4/0	.0125	.0250	.037	.050	.063	.075	.087	.100	.113	.125	1%
3/0	.0157	.0315	.047	.063	.079	.095	.110	.126	.142	.158	
2/0	.0198	.0397	.059	.079	.099	.119	.139	.159	.179	.199	
1/0	.0250	.0500	.075	.100	.125	.150	.175	.200	.225	.250	
1	.0315	.0630	.095	.126	.157	.189	.221	.252	.284	.315	
2	.0397	.0795	.119	.159	.199	.238	.278	.318	.357	.397	3%
4	.0632	.1265	.190	.253	.316	.379	.442	.506	.569	.633	
6	.1007	.2015	.302	.403	.504	.605	.705	.806	.907	1.007	
8	.1603	.3205	.481	.641	.801	.961	1.122	1.282	1.442	1.603	
10	.2550	.5100	.765	1.020	1.275	1.530	1.785	2.040	2.295	2.550	
12	.4050	.8100	1.215	1.620	2.025	2.430	2.835	2.240	3.240	3.645	

(1% at left between AWG 6 and 8; 3% at left below AWG 12)

Voltage Drop at 100 Amps
Distance Run in Feet

AWG	5	10	15	20	25	30	35	40	45	50	
4/0	.0250	.0500	.075	.100	.125	.150	.175	.200	.225	.250	1%
3/0	.0315	.0630	.095	.126	.157	.189	.220	.252	.284	.315	
2/0	.0397	.0795	.119	.159	.198	.238	.278	.318	.357	.398	3%
1/0	.0500	.0100	.150	.200	.250	.300	.350	.400	.450	.500	
1	.0630	.1260	.189	.252	.315	.378	.441	.504	.567	.630	
2	.0795	.1590	.238	.318	.397	.477	.556	.636	.715	.795	
4	.1265	.2530	.379	.506	.633	.759	.895	1.012	1.138	1.265	
6	.2015	.4030	.605	.806	1.007	1.209	1.410	1.612	1.813	2.015	
8	.3205	.6410	.961	1.282	1.603	1.923	2.243	2.564	2.884	3.205	

(1% at left between AWG 4 and 6; 3% at left below AWG 8)

Voltage Drop at 150 Amps
Distance Run in Feet

AWG	5	10	15	20	25	30	35	40	45	50	
4/0	.0375	.0750	.112	.150	.187	.225	.262	.300	.337	.375	1% 3%
3/0	.0472	.0945	.142	.189	.236	.283	.330	.378	.425	.472	
2/0	.0596	.1192	.178	.238	.298	.357	.417	.477	.536	.596	
1/0	.0750	.1500	.225	.300	.375	.450	.525	.600	.675	.750	
1	.0945	.1890	.283	.378	.472	.567	.661	.756	.850	.945	
2	.1192	.2385	.357	.477	.596	.715	.834	.954	1.073	1.192	
4	.1897	.3795	.569	.759	.948	1.138	1.328	1.518	1.707	1.897	

(1% at left between AWG 2 and 4; 3% at left below AWG 4)

(continued on next page)

Voltage Drop at 200 Amps

Distance Run in Feet

AWG	5	10	15	20	25	30	35	40	45	50	
4/0	.0500	.1000	.150	.200	.250	.300	.350	.400	.450	.500	1%, 3%
3/0	.0630	.1260	.189	.252	.315	.378	.441	.504	.567	.630	
2/0	.0795	.1590	.238	.318	.397	.477	.556	.636	.715	.795	
1/0	.1000	.2000	.300	.400	.500	.600	.700	.800	.900	1.000	
1	.1260	.2520	.378	.504	.630	.756	.882	1.008	1.134	1.260	
2	.1590	.3180	.477	.636	.795	.954	1.113	1.272	1.431	1.590	
4	.2530	.5060	.759	1.012	1.265	1.518	1.771	2.024	2.277	2.530	

1% (at left of row 1) — 3% (at left of row 4)

Voltage drop is not as important with low-amperage equipment, such as lights, because small-gauge wire can handle the low-amperage load. It is with high-amperage equipment that voltage drop is crucial. As an example, the total difference between a charged and a discharged battery is less than 1 volt, and it takes a minimum of 13.7 voltage potential to fully charge a battery. If the voltage drop in the wire is so great that the charge voltage reaching the battery is less than 13.7, a reasonable charging capability is virtually nonexistent.

It is with high-amperage equipment that voltage drop is crucial.

Voltage drop in a 12-volt DC circuit differs considerably from that in a 120-volt AC circuit. In an AC circuit, a 10-gauge wire, 120 feet long, carrying 30 amperes, would have a drop of only 3.672 volts, slightly more than 3 percent of 120 volts (3.6 volts); a 60-foot, 10-gauge, 2-wire (10/2) extension cord would have the same voltage drop. This is why there is no unacceptable voltage drop in an RV's typical shore-power cable, which is 10-gauge wire and 25 feet long. In fact, a 35-foot extension could be added to the shore-power cable without a significant voltage drop.

Many excellent converter/chargers are on the market—some even have a charging capability of 45 amperes or more—but they will never perform at optimum efficiency until RV manufacturers install them using an adequate length of proper-gauge wire. (Wire types, ratings, and insulation coverings are discussed in Chapter 7.)

Voltage Drop from Alternator to House Batteries

The voltage drop from the alternator in a motorhome or tow vehicle to the house batteries is just as important to consider as the voltage drop from a converter/charger to the batteries. For the most efficient house-battery charging by the alternator, the wire run should be as short as possible. Most trailer manufacturers recognize this and put the batteries at the front of the trailer (some also are wise enough to locate the converter/charger close to the batteries), but even at the front, the batteries are a considerable distance from the tow vehicle's alternator.

A regular-cab pickup truck is about 17 feet long. If the trailer is a fifth-wheel and the batteries are in a compartment just behind the gooseneck (i.e., the raised front section), when the trailer is hitched, the distance in a straight line from the alternator is about 22 feet. On a conventional trailer with the batteries at the front on the tongue, a straight line from the alternator to the batteries is about 20 feet. When the turns and angles of the wire routing are considered, the wire run can be several feet longer.

House batteries (and the converter/charger) should be located at the front, near the engine, in a conventional motorhome; at the rear in a diesel-pusher model. Because batteries are subject to premature deterioration when exposed to high temperatures, they should not be *in* an engine compartment, only near it.

An important factor to consider in alternator-charging of house batteries is the alternator output. The higher the amperage, the better job of charging, but only if the proper-gauge wire is used in the charging circuit.

Table 4-3 can also be used to determine the wire gauge needed from the alternator to the house batteries or the SLI battery. If the alternator's output is 50 amperes, for example, 4-gauge wire would be needed for a 10-foot run to prevent a voltage drop greater than 1 percent of 14 volts. Some motorhomes, particularly bus conversions, have a 24-volt battery system. To apply Table 4-3 to a 24-volt system, use 28 volts (14 volts doubled) for the charging voltage. With a voltage drop of 0.28 (1 percent of 28 volts) and the same 50-ampere alternator output, Table 4-3 indicates that using up to 20 feet of 4-gauge wire, or 10 feet of 6-gauge wire, would be satisfactory.

Table 4-3 can also be used to determine the wire gauge needed from the alternator to the house batteries or the SLI battery.

Voltage drop is not a constant; it varies with the amperage. Both converter/chargers and alternators begin charging at a high amperage rate, but very quickly the amperage begins to drop. As it does, the voltage drop in the wire also diminishes, even though the wire's resistance remains the same. When the wire gauge is too small for the maximum amperage output of the charger, the batteries may become charged over a long period, but they can never receive the benefit of the initial high amperage that provides quick battery charging. If adequate wire size isn't used to accommodate this high initial charging, the charging unit (either a converter/charger or an alternator) can be reduced to nothing more than a trickle charger since full capacity cannot be utilized.

We saw a Class A diesel-pusher motorhome with the house batteries located behind the front grille and the converter/charger/fuse panel at the rear of the coach—almost as if the manufacturer had deliberately put it as far from the batteries as possible. On this 35-foot-long unit, the wire from the 100-ampere alternator (located in the engine compartment in the rear) to the house batteries was 8 gauge.

On Class C motorhomes, it is common practice to locate the batteries under the entrance steps in the doorway; however, if the doorway is in the back of the coach, as it is on many units, the wire run can be excessive.

Inexplicably, the wire from the batteries to the converter/charger, with its much lower amperage output, was heavier 6-gauge wire. The runs for both wires had to be at least 60 feet (30 feet doubled). With this layout, the alternator could provide only a small charge, and the wire gauge needed to keep voltage drop at or below 1 percent would be so large it would be impractical for use. In addition, the ampacity of 8-gauge wire is 55 amperes, so trying to force 100 amperes through the wire would create excessive heat, which is an unsafe condition. All these problems could be avoided if the batteries were located in the rear.

On Class C motorhomes, it is common practice to locate the batteries under the entrance steps in the doorway; however, if the doorway is in the back of the coach, as it is on many units, the wire run can be excessive.

Battery Monitoring

An important part of a 12-volt system is a means of monitoring what is going on in the system. The subject of monitors and their various functions is complex and is covered fully in Chapter 10.

The Distribution Panel

The *distribution panel* is the correct name for what is commonly called the *fuse panel*, or *fuse block*, if fuses are used, or the circuit-breaker panel if circuit breakers are used. Whether the distribution panel is incorporated into a converter/charger (most are the fuse type) or whether it is a separate unit, it should be as close as possible to the battery so wire runs are short. The panel should not be located in the battery compartment because of the corrosive atmosphere. At least 6-gauge wire should be used for both the positive and negative conductors between the battery and the distribution panel.

Many distribution panels used in RVs, especially trailers, are simply fuse blocks that accommodate either automotive-glass-cylinder (AGC) fuses, or automotive-spade fuses to protect the different circuits connected to the panel. If the fuse block is incorporated into some converter/chargers, DC power can be provided to the RV's circuits without a battery even being connected to the system.

Fuse blocks carry the individual wire connections, located on the *bus bar* (a conducting bar that carries heavy currents to supply several electric circuits), for the positive wires for each 12-volt circuit in the RV. Some fuse blocks also have a bus bar for the negative wires of each circuit or, perhaps, a single lug connection. Some built-in fuse blocks don't have provision for new equipment, so if additional 12-volt circuits are added, an extra fuse panel may be needed.

It is more convenient to have circuit breakers on the distribution panel—flicking a switch is easier than removing and replacing a fuse—but circuit-breaker panels are more expensive than fuse panels, so they aren't found in most RVs. It doesn't require much electrical knowledge to upgrade to a circuit-breaker panel. Simply remove each wire from the fuse panel, label the positive and negative wires for each circuit, remove the fuse block, install the circuit-breaker panel in its place, and reconnect the wires. Circuit-breaker panels are available with LEDs that indicate whether the circuits are on or off.

Flicking a switch is easier than removing and replacing a fuse—but circuit-breaker panels are more expensive than fuse panels, so they aren't found in most RVs. It doesn't require much electrical knowledge to upgrade.

RVs generally are wired so that one circuit services a specific area. Perhaps all lights in the rear of the RV are on one circuit; this same circuit also may include a stereo and other 12-volt equipment located in the vicinity. Often a circuit includes all 12-volt equipment on the right side of the RV; another circuit handles the equipment on the left. Different rooms in the RV may have individual circuits. High-amperage appliances, such as the furnace, water pump, and refrigerator, should be on separate circuits. TV amplifiers, receptacles for

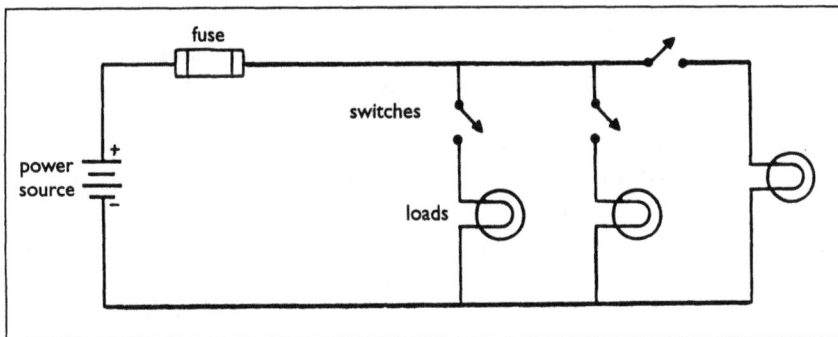

Figure 4-1. Schematic of 12-volt parallel-wired circuit with three different loads.

12-volt TVs and video-cassette players, and stereos should be on the same circuit, but often they are not. If this equipment is on one circuit, isolated from other equipment, electrical interference is less likely; if it does occur, tracking it down and correcting it is easier when dealing with only one circuit. All 12-volt circuits are wired in parallel (Figure 4-1, pg. 75).

Battery-charging Wiring Harnesses

Motorhomes have always needed a 12-volt system for automotive functions, but trailers, which don't have an engine, have lagged behind in the development of 12-volt systems. Our own trailer is an example. Shortly after we took delivery of our fifth-wheeler, the deficiencies became apparent. While installing the deep-cycle batteries, we discovered that the ground wire and the wire connecting the batteries to the fuse panel were only 10 gauge. The 10-gauge wire from the batteries connected to a 30-ampere automotive-spade-type fuse on the distribution panel—the main fuse for the trailer's entire 12-volt system; this was all according to the NEC. Just opposite the 30-ampere fuse, in addition to the bus-bar connections to the trailer's various circuits, was the connection for the battery-charging wire coming from the pin box. The wire running from this fuse-panel connection to a terminal stud in the pin box is 6-gauge wire. At the stud, it is connected to the TECC, which is plugged into the receptacle in the truck bed when the trailer is hitched.

For all this distance—a total of 36 feet from alternator to batteries— the manufacturer-installed wiring was expected to provide enough amperage to charge the house batteries, but of course it didn't.

The TECC is only 14-gauge wire (in later models, the TECC charging wire has been upgraded to 10 gauge). When the TECC plug is inserted into the receptacle in the truck bed, it connects to the 8-gauge wire that runs the 20 feet to the alternator. For all this distance—a total of 36 feet from alternator to batteries—the manufacturer-installed wiring was expected to provide enough amperage to charge the house batteries, but of course it didn't.

We had experienced this problem before: Years ago, shortly after we took delivery of our first fulltiming RV, a 23-foot conventional trailer, we had problems with the tow-vehicle wiring harness, which had been installed by the dealer. The day after we first camped overnight without an electrical hookup, we found that the batteries weren't being charged by the alternator, even after many hours of driving. The alternator was checked and found to be functioning properly. An RV dealer checked the wiring and opined that the 12-gauge charging wire was suitable for charging the batteries. He also stated that wire size was unimportant—any size wire would do the job! After all this, we deduced we had a voltage-drop problem that could be solved by installing a heavier-gauge charging wire, and we decided to do the job ourselves. As we were replacing the wire with some 8-gauge wire, the heaviest we could find in the small town where we had stopped, we found many other things wrong with the wiring setup. The charging wire was connected directly to the alternator with no means of isolation from the starting battery, and there was no circuit breaker in the system. We located a suitable isolator and circuit breaker, and they were duly installed. While we were at it, we decided to wire in an automotive-type ammeter under the dashboard to monitor the charge rate. We greatly improved our charging system but it was still a long way from ideal.

We no longer had a problem with battery charging if we only stayed overnight without an electrical hookup and the next day drove long enough to put a good charge into the batteries. If we wanted to stay longer in primitive campsites, we could not charge the batteries sufficiently, even though each morning and evening we hooked up the TECC and ran the truck's engine for about 30 minutes. This only restored a partial charge, so after three or four nights in the same campsite without an electrical hookup, the batteries would be flat no matter how long the engine was run—at idle speed there wasn't enough amperage to ever fully charge them.

Now, to return to the poor wiring on our fifth-wheel trailer: We envisioned having the same problems we had with the previous trailer. Before we purchased the fifth-wheeler, we acquired a different pickup truck with a 60-ampere stock alternator. It was larger than the one in our previous truck, but still not a very high-output unit for battery charging. The only way we could have a decent charging system was to rewire the trailer.

The 10-gauge battery wire was replaced with 6-gauge wire; 4-gauge wire would have been used except that the fuse panel would not accommodate wire with such a large diameter. (Eventually we intend to replace the fuse panel with a circuit-breaker unit that will accept larger wires.) The truck charging line from the alternator back to the TECC was changed to 6-gauge wire. We could not replace the ridiculously small 14-gauge wire in the TECC; except for that, the charging line was now 6 gauge. For the times when we wanted to charge the batteries without driving, the TECC, with its 14-gauge wire, was bypassed with an extension charging cable we made from a 12-foot, 6-gauge battery jumper cable. The alligator clips were removed, and a male Bargman plug was put on one end and a male plug of the type used for an electric range on the other (Figure 4-2, pg. 78). To accommodate the plug, a weatherproof outlet box with a female range receptacle was installed on the pin box and wired to the single-stud terminal block, to which the 6-gauge wire from the fuse panel is attached (Figure 4-3, pg. 78). The length of the extension cord is twice that of the TECC, so we can reach the truck receptacle without having to maneuver the truck in close to the trailer. TECC is usually so short that it is difficult

Figure 4-2. Authors' extension charging cable made from a battery jumper cable, with a TECC plug on one end and a range plug on the other.

Figure 4-3. Receptacle on pin box to accommodate extension charging cord shown in Figure 4-2.

to plug into the tow vehicle's receptacle without actually hitching up.

When the engine was started in the morning, the 60-ampere alternator would charge for a maximum of about 30 amperes (50 percent of the alternator's rating) before it rapidly tapered off to 10 amperes or so. To take full advantage of the high initial rate, we never started the engine until the TECC was plugged in. Running the engine for 30 minutes put a partial charge into the batteries, particularly if they were not discharged more than about 20 percent. A half hour of running later in the day also helped, but the batteries still would not recharge fully with this system unless the engine was run for 8 to 10 hours. The engine was never run for this long while we were parked, of course. It's not good to idle an engine for such a long period, and we couldn't have stood the noise—the noise was bad enough for 30 minutes at a time. (Even if we had the ability for charging at a higher rate, it would be ineffective because, until we rewire the fuse panel, the charging current must still go through the 30-ampere master fuse. We now have an alternate—much superior—charging system, described in Chapter 6.)

Newer trucks and vans have alternators with outputs higher than 60 amperes and, for proper charging, require charge lines of at least 4-gauge wire, perhaps even larger, depending on the alternator's output.

A Separate Charge Line

In standard automotive wiring, the practice is to ground the alternator to the chassis and the engine block, then use the chassis for the return wires to the battery and from all electrical equipment such as lights. Often the ground-wire connections become corroded and add to the resistance of the system, creating more voltage drop than already exists. The TECC receptacle on the tow vehicle most likely will have a short jumper ground wire from the ground terminal on the receptacle to a screw stud either on the bumper or in the bed of the tow vehicle (if it is a pickup truck). The screw stud is often a bolt screwed into the chassis; eventual rusting results in a bad electrical connection. On our trailer, the charging ground wire on the TECC is grounded to the pin box and the battery is grounded to the trailer chassis through a lug, thereby using the chassis for the negative portion of the circuit between the pin box and the battery.

All these various connections are potential sources of trouble because of possible corrosion or poor electrical contact due to dirt or painted surfaces. To eliminate these problems, a better arrangement is to run a separate ground wire between the batteries and the TECC plug, and another wire directly from the alternator to the TECC receptacle. But first consider the advantages of bypassing the TECC entirely and running a completely separate charge line that incorporates both the positive and negative ground wires. In a separate charge line the proper gauge wire could be used because, as we have pointed out, the wire holes in the TECC are too small to accommodate wire of an adequate size for a charging line.

Consider the advantages of bypassing the TECC entirely and running a completely separate charge line that incorporates both the positive and negative ground wires.

The wires for a separate charge line should run from the alternator to the isolator, to a circuit breaker, and then back to the vicinity of the TECC receptacle, where they would terminate in a female plug. Do not use the alternator's bracket as the ground connection even if the alternator is grounded that way. If it is not possible to make a direct connection to the alternator, use the SLI battery's ground strap connection.

From the trailer, the battery ground wire comes from the chassis terminal stud; the positive wire originates at the battery's positive terminal. These wires, which terminate in a male plug, are connected to the wires from the alternator. (A distribution post or bus bar can eliminate having multiple wires attached directly to the battery. One heavy wire connects the battery to the distribution post, and wires for various circuits are attached to the post. A distribution bus bar is composed of several posts.) When calculating voltage drop (use Table 4-3), include the length of the ground wire as well as the length of the positive wire.

It is good practice to run the positive and negative wires together using twin cable (i.e., two wires in one casing) if it can be obtained in the necessary gauge. Polarized, two-wire connectors of the type shown in Figure 4-4 (pg. 80) can be used.

79

Figure 4-4. Polarized two-wire connectors for separate charging lines. They are available in sizes to accommodate up to 4/0-gauge wire. (Photo courtesy of Wrangler Power Products)

For charging lines, these connectors are far superior to the usual connectors on TECCs. The twin cable and the connectors are available from Wrangler Power Products and welding supply shops.

Once there is a separate charging line, the TECC charging line is disconnected; however, the TECC must still be used to operate the trailer's brakes, turn signals, and running lights.

A word of caution: On some late-model vehicles, much of the electrical circuitry is computerized, including the circuitry of the alternator, which affects the attaching of trailer charge lines. On some vehicles, the alternator regulator is located in the computer instead of being internal in the alternator or a separate external unit. If this is the case, it may be necessary to split the charge line at the SLI battery and, at this point, attach the isolator and trailer battery charge line—instead of connecting to the alternator's output post—so the charge line is downstream from the computer system. Heavy-gauge lines must be routed so the high inductance around them will not affect other circuits; keep them away from other wires and components. To prevent damage to the computer system, check with the manufacturer of your vehicle for recommendations.

Battery Sense Lines

With an alternator that has connections for two battery sense lines on the regulator, one for each battery bank, one line must be connected in the vicinity of the TECC receptacle on the tow vehicle. A small, single-pin plug and receptacle, or a two-pin polarized plug and receptacle, should be used for the trailer battery sense line. Flat, polarized 12-volt connectors, manufactured by Cole Hersee, are available from RV suppliers.

Battery sense lines measure battery voltage and do not carry a large load, but the wire should not be smaller than 16 gauge. A battery sense line should be fused for 1 or 2 amperes, depending on the regulator manufacturer's recommendation.

Attach separate charge lines and battery sense lines to the TECC by using tape or plastic electric cable ties so that all the necessary hookups can be conveniently made at the same time when hitching up.

Schematics and Block Diagrams

A *schematic* is a drawing of an electrical circuit (or circuits) showing the routing of all wires and how all the components are joined together (see Figure 4-1, which is a schematic of a 12-volt parallel-wired circuit). Some schematics include wire size and color coding.

A *block diagram* shows how various large devices—panels, motors, and chargers—relate to one another electrically (Figure 4-5). A block diagram

Although owners should have a schematic, or at least a block diagram, to aid them in tracing shorts and bad connections and isolating other problems, only a few RV manufacturers provide either.

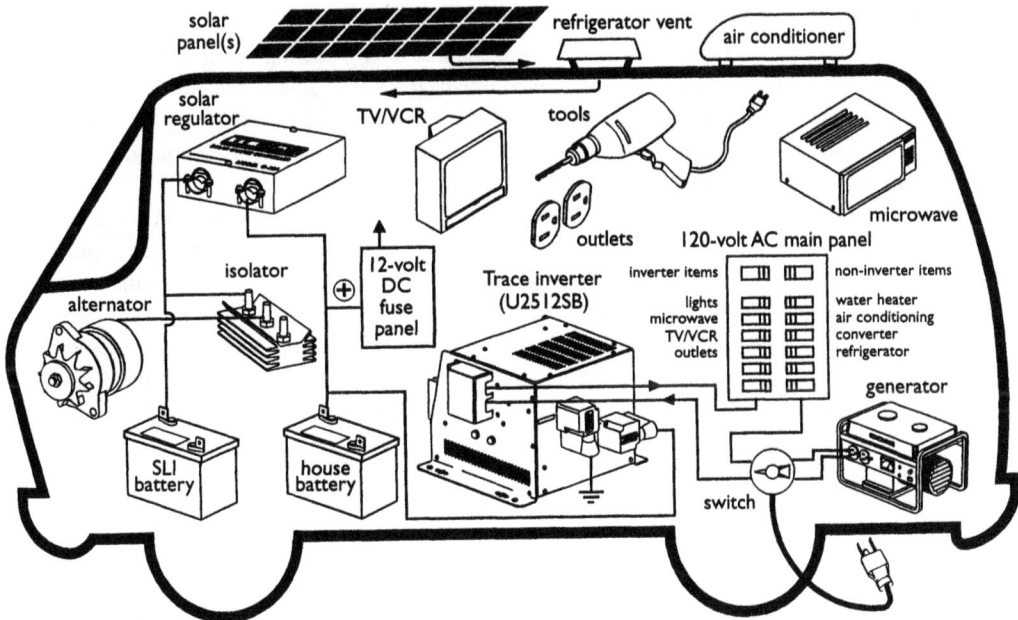

Figure 4-5. Block diagram of the various electrical components in a motorhome.
(Illustration courtesy of Trace Engineering Corporation)

12-Volt Circuits and Wiring

does not necessarily show the actual wiring of individual circuits; nonetheless, it is useful for troubleshooting and for making changes or additions to the electrical system.

Although owners should have a schematic, or at least a block diagram, to aid them in tracing shorts and bad connections and isolating other problems, only a few RV manufacturers provide either.

On a schematic, each component is represented by a different symbol (Figure 4-6, pg. 83).

Battery Symbol

As shown in Figure 4-6, the symbols for both single-cell and multiple-cell batteries have a line on each end. In a schematic, each end line is connected to the circuit being illustrated and is usually identified as having either plus or minus polarity.

Sometimes a battery may be represented by just a rectangular box and labeled "battery." Other power sources—generators, converter/chargers, inverters, and shore power—are represented by rectangular boxes or circles.

Ground Connections

The ground symbol in a schematic is a sort of engineering shorthand. It eliminates the need to draw a negative return line to the minus side of the power source in the circuit. Of the two ground symbols shown in Figure 4-6, the triangular-shaped one is most commonly used to show the negative connection to the minus side of the battery in a 12-volt circuit.

Technically, the rake-like symbol represents a chassis ground and the triangular-shaped symbol indicates an earth ground. When the symbol for ground appears in the schematic for an electrical device such as a converter, it usually means the circuit is connected to the chassis, which in turn is connected to the negative side of the power source. The ground symbol appears in schematics of regulators to show this negative connection to the alternator. An earth-ground symbol is used in two-way radio schematics to indicate antenna grounding, or to indicate grounding of household AC circuits like those found in campground electrical hookups.

Wire Connections

When a schematic is created, it is often necessary to show two wires of different circuits crossing each other. It must be clear whether or not the crossing is an actual electrical connection. The usual practice is to make a dot at the crossing to indicate that the wires are actually connected. If they are not connected, they are shown just crossing each other; sometimes a half-moon shape is drawn on one line at the crossing.

wire connections

single-cell battery · multi-cell battery · earth ground · chassis ground · no connection · connection · no connection · connection

double-pole double-throw relay

single-pole single-throw switch

double-pole double-throw switch

5-pole rotary switch

double-pole single-throw switch

fixed resistor · variable resistor · adjustable resistor · photo resistor · thermistor · single-filament lightbulb

fixed capacitor · variable capacitor · polarized electrolytic capacitor · air-core inductor · iron-core inductor · adjustable inductor

air-core transformer · iron-core transformer · primary tapped transformer · fuse · circuit breaker

diode/ rectifier · Schottky diode · zener diode · light-emitting diode (LED) · photo diode · solar cell (diode)

triac · thyristor (SCR) · P-channel bipolar transistor · N-channel junction FET · N-channel single-gate MOSFET · metal-oxide varistor (MOV)

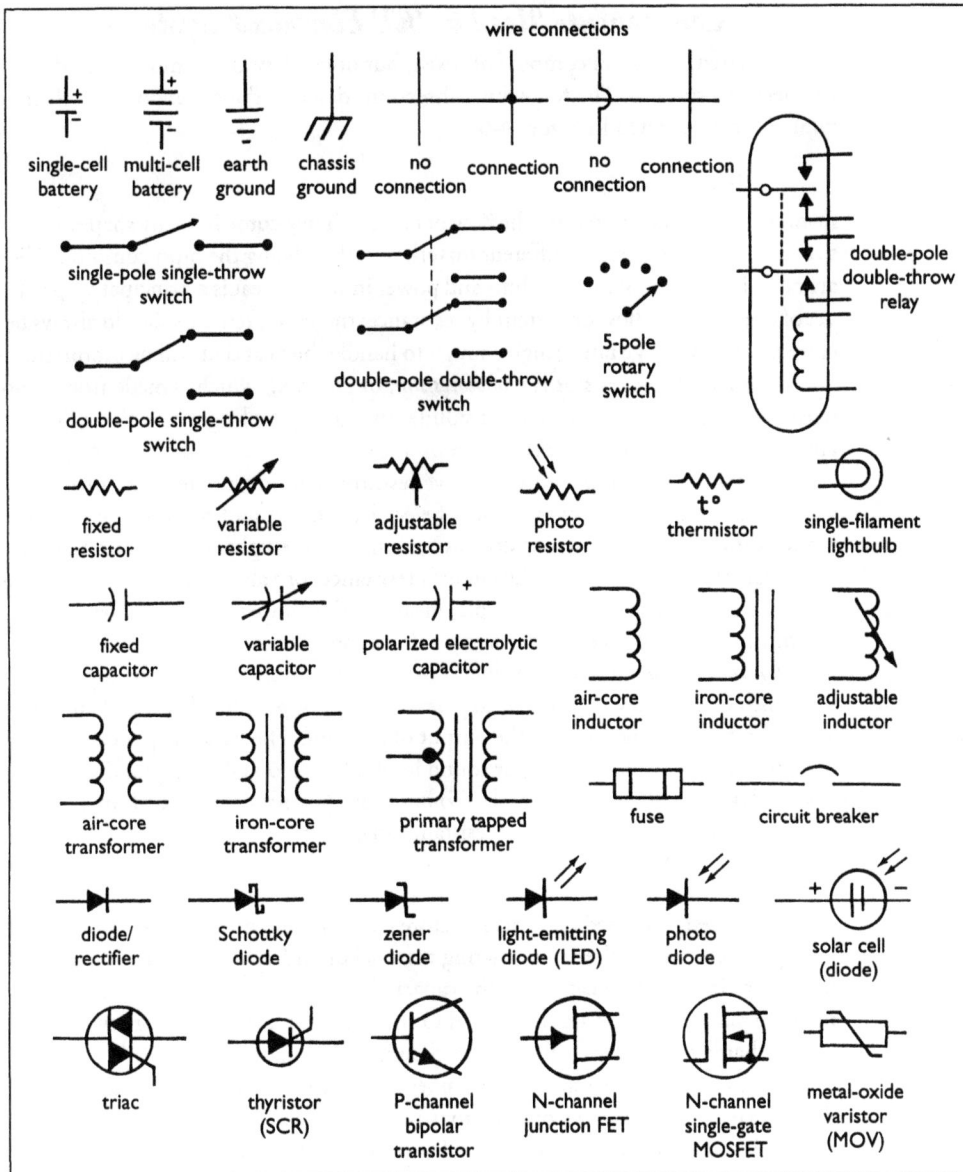

Figure 4-6. A selection of schematic symbols of components commonly found in RV electrical systems.

Components Used in RV Electrical Systems

Many different electrical components exist, but only a few are commonly used in RV electrical systems. The following subsections describe these components; their symbols are illustrated in Figure 4-6.

Resistors

Resistors are designed to reduce the flow of current. They come in many shapes and sizes and are made of many different materials, carbon being the most common. They are rated by their resistance in ohms and power in watts. Heat is a principal by-product of opposing the flow of current by resistance; therefore, resistors should always be chosen with a wattage rating high enough to handle the heat that will be produced.

Another type of resistor is a *photoresistor*, or *photocell*, which is made from light-sensitive materials such as cadmium sulfide. Increasing the brightness of the light falling on the photocell decreases the resistance.

Thermistors are temperature-sensitive resistors that measure temperature and vary resistance to prevent overheating of electrical devices and components. As the temperature rises, the resistance decreases, similar to the light reaction of photocells. When the temperature varies, the circuit's resistance, or value, is changed. A thermistor in a battery sense line, for example, measures the temperature of the battery. Thermistors are also used in alternator and regulator circuits.

Variable resistors adjust the value so that different resistances can be present in the same circuit. They are also called *potentiometers*, or *pots*, for short, and are used wherever it is necessary to vary the output of a circuit. The various applications include controlling the volume, or sound level, of a radio and changing the brightness of dashboard lights in a vehicle. *Trimmers* are potentiometers used for a semipermanent adjustment of the resistance in circuits.

Capacitors

Capacitors, best described as devices to store electrons, are made of two conductors, or large plates, with either an insulating material or air between them. As current flows in a circuit with a capacitor, the capacitor collects and stores electrons on the negative plate until they are discharged to the positive plate. Capacitors eventually self-discharge as electrons leak through the insulating material to the other plate. When the other plate has an equal number of electrons, or charge, the capacitor is discharged. This ability to store electrons is called *capacitance* and is measured in *farads*. Because most capacitors have values of much less than a single farad, they are usually rated in *microfarads* and *picofarads* (millionths and trillionths of a farad, respectively). Construction of capacitors varies, but a common method is to place in a cylinder two foil sheets rolled together with an insulator between them. A wire lead is connected to each sheet so the wires protrude from one end of the cylinder.

Capacitors are used in power-supply filters to smooth out the ripples in DC current and in ferroreso-nant converter/chargers to regulate voltage output (see Chapter 5). Capacitors may be either fixed or variable. Variable capacitors are used in radio tuners.

WARNING! Use caution when touching a capacitor in a circuit. Because of its ability to store electrical energy, the capacitor can deliver a potentially lethal shock—even after power to the device is turned off.

WARNING! Use caution when touching a capacitor in a circuit. Because of its ability to store electrical energy, the capacitor can deliver a potentially lethal shock— even after power to the device is turned off.

Inductors

As discussed in Chapter 1, inductors are the coils that cause the electromagnetic fields in transformers to produce alternating current. They are the basis of the functions of motors, solenoids, electromagnets, alternators, converter/chargers, and battery charg-ers. Inductors used in conjunction with capacitors create resonant circuits that control output in many converter/chargers and battery chargers.

Fuses

Fuses in RV circuits can be the AGC type rated at ¼ ampere to 50 amperes or the automotive-spade type rated at 5 to 30 amperes. Fuses might also be the large, tubu-lar, household type rated at up to 300 amperes. Some type of fuse is available in any amperage size desired.

All fuses work similarly: When current exceeds a predetermined amperage, a thin metal strip or wire melts and breaks the circuit. Fuses can protect a circuit for just a single light or an entire 12-volt system (see "Disaster Fuses" later in this chapter).

Fuses may be either the fast-acting or slow-blow type. A fast-acting fuse blows whenever an excessive amount of current flows through the circuit, and is best used to protect equipment and circuits containing semiconductors. Slow-blow fuses with-stand an excessive amount of current for a given time before they blow—usually at the point before the wiring begins to burn. Slow-blow fuses are used in circuits for motors because, when motors start, there is a large amount of surge current before the current settles down to the normal flow. This surge can cause fast-acting fuses to blow before the equipment is operating normally. An initial surge can also occur in electronic equipment without semiconductors. For any equipment, always use the type of fuse specified by the manufacturer.

All fuses have a voltage rating. A fuse with a higher rating than the voltage of the circuit can be used if the fuse has the proper blow characteristics. Fuses usually blow at 125 percent of their rating, so a size just above the rating of the equipment to be protected should be selected. The rating of the fuse, however, should never be higher than the ampacity of the wires in the circuit it protects.

Circuit Breakers

Instead of fuses, circuits can be protected with circuit breakers. Circuit breakers are temperature sensitive. When they become hot from an excessive amperage load, the switch type opens and breaks the connection and must be reset manually; the heat-sensitive type stops the current flow, which resumes automatically when the breaker cools. Circuit breakers are rated for either AC or DC service or for both AC and DC. When selecting a breaker, it is important to choose the right type for the application.

All circuits in an RV should be protected by either a fuse or a breaker, but often they are not. Prudent RVers should install fuses or breakers on any unprotected circuits.

All circuits in an RV should be protected by either a fuse or a breaker, but often they are not. Prudent RVers should install fuses or breakers on any unprotected circuits including, and especially, inverter lines and charge lines from alternators or converter/chargers and circuits from solar panels.

Switches

Switches are available in many sizes, styles, and amperage ratings. They can be slider-, toggle-, lever-, button-, or rotary-operated. Simple switches are single-pole, single-throw (SPST): the switch has two connections, one for the power source and one for the circuit. The lever moves between two positions: on and off. A single-pole, double-throw (SPDT) switch has three connections: one for a common power source and one each for two different circuits. The lever can be moved into one of three positions. The middle position is off for both circuits; the top and bottom, or left and right, positions (depending on how the switch is mounted) are each for one circuit. An SPDT switch is the type used for switching between two batteries or banks.

Double-pole, double-throw (DPDT) switches work in the same manner as SPDT switches, but turn the positive and ground lines on and off at the same time, thus isolating the two different circuits from each other. This type of switch in a 30-ampere size is often used in RVs for switching between the incoming AC shore power and a generator, or between the inverter and the AC distribution panel.

The rotary multi-pole type of switch is used in radios, monitoring meters, and multimeters.

Relays

A *relay* is nothing more than a switch controlled by an electromagnet (i.e., a coil with a metal core). As current is turned on and flows through the coil, the core becomes magnetized and pulls the spring-loaded arm of the switch toward it. As this brings a contact on the arm together with another contact, the relay's main circuit is on and its current flows. When current to the coil is turned off, the magnetic field collapses and the arm with the contact springs open, breaking the circuit.

A relay can close or open one circuit or many circuits at the same time. Relays have poles as do other switches, so they also can be SPST, SPDT, or DPDT. A relay can close two circuits at a time and, upon opening them, the arms move and close two other circuits—the basis for transfer switches (see Chapter 7). A relay can either make or break a contact, depending on whether it is normally open or closed.

Semiconductor Devices

Solid-state semiconductor devices are the most advanced form of electronic components. They are made of silicon, the most common material, or germanium, which acts as either a conductor or a non-conductor, depending on the conditions present. Silicon can be combined with other materials to have different properties. A silicon mixture can be grown into large crystals, which can then be sliced into chips for making electronic parts.

A mixture of silicon and boron produces what is called a *P-type silicon chip;* a mixture of silicon and phosphorus produces an *N-type silicon chip.* Silicon has the property of freely sharing its electrons with other substances. An atom of phosphorus has five electrons while an atom of boron has only three; the silicon-boron P-type chip with fewer electrons is said to be electron deficient, and this deficiency creates a "hole" into which other electrons from the silicon can "fall." As one electron falls into a hole, the space that electron occupied is now vacant, so another electron can fall into that hole, and so on.

The phosphorus-silicon N-type chip has an extra electron that moves through the chip with ease, thus creating a current flow. P-type chips also can have a current flow through the movement of both holes and electrons. Both types conduct electricity and, because their resistance is determined by the number of electrons or holes they have, they also function as resistors. The N- and P-type compositions are the basis for almost all semiconductors. In certain combinations or configurations with various leads, either type can create diverse electronic components (e.g., transistors) that have various electrical results, depending on the voltages or amperages applied.

Diodes

Diodes, which pass current in only one direction, are the simplest of all semiconductor devices and are used in many RV applications. When one P-type and one N-type silicon chip are combined, electrons flow in only one direction, creating a diode. The interface where the two chips join is the *PN junction.*

The usual method of connecting a diode is to place the N material on the negative side of the circuit and the P material on the positive side. On each end of the diode is a lead; the lead from the plus end is the *anode,* the other is the *cathode.* On smaller diodes the cathode end is marked with a dark band.

The voltage potential of the positive pole of the power source (battery) normally attracts electrons, but it will not do so through a diode circuit until the voltage across the diode rises to the threshold point of the diode. (With silicon, that point is 0.6 volt; therefore, 0.6 is the voltage drop across the diode.) At this point, electrons cross the PN junction from the N material to the P material. As current flows, holes are created in the N material by the electrons flowing to the P material. This current is called *forward-biased* because current cannot normally flow in the reverse direction; voltage potential from the battery attracts the electrons away from the PN junction and stops reverse flow. A reverse current flow, if one exists, is called *reverse-biased.* This forward/reverse flow is the basic principle of semiconductors.

Diodes are used in isolators to separate the charging lines between the SLI battery and house batteries and in alternator circuits to convert AC to DC (in this application, diodes are known as power rectifiers). Other types of diodes commonly used in RVs are light-emitting diodes (LED), *zener diodes,* and *photodiodes.* LEDs are often used for pilot lights, indicator lights on circuit boards, lighted switches, and digital displays of electronic equipment. Each segmented numeral and letter on this type of digital display is composed of seven LEDs. A zener diode is a diode in which a large, reverse-biased voltage changes the resistance across the PN junction from a large value to a small value, allowing current to flow in the reverse direction. *Solar cells* are PN-junction photodiodes that use sun power to generate voltage (see Chapter 6).

Transistors

Transistors are solid-state devices made of combined P- and N-type silicon chips. They have three leads. A very small voltage, or current, at one lead controls a larger current flowing through the other leads. Transistors function as switches or amplifiers, and are used in regulators, high-powered amplifiers, and power supplies. Transistors, like all semiconductor devices, are heat-sensitive and can be damaged or destroyed by excessive heat.

The two types of transistors are *bipolar transistors* and *field-effect transistors (FETs).* Bipolar transistors are composed of three chips, either two P and one N, or two N and one P, arranged in a sandwich configuration of NPN or PNP. The middle layer controls the current moving through all three layers. The three leads of the transistor are designated the *emitter, base,* and *collector;* the base conducts the controlling current. A bipolar transistor's function is to use a small amount of current to control the flow of a large amount.

FETs require practically no current to operate, just an applied voltage to control the large flow of current. The two types of FETs, the *junction FET (JFET)* and the *metal-oxide semiconductor FET (MOSFET)*, are constructed differently than bipolar transistors. Instead of a three-layer sandwich, JFETs use a single piece of either N- or P-type material with two pieces of the opposite material attached to its sides. The central piece channels the current through two leads, the *source* and the *drain*, one at each end of the JFET. A single common lead, the *gate*, is attached to both side pieces. One advantage of a JFET is that little or no current flows in the gate circuit, so it consumes little power. JFETs are not suitable for high-power needs and are used mostly in low-power amplifier circuits and as switches.

MOSFETs differ from JFETs because they have a capacitor at the gate lead. The gate lead is attached to a metal plate that is separated from the rest of the device by an insulator. Since there is no direct electrical connection, high resistance is created in the input of the device.

MOSFETs can be extremely small and are used in most microcomputer and memory circuits. They also switch on and off very high currents in fractions of a second and function as a voltage-controlled resistor.

Thyristors

Thyristors, which may be either *silicon-controlled rectifiers* (SCRs) or *triacs*, have three leads similar to transistors; however, the controlling current is either on or off, so they function as solid-state switches.

SCRs have a fourth layer of material creating three PN junctions. They are sometimes referred to as four-layer diodes with three leads: anode, gate, and cathode. An SCR acts as a switch that passes only the rectified DC when the proper phase of AC is present. The phase triggers the SCR into being conductive; the SCR shuts off after the phase has passed and then waits for the proper phase to return. SCRs are rated by the amount of current they can switch. High-current SCRs handle up to 2,500 amperes at thousands of volts, and are used to control motors, lights, battery chargers, and appliances.

Triacs are two SCRs connected in parallel. They are composed of material arranged NPNPN, with an additional bit of N material on one of the P layers, which is the gate lead. Triacs conduct both AC and DC, and are also rated by the amount of current they can switch.

Varistors

Metal-oxide varistors (MOVs), solid-state devices with large junction areas capable of dissipating great amounts of AC and DC power very quickly, are designed around a

89

specific operating voltage. When subjected to a surge or spike voltage exceeding this amount, the MOV passes the current. MOVs are a component of surge protectors (see Chapter 8).

Integrated Circuits

Integrated circuits (ICs) are entire circuits combining transistors, resistors, diodes, and capacitors, all contained on a tiny chip that can be as small as a quarter-inch square. ICs can be designed for just about any purpose and are used in radios, TVs, computers, and, of course, alternator regulators.

Wiring Circuits

Most RV wiring is composed of simple circuits, which are basically all the same whether they are for the 12-volt DC system or the 120-volt AC system. The simplest circuit contains a power source with a voltage potential (battery); from this source a single wire is routed to the load and then back to the power source. Figure 4-7 shows this simple circuit with a fuse and switch added.

Most RV wiring is composed of simple circuits, which are basically all the same whether they are for the 12-volt DC system or the 120-volt AC system.

In a DC circuit, the first wire starts at the positive connection on the power source, which is probably a battery. This line goes to a fuse with an amperage rating slightly higher than that of the device to be powered. Next, the wire goes to a switch so the device (or load) can be conveniently turned on and off. Finally, the wire reaches the device. This wire is the positive or hot wire of the circuit. The wire that returns to the power source from the device is the negative or ground wire. This routing, with the fuse after the power source and the switch following, estab-

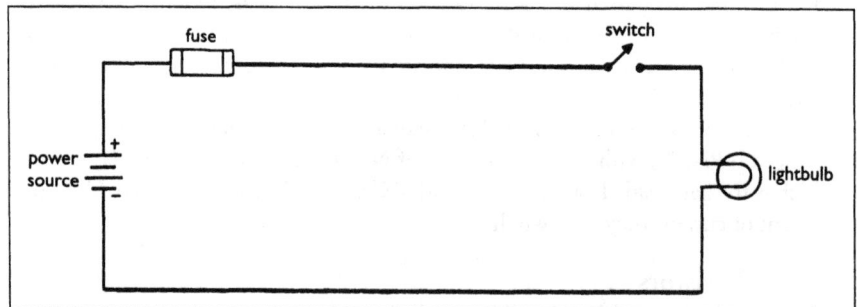

Figure 4-7. A circuit with a battery, fuse, switch (open), and lightbulb to represent the load.

lishes proper polarity for the circuit. Because many DC devices can be ruined if they are wired with the wrong polarity, the positive wire must always go to the positive pole, or terminal, of the device (pole identification is either on the device or in the instruction manual).

The wiring for alternating current is exactly the same as for direct current. Years ago, it was not necessary for equipment to be wired for polarity since AC flows both ways in the circuit; however, with today's sophisticated electronic equipment, AC circuits also need to be polarized. That's why one of the blades on an AC plug is wider than the other—take a look at the plug on your TV. The plug can only be inserted into a receptacle one way, and that way provides the correct polarity.

With today's sophisticated electronic equipment, AC circuits also need to be polarized. That's why one of the blades on an AC plug is wider than the other—take a look at the plug on your TV.

Think of a circuit as a path along which the current flows: from the power source to the fuse, to the switch, through the electrical device, and then back to the source, completing the circuit. For a circuit to work, there must be a complete, unbroken path from beginning to end. Whenever the path is broken the circuit is opened, and the device will not work. A switch causes a break in a circuit. A fuse can also open a circuit. If the current exceeds the ampere rating of the fuse, the metal strip in the fuse melts. When it melts through, the circuit is broken.

Disaster Fuses

An important item—usually missing—is a fuse or circuit breaker to protect the RV from possible destruction in the event of a major electrical problem. Batteries can short out internally from excessive heat or overcharging, literally melting down. If converter/chargers and inverters short out, the resultant rush in current flow can cause wiring to become so red hot that insulation melts. These situations can result in fires, and a fire can quickly consume an RV.

A fuse to prevent these occurrences is aptly named a *disaster fuse*. The amperage of the disaster fuse should depend on the number of batteries in the system or the maximum current output of the equipment it is to protect. (Manufacturers recommend that one Group 27 battery should not sustain a load of more than 50 amperes for more than a short interval.) We use a 100-ampere fuse to protect our system because we have two Group 27 batteries (i.e., 50 amperes for each battery).

The disaster fuse should be mounted in the negative line going from the battery bank's minus post to the chassis ground post (Figure 4-8, pg. 92). The ground wire

Figure 4-8. Authors' disaster fuse installation. On each end of the cylindrical-shaped fuse is a copper blade with a hole; one hole is for attaching the battery's negative wire lug; the other hole is for bolting the fuse to the chassis.

from the fuse block is attached to the chassis post, not the battery side of the fuse. This fuse-block ground wire should be no smaller than 8-gauge wire. The fuse located between the batteries, chassis post, and fuse panel must be for DC use because an AC fuse won't provide enough protection. A fuse manufactured by Cooper Bussman Industries, either the Buss FWA (70- to 800-ampere rating) or FWX (35- to 800-ampere rating) series or the equivalent, is suitable since it is fast-acting and designed to prevent excessive heat from reaching the semiconductors in inverters and converter/chargers.

If bolting is not feasible, a fuse block may suffice. Cooper Bussman makes modular fuse blocks with dovetail interlocks, allowing two or more to be connected together. The two terminal connections on each end accommodate 6-gauge or larger wire. Lugs are not needed since each wire slips into a hole and is held in place with a set screw. Depending on size, Buss designations are 1BS101, 1BS102, and 1BS103.

A similar fuse should be in the positive line from an inverter or converter/charger of a size no larger than 125 percent of the current draw of the equipment, and in any other circuits that carry a large amount of current. We have a 100-ampere fuse in the positive line to our 600-watt inverter. Higher wattage inverters require higher amperage fuses (see Chapter 9).

Expect to pay $35 minimum for a DC fuse. They are available from electrical supply stores, usually on special order, or from Ample Power Company.

12-Volt Plugs and Receptacles

Cigarette-lighter plugs and sockets are what the RV industry uses as 12-volt electrical connections. We have never liked these connectors because after some use they become too loose to make good contact. We also think they are a potential safety hazard. The open hole is an invitation for a child to poke something into it. If that something is metal, an arc can occur when the center contact is shorted out to the sides of the socket; fire could result. A wire or bent paperclip inserted in a socket can become red hot in a fraction of a second, causing a severe burn to the hand holding it.

We replace all cigarette-lighter connectors with two-pronged polarized plugs and sockets, which resemble miniature 120-volt AC connectors (Figure 4-9) and are rated at 7.5 amperes so they can handle most 12-volt loads. The plugs and cord sockets are available at Radio Shack (Catalog Nos. 274-201 and 274-202) and electronics stores. Panel-mount sockets are no longer sold by Radio Shack, but they are available at other electronics stores. Soldering, rather than crimping, must be done to attach wires. The soldered tab holes accommodate 14-gauge wire or smaller.

Figure 4-9. On the authors' trailer all cigarette-lighter plugs and sockets have been replaced with the safer, more efficient type of plugs and receptacles shown.

Many 12-volt appliances have a fuse incorporated in the cigarette-lighter plug. If this is changed to another type of connection, a fuse must be wired into the cord. We use in-line fuseholders because they can be soldered to one side of the replacement plug and then to the appliance's cord in the positive lead wire. If the positive wire is made shorter by the length of the fuseholder, the fuseholder and the negative wire can be taped together after installation to make a neat package.

On certain equipment, such as a DC TV, the fused cigarette-lighter plug can be utilized if an adapter is made with a polarized plug on one end and a good-quality cigarette-lighter socket on the other (Figure 4-10).

Dinghy Harness Wiring

When a motorhome is purchased, the owner usually wants it to be wired for towing an auxiliary vehicle (called a *dinghy* or *tag-along*). Unless the wiring was installed by the manufacturer, it will have to be added.

Figure 4-10. A pigtail cigarette-lighter socket with a polarized plug.

A four-way socket should be mounted under the motorhome's rear bumper, to the left of the hitch receiver, so the wires from the socket can be conveniently tapped into the taillight's wiring. The connections can be spliced into the existing wiring with solderless, snap-on tap-ins.

Another four-way socket has to be installed on the front bumper of the dinghy so the two vehicles can be hooked together using a four-wire harness with a four-way plug on each end. In a four-wire hookup, one wire is for the taillights, two for each of the different turn signals, and one for the ground. If a single bulb is used for both the brakes and turn signals, the brake lights are activated by the turn-signal wires. Using a multimeter to check the motorhome's wiring shows which wires perform which functions (see Chapter 11).

On the motorhome's socket, usually the upper-left pin is for the left signal and the upper-right pin is for the right signal. The taillight is wired to the lower-left pin and the ground wire to the remaining lower-right pin. The ground wire can be attached to the motorhome's frame with a ring connector on a wire fixed to the lower-right pin. To attach the ring connector, drill and tap a hole in the chassis to take a 10/32 machine screw or, if the chassis metal is thin enough, use a self-tapping sheet-metal screw. The screw, a metal washer, and the ring connector make a proper ground connection if the installation area is free of dirt and the paint is scraped off until the metal is shiny. Coat the various parts of the connection with dielectric grease to ensure a good electrical contact.

If the dinghy is a newer vehicle with lamp burnout warning indicators, amber turn signals, and an electronic fuel-injection system, wiring problems can exist. Diodes may have to be installed in the dinghy circuits to prevent current from the motorhome from feeding back into the dinghy's electrical system, which can result in all the dinghy's lamps flashing at once or burnout of LEDs.

Dinghy wiring requires research and careful planning to ensure the installation won't damage the dinghy's electrical system. Wiring can be eliminated if a light bar or add-on lights are used.

Dinghies with a two-light system—independent amber turn lights—require a five-wire harness and five-way plugs and receptacles. The first wire goes to the left amber turn light, the second to the right amber turn light, the third to the brakes, and the fourth to the taillights; the fifth is the ground. This is the usual setup for most foreign and some domestic vehicles. If the wiring on the motorhome is a single-light arrangement, an adapter is needed to convert to the two-light system of the towed vehicle. The same adapter can be used if the motorhome has a two-light system and the dinghy has a single-light system.

Wiring harnesses are available from RV supply stores, as well as Automatic

Equipment Manufacturing Company, Remco, and Roadmaster, Inc., or you can purchase the components and make up your own. In some cases, a separate diode assembly, called a *converter*, may have to be purchased. In any wiring installation, be sure that no wires chafe against metal edges or drag on the pavement.

Dinghy wiring requires research and careful planning to ensure the installation won't damage the dinghy's electrical system. Wiring can be eliminated if a light bar or add-on lights are used. These perform the taillight functions, so tapping into the dinghy wiring is unnecessary. Many manufacturers of dinghy-towing apparatus offer light bars or add-on lights as options.

FIVE

Converter/Chargers and Battery Chargers

After the alternator, the second most important component of the 12-volt charging system is the converter/charger. A converter changes one voltage to another; when an RV is connected to shore power, it converts 120-volt AC to the DC power needed to operate the 12-volt equipment. Most converters deliver between 10.8 and 13.0 volts, which is not enough to charge a battery; therefore, the charger part of the converter/charger, with its regulated, controlled, higher voltage output, is needed to maintain the house batteries at full charge.

A unit that is only a converter may be installed in older RVs. Converters provide power only for DC equipment and do not produce a regulated voltage high enough for battery charging. A typical 30-ampere converter might operate at 10.8 volts under a 30-ampere load and only at 12.8 volts under a zero load—more than sufficient to power 12-volt equipment, but too low for battery charging—the batteries will eventually self-discharge if they are not maintained with a charge from some other source.

Charger options are often offered by converter manufacturers. The charger can be either built-in or installed as a separate unit. Converters with a built-in charger usually have two separate outputs: one supplying the power for the RV's 12-volt equipment, the other going to the battery for charging purposes. Charger options have regulators with solid-state technology utilizing SCRs to maintain a constant voltage of 13.8 to 14.0 volts. They are usually rated at between 5 and 20 amperes and, because of this generally low amperage, are intended only to top off batteries rather than completely recharge depleted deep-cycle batteries. Complete recharging could be done, but it would take a long time.

During charging, the output tapers off quickly to just a few amperes, as with stock alternators. The charging rate is usually included in the total ouput rating of the converter. For example, if the converter is rated at 30 amperes with a 5-ampere charger and the full 5 amperes is used for charging, 25 amperes is left to

96

provide 12-volt power for operating the equipment. Straight converters are being phased out by many manufacturers. Most recently built RVs are equipped with a converter/charger.

Before we go any farther, we must clarify the terminology about these various units because the line between converters and battery chargers is becoming more and more blurred. Manufacturers call these units by many different names: converter and battery charger, battery charger/conditioner, or sometimes just converter or charger even though the unit may convert and charge. To avoid ambiguity, we refer to a unit incorporating a battery charger as a converter/charger.

The Workings of a Converter

Simply described, a converter is a step-down transformer that lowers 120 volts to 12 volts and, because the voltage is still AC in form, rectifies it into DC voltage by means of diodes in a rectifier circuit. (This is also what happens to voltage produced by an alternator.) The produced DC has AC ripples imposed on it, and the ripple effect is quite pronounced. This is a simplified description of a *linear unregulated converter*.

Linear Unregulated Converters

Converter/chargers and units that are either converters or chargers are alike in the way they convert 120-volt AC to 12-volt DC. They differ only in the method in which they regulate the output voltage; some units are simple and some are quite sophisticated.

Linear unregulated converters include either a fuse or a circuit breaker, mainly to protect against excessive current flow; most have thermal protection to shut down the unit if it becomes overheated. They may have a filter circuit to lessen radio frequency interference (RFI).

Another common feature in many units is a *transfer switch* (i.e., electromagnetic relay), which automatically disconnects the battery circuit from the RV's main house circuits whenever the shore-power cable is plugged in. This completely isolates the batteries from the DC circuits so the batteries cannot discharge. When the shore-power cable is disconnected or a power failure occurs, the transfer switch kicks over so the batteries come on line. With this type of

Converter/chargers and units that are either converters or chargers are alike in the way they convert 120-volt AC to 12-volt DC. They differ only in the method in which they regulate the output voltage.

Converter/Chargers and Battery Chargers

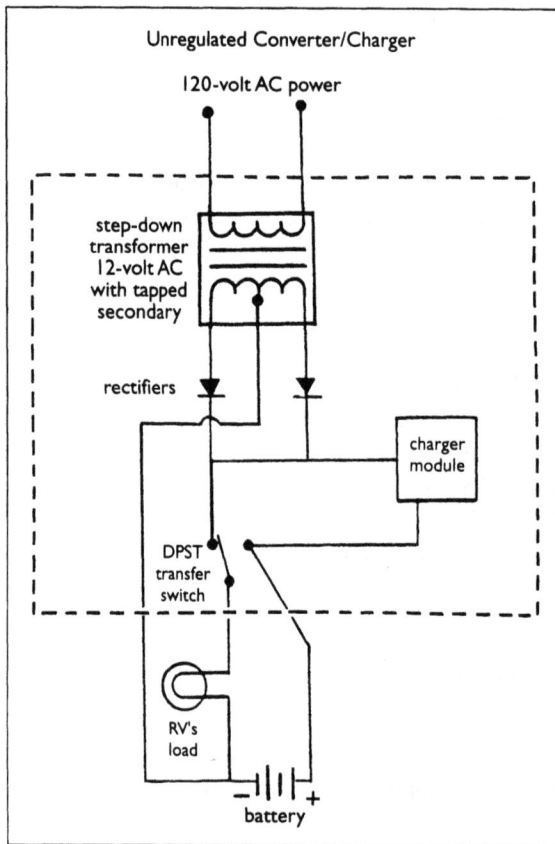

Unregulated Converter/Charger

120-volt AC power

step-down
transformer
12-volt AC
with tapped
secondary

rectifiers

charger
module

DPST
transfer
switch

RV's
load

battery

Figure 5-1. A simplified version of the circuitry of a linear unregulated converter with regulated charger, including a built-in transfer switch.

converter/charger, the charger circuit bypasses the transfer switch and maintains the batteries at full charge (Figure 5-1). Small-output converter/chargers found on some RVs may have a manual switch instead of an automatic transfer switch. Either switch does the job, but the manual switch requires the user to remember to turn it on and off as needed.

Many manufacturers also incorporate a DC fuse block that serves as a distribution panel for the RV's entire DC system. Sometimes a main fuse protects the unit and the system, and individual automotive-type fuses protect each circuit. Some models have an AC panel board with a main circuit breaker and breakers for each AC circuit (Figure 5-2). Linear units range in size from 6- to 50-ampere outputs.

For many years, unregulated converters have been popular original equipment for RVs primarily because they are so inexpensive. They are rugged and there are few parts to wear out, but these high-efficiency, reliable devices have one drawback. Because the input AC voltage controls the output DC voltage, it affects the power available for operating 12-volt equipment. If input voltage is low, output voltage is correspondingly low; the same situation occurs with high voltage: high input, high output. Voltage spikes are transmitted in the same manner. Voltage-sensitive appliances, such as furnaces, may be affected by unstable input voltage reaching a linear-type unit, and voltage spikes can adversely affect stereos and other electronic equipment.

Unregulated, unfiltered output voltage produces an annoying hum in most radios. To counteract this problem, most linear converters have one or two filtered radio circuits that bypass the converter and run directly off the battery.

Ferroresonant Converter/Chargers

Ferroresonant converter/chargers are more advanced in voltage regulation than the unregulated linear type and do not have transfer switches. They are capable of handling large variations of AC voltage input with little change in DC output. This is not as efficient as it might seem, however, because part of the input current is used to maintain the regulation, slightly diminishing the overall output current.

A high-amperage output is developed at the unit's lowest voltage output; the lowest amperage occurs at its highest voltage rating. Output is tapered, similar to that delivered by alternators with automotive-type regulators. As a converter, a unit can handle high DC loads.

The technology of a ferroresonant converter is complex, but, briefly, it is based on a modified step-down transformer with an extra coil combined with the secondary coil. The transformer transfers energy from the primary coil to both secondary coils by induction, aided by an iron or laminated ferrous core in the middle of both coils. The presence of the cores greatly strengthens the transformer's electromagnetic field. The cores are in many forms and shapes, the most common resembling a square donut with the windings of one coil wrapped around one side of the donut and the windings of the other two coils around the opposite side.

The leads of the transformer's extra coil are connected to a capacitor of a certain value, which forms a *resonant circuit.* As current flows through the extra coil winding and the capacitor, they resonate at the 60-Hz AC frequency input (Figure 5-3, pg. 100).

When the coil reaches its *saturation point* (i.e., when a magnetic field builds in a coil and reaches its maximum), any increase in the input AC voltage does not cause any further increase in the magnetic field, so the voltage is prevented from rising higher. The resonant circuit causes the transformer to saturate, achieving a form of regulation. This simplistic description of the circuits in ferroresonant converters

Figure 5-2. MagneTek's 6300 Series Power Electrical Center incorporating a converter/charger and AC and DC distribution panels. Cover has been removed to show interior.
(Photo courtesy of MagneTek)

99

Ferroresonant Converter/Charger

120-volt AC power

step-down transformer with two secondaries

resonant circuit

rectifiers

+ —

12-volt DC

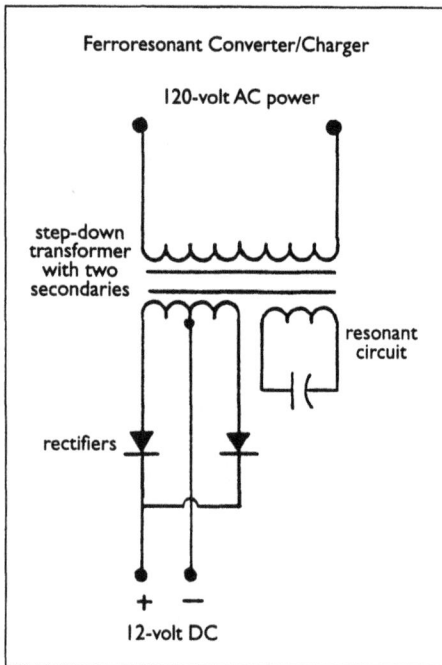

Figure 5-3. A simplified version of the circuitry of a ferroresonant converter/charger.

doesn't begin to cover their sophistication or complexity, but rather is an overview of how they work.

The output voltage of ferroresonant converter/chargers ranges from 12 volts at full load to 14 volts at no load. They have overload and thermal circuit-breaker protection, as well as a regulated filtered output. Unlike linear unregulated converter/chargers, in a ferroresonant unit the battery must be connected to provide filtering for the system.

With ferroresonant converter/chargers, sensitive electronic equipment and AM radio reception is less likely to be affected. These units naturally produce a somewhat smoother DC current with a clipped, flattened ripple, rather than the more pronounced undulation of linear converters. The current is "floated" across the terminals of the battery, which functions as a giant capacitor. With voltage across the battery, the ripples of the current are smoothed out.

Phase-controlled Converter/Chargers

Current and voltage regulation in *phase-controlled converter/chargers* is achieved with semiconductor switching. Two or more SCRs (solid-state devices that use AC voltage to pass large amounts of direct current through them) are used. The SCR is in the off mode until, at a given point, a small AC voltage triggers it to allow a large amount of direct current to flow through it. The frequency of the alternating current, which goes through two alternations of 60 Hz for a total of 120 times a second, controls the SCR's triggering at each phase of the current with a special circuit. Other regulating circuits vary the period of SCR conductivity until a constant voltage is present at the output. SCRs produce a high-current pulsation requiring the battery to average the voltage, which can cause the battery to heat (Figure 5-4).

Because it's difficult to eliminate or reduce RFI, it's better to turn off the converter/charger while operating the radio than to live with the noise.

Each time an SCR is triggered, a voltage spike occurs. If not properly filtered, the spike can create a hum that affects radio reception. Because it's difficult to eliminate or reduce RFI, it's better to turn off the converter/charger while operating the radio than to live with the noise. (We have this problem, which affects AM and FM reception and even the cassette player. We have tried many methods of correcting it, but to no avail.)

Phase-controlled converter/chargers have much better regulation than the ferroresonant types. On a smaller scale, this form of regulation is used in the battery-charging component of linear unregulated converter/chargers with a transfer switch. With phase-controlled technology, it is easy to design a regulator that provides the same form of multistage charging available in alternator regulators—where the regulation can be either constant voltage or constant amperage, or a combination thereof.

One disadvantage of phase-controlled regulation is that it does not produce its full rating with low AC voltage input. When high-wattage equipment is in use, such as an air conditioner or electric heater, that pulls down the AC voltage, the DC voltage should be monitored to ensure that the batteries are receiving enough voltage to charge them. On our previous trailer we had a converter with a built-in phase-controlled charger and, sometimes, when the air conditioner or electric heater was in use, we noticed the 12-volt lights were dimmer than normal. The batteries were not being charged because the input AC voltage was too low. Turning off the air conditioner or heater usually solved the problem.

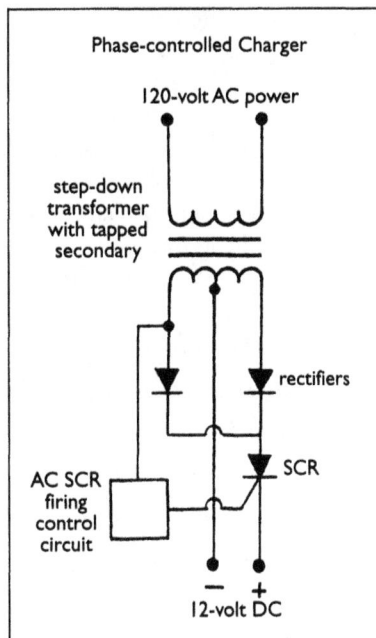

Figure 5-4. An extremely simplified version of the circuitry of a phase-controlled charger showing how a typical SCR is wired. This type of charger can have many wiring variations other than the one illustrated.

High-Frequency Switching Converter/Chargers

High-frequency switching converter/chargers (also referred to as a *pure DC charger* or *pulse-width modulated (PWM) switch-mode power supply*) are the next generation up from the phase-controlled type and use either FETs or MOSFETs. MOSFETs are used most often because they can switch high currents at high speeds; FETs are not as good at handling high power. Since both require little current to operate, converter/chargers with these types of transistors are very efficient.

A circuit that creates a high frequency, between 15 and 45 kilohertz, controls the MOSFETs in high-speed switching of the rectified direct current. The direct current is switched on and off at up to 45,000 times a second, resulting in a very

101

smooth current with no apparent ripples—a pure direct current.

The output has a taper that develops the maximum rated current at a voltage lower than the rated voltage, and minimal current at the upper voltage. If the converter/charger is rated at 40 amperes, the no-load voltage is 14 volts, and the battery is severely discharged, the converter/charger will deliver the 40 amperes, but the initial voltage may be as low as 12.5 volts. Once the battery voltage starts to rise and the amperage rate begins to taper off, the converter/charger voltage rapidly rises toward its maximum. Some units hold a high voltage (13.6 to 14.0) from no load to about 85 percent of the maximum load before the voltage tapers off at maximum load.

High-frequency switching converter/chargers should comply with Federal Communications Commission requirements so they do not interfere with radio and TV broadcasts, cellular telephones, and radio navigation transmissions. Because of the high frequencies involved, mostly in the radio high-frequency range, a special case is needed to prevent radio-frequency emissions. Because the case tightly encloses the sensitive electronics, a small fan is sometimes used for ventilation to prevent overheating. Some units use a variable-speed fan that creates hardly any noise; these pure DC units are the quietest of all converter/chargers. They are protected against high-input voltage and excessive temperature.

We have a high-frequency switching converter/charger that has proven to be efficient and trouble free. Our only complaint stems from the constant 14 volts the unit maintains. This voltage is too high for the lightbulbs used in 12-volt fixtures, so bulbs burn out prematurely.

We have a high-frequency switching converter/charger that has proven to be efficient and trouble free. Our only complaint stems from the constant 14 volts the unit maintains. This voltage is too high for the lightbulbs used in 12-volt fixtures, so bulbs burn out prematurely. The voltage can't be lowered since there is no provision for voltage adjustment (how we overcame this problem is discussed in Chapter 6). One manufacturer makes a unit that develops maximum-load voltage of 13.2 volts and no load at 14.0 volts. Whenever a load of 1.5 amperes or more is applied, the voltage drops to 13.6 volts to prevent premature bulb burnout.

The Opti-Charge battery charge controller made by Opti-Chip Technologies, Inc., solves some of the problems caused by high, constant voltage from converter/chargers. It measures battery voltage and turns off the converter or charger when a high-voltage set point is reached, and turns on again when the voltage drops to another set point (the set points are adjustable). This allows the batteries to rest between charges and avoids the continuous application of a high, constant voltage, which causes electrolyte loss, thus shortening battery life. The On/Off control is regulated by a special adapter that is plugged into the AC receptacle, and the converter/

charger is plugged into the adapter. The Opti-Charge can be used with any type of converter/charger.

High-frequency switching converter/chargers are the lightest, smallest, and most efficient units on the market.

Multistage Charging in Converter/Chargers

Certain phase-controlled and high-frequency switching converter/chargers and inverters with built-in battery chargers are available with multistage charging (Figure 5-5). The charge is similar to that of multistage regulators used with alternators, with the usual bulk, absorption, and float stages; the equalization stage is an option on some units.

A multistage charger has several safety features. The system shuts down if voltage in the battery or the charger is too high or too low, if there is excessive amperage, if the unit's temperature becomes too high,

A converter/charger services the RV house batteries, which should be deep-cycle, and multistage charging is the best method of charging deep-cycle batteries.

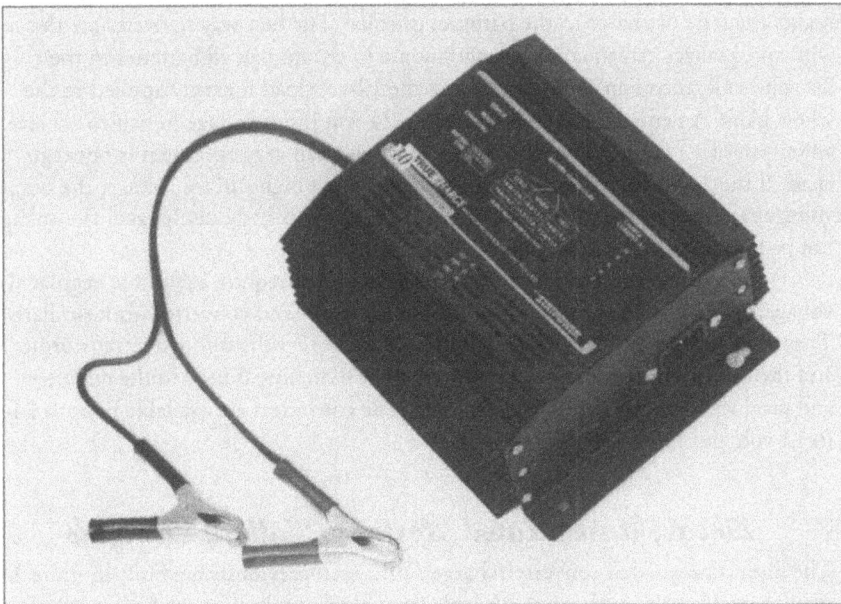

Figure 5-5. Statpower's Truecharge 10 multistage converter/charger.
(Photo courtesy of Statpower Technologies Corporation)

Converter/Chargers and Battery Chargers

or if certain other problems occur. Some chargers have an optional remote control that turns the charger on or off and provides status data of the charger, battery, and entire system.

Because a converter/charger services the RV house batteries, which should be deep-cycle, and because multistage charging is the best method of charging deep-cycle batteries, a converter/charger or inverter/charger with this feature provides excellent charging capability.

DC-to-DC Converters and Equalizers

While *DC-to-DC converters* and *equalizers* are not actually chargers, they deserve mention because they are frequently used in 24-volt systems in the charger circuits. Many of the bus conversions, which are becoming increasingly popular as RVs, have a 24-volt system, but they still require a 12-volt system for lights and other 12-volt equipment used in most RVs.

Because most 24-volt systems consist of either four 6-volt or two 12-volt batteries wired in series, one way to obtain 12-volt service is to utilize just one of the 12-volt batteries or one of the 12-volt sides of the battery bank; however, doing so makes the state of charge in the batteries unequal. The best way to overcome this is with an equalizer. An equalizer's functions are to ensure that all batteries in the entire 24-volt bank receive an equal charge and the 12-volt load is evenly applied to the whole bank. An equalizer actually splits the 24-volt input voltage in half to achieve an output of 12 volts; however, the output voltage can vary because it is not regulated. If the 24-volt batteries are at full charge with a high surface voltage, the output voltage can be higher than needed; if the batteries are slightly discharged, the voltage can be lower than what is desirable.

For electronic equipment or other appliances that require a constant regulated voltage, a DC-to-DC converter is used. The equalizer and converter work similarly: They convert 24-volt DC into AC, step it down to 12 volts through a transformer, and then rectify it back to DC. High-frequency switching is used in the circuitry and produces pure DC on the output side. The converters are available in both 24- to 12-volt and 12- to 24-volt versions.

Linear, Unregulated, Portable Battery Chargers

The linear unregulated converter/chargers discussed previously are built-in units, but many portable battery chargers available from auto supply stores and mass merchandisers are also linear and unregulated (Figure 5-6). Charging rates range from 3 to 50 amperes. Portable battery chargers are usually equipped with a switch/circuit breaker to protect the unit and an ammeter to indicate the charging amperage.

Because it is unregulated, the voltage steadily increases as the battery charges until the electrolyte boils. To prevent overcharging, charging time and amperage must be monitored. A 10-ampere charger develops its maximum charge rate at around 12.8 volts; the charge tapers off as the voltage rises to about 14.2 volts, at which point little charge amperage will flow. The voltage continues to climb, however, until it reaches approximately 17.0 volts. The voltage varies according to the ampere rating of the charger. An 18-ampere charger reaches maximum load at 13.02 volts; a 40-ampere charger at 13.38 volts.

Figure 5-6. Schauer's unregulated 6-ampere portable battery charger.
(Photo courtesy of Schauer Manufacturing Corporation)

Some portable battery chargers have the same type of regulator as phase-controlled converter/chargers. With this type of regulation, overcharging is not a problem.

An unregulated charger can be used for an equalization charge if it is properly monitored. Some chargers have a timer to limit the charge cycle to a specific period to prevent battery damage. Some models have an automatic feature that allows a regulated tapered charge up to 13.8 volts; the unit then shuts off until the voltage drops to 12.8 volts, when it again turns itself on. They may also have a switch that selects 14.2 volts as the set point for deep-cycle batteries. Chargers with the higher amperage ratings have a feature that allows for a temporary high-amperage boost for engine starting. Some chargers have temperature-sensitive breakers that protect both the charger and the battery (assuming that both are in the same temperature environment).

Because a portable charger is so efficient, because it is not fussy about the quality of the AC input voltage (as are the more elaborate chargers), and because it can tolerate voltage drops and surges, it is very effective for charging when a portable gasoline generator is the AC power source.

A portable battery charger quickly delivers a bulk charge if it has a suitable ampere rating. Because a portable charger is so efficient, it is not fussy about the quality of the AC input voltage (as are the more elaborate chargers), and because it can tolerate voltage drops and surges, it is very effective for

Converter/Chargers and Battery Chargers

charging when a portable gasoline generator is the AC power source.

A portable battery charger should not be used in place of a converter/charger. The Underwriters Laboratories (UL) do not list these devices for permanent mounting in RVs. They must be used in an open-air environment with ample ventilation and in a dry, noncorrosive location.

Table 5-1 (pg. 108) lists manufacturers of all types of the equipment described. Included are manufacturers that make inverters with a battery charger. An inverter's primary function is to operate 120-volt AC equipment from 12-volt battery power (discussed in Chapter 9).

There are many different ways of achieving a fully charged house battery bank and providing power to the DC electrical system other than from the batteries. An RV with both 12- and 120-volt electrical systems will have some type of converter/charger, or perhaps just a converter, installed at the factory and, in most cases, owners will live with whatever type of equipment is standard. This information is provided to help those who need to replace failed equipment or who wish to upgrade to newer, more efficient equipment.

Battery Charging with Alternating-Current Generators

A genset, an AC generator permanently mounted in an RV, handles battery charging with ease in conjunction with a converter/charger or an inverter with a charger. Gensets usually produce clean AC with a smooth sine wave free of spikes and surges.

If a genset is used with a multistage charger to take care of battery charging needs, upgrading to a high-output alternator may not be necessary to have a topnotch charging system.

When boondocking, using a genset is a satisfactory method of charging batteries. The genset can charge the batteries at the same time current is being used for other purposes, such as operating the microwave or the air conditioner. Charging through a genset is more efficient than charging while driving by using the engine alternator in the motorhome or tow vehicle, and may be less noisy. Coupled with an AC-operated multistage charger, a genset does as good a job of charging as a high-output alternator with a multistage regulator, and is far superior to charging with a standard alternator. If a genset is used with a multistage charger to take care of battery charging needs, upgrading to a high-output alternator may not be necessary to have a topnotch charging system.

Portable AC generators also can be used for battery charging. Most portable generators have some sort of DC output built in, which may be 8, 10, or 15 amperes. Units with the lower amperage ratings are usually unregulated with a constant amperage, whereas 15-ampere units are regulated with a tapered output. While the built-in charging feature has some merit, it does not provide fast charging. If the batteries were discharged to about 50 percent of capacity, it might take 5 or 6 hours of running to restore them, depending on the ampere-hour capacity of the battery bank. Portable generators can certainly provide a reasonable bulk charge, but, for efficiency and to avoid running the noisy generator for 5 or 6 hours, the balance of the charging should be finished off by other means.

A portable generator can be used to run a portable battery charger with a higher amperage output than that provided by the generator's DC output. The generator can certainly power a 10- to 30-ampere (or more) unregulated, or manual, battery charger, which can do fast charging at a constant amperage rate. To prevent overcharging, however, the battery voltage must be monitored constantly with a voltmeter or the built-in ammeter of the charger. When the amperage drops to 1 or 2 amperes on the ammeter, the battery is usually charged. The noise of the generator will be a constant reminder to do the monitoring.

A 300-watt generator would power a 10-ampere charger and, while a 600-watt unit would marginally run a 30-ampere charger, a 1,000-watt generator would be better. Use a generator with a wattage rating one-third higher than that of the input AC wattage or amperage of the charger. For efficient charging, the proper type of charger is needed. Automatic chargers are regulated to some extent with a tapered output, which does not provide as fast a charge as the manual, unregulated, constant-amperage type.

The shore-power cable can be connected to a portable generator to utilize the RV's built-in converter/charger for the charging. If the RV is equipped with a converter with a low-ampere-rated charger, charging may not be any faster than if the DC output of the generator were used, particularly since the converter's charger is regulated and its output will taper off. The generator's output is constant amperage with no tapering off.

Whenever the shore-power cable is plugged into a generator's AC output, it is important to make sure that all AC equipment is turned off in order to prevent an overload during the charging process.

Although a portable generator may have a high-enough wattage rating to run a converter/charger at 40 to 75 amperes, it may not be able to do the job. Most portable generators do not produce a clean sine wave free of voltage spikes and surges. This so-called "dirty electricity" should not be used to power sophisticated converter/chargers such as the phase-controlled or high-frequency switching types. The spikes and surges interfere with the delicate circuitry of these highly complex

Converter/Chargers and Battery Chargers

chargers, particularly the multistage types, and may damage the unit. The Heart Interface Corporation people conducted tests with portable generators of over 1,000 watts for running their Freedom 10, multistage, 50-ampere inverter/charger. The

Table 5-1.

Converters and Chargers					
Manufacturer	**Model**	**Type**	**Function**	**Amperage**	**Voltage Output**
Carson Manufacturing Company, Inc.	CP-20 FKCR-2	converter/ charger	linear converter with regulated tapered charging	20-amp converter, 3-amp charger	12.5 volts
	CP-20 FKCS-2	converter/ charger	linear converter with regulated tapered charging	20-amp converter, 3-amp charger	12.5 volts
Heart Interface Corporation	Freedom 10*	inverter/ charger	high-frequency switching, multi-stage charging	50 amps	13.5–14.4 volts
	Freedom 25*	inverter/ charger	high-frequency switching, multi-stage charging	130 amps	13.5–14.4 volts
MagneTek	3200 Series	converter/ charger	linear converter with phase-controlled regulated tapered charging	20, 30, or 40 amps depending on model	14 volts
	6300 Series	converter/ charger	linear converter with phase-controlled regulated tapered charging	converter—25, 32, 36, 45, or 50 amps, charger—6 or 12 amps depending on model	14 volts
	900 Series	converter/ charger	ferroresonant tapered charging	30, 40, 50, or 75 amps depending on model	14.1 volts
	7200 Series	converter/ charger	high-frequency switching, tapered charging	40 or 55 amps depending on model	13.6/14 volts

NOTES:
Except for the portable chargers, all chargers can be used as converters.
*See Table 9-3 for inverter information on these models.

RV Electrical Systems

portable generators were unsatisfactory. They found that only genset-quality generators of about 2,000 watts produced clean-enough electricity to do the job. (See also The Power Factor in Generator Battery Charging in Chapter 9.)

Voltage Adjustable	DC Distribution Panel	AC Distribution Panel	Comments
no	3-circuit fuse block	15-amp GFCI circuit	
no	one 15-amp, two 7.5-amp circuits	two 15-amp GFCI circuits	
fully	no	no	equalization charge possible
fully	no	no	equalization charge possible
no	4-circuit fuse block	no	built-in DPST transfer switch
no	4- or 6-circuit fuse block	30-amp circuit breaker with one 15-amp GFCI and three breaker-protected circuits	built-in DPST transfer switch, unit is a complete power center
no	no	no	35-amp 24-volt model available
no	no	no	fan-cooled true DC charger with voltage cutback for lightbulb protection

(continued on next page)

Manufacturer	Model	Type	Function	Amperage	Voltage Output
Newmark Products, Inc.	PCS-RAC Series	converter/ charger	linear converter with phase-controlled regulated tapered charging	converter— 20, 30, or 40 amps depending on model, charger—5 amps	14 volts
	RAC Series	converter/ charger	linear converter with phase-controlled regulated tapered charging	converter—20, 30, or 40 amps depending on model, charger—5 amps	14 volts
	30F and 50F Series	converter/ charger	ferroresonant tapered charging	30 or 50 amps	14 volts
Schauer Manufacturing Corporation	M51, M72, and MV10612	portable battery charger	linear unregulated constant-amperage charging	5 and 1 amps, 7 and 2 amps, variable 1 and 3 to 10 amps	14.2 volts
	R72 and RCC10	portable battery charger	linear phase-controlled regulated tapered charging	7 and 2 amps, and 10 amps	14.2 volts
Schumacher Electric Corporation	SE82-6 and SE1010-2	portable battery charger	linear unregulated constant-amperage charging	6 and 2 amps, 10 and 2 amps	13.8 volts
	SE1012D	portable battery charger	linear unregulated constant-amperage charging	10 amps	14.2 volts
	SE50MA-2	portable battery charger	linear phase-controlled regulated tapered charging	2 and 10 amps	13.8 volts
Statpower Technologies Corporation	Truecharge 10, 20, and 40 Series	converter/ charger	high-frequency switching multistage charging	10, 20, or 40 amps depending on model	13.1–14.8 volts

NOTES:
Except for the portable chargers, all chargers can be used as converters.
*See Table 9-3 for inverter information on these models.

Voltage Adjustable	DC Distribution Panel	AC Distribution Panel	Comments
no	up to 8-circuit fuse block	30-amp circuit breaker, up to 5 circuits	built-in DPST transfer switch, unit is a complete power center
no	up to 5-circuit fuse block	no	built-in DPST transfer switch
no	4- or 6-circuit fuse block	no	
no	no	no	not for permanent mounting, switchable dual output for maximum or trickle charge, variable 10-amp model has either 6- or 12-volt output, units have ammeters
no	no	no	not for permanent mounting, switchable dual output for maximum or trickle charge, 10-amp model has automatic shut-off when charged, units have ammeters
no	no	no	not for permanent mounting, switchable dual output for maximum or trickle charge, units have ammeters
no	no	no	not for permanent mounting, for charging deep-cycle batteries only, unit has ammeter
no	no	no	not for permanent mounting, switchable dual output for maximum or trickle charge, 10-amp model has automatic shut-off when charged, unit has ammeter
fully	no	no	battery type selector switch, dual battery charging, optional temperature sensor, provision for equalization stage on 20- and 40-amp models, units have LED charging current display, optional remote display panel

(continued on next page)

Converters and Chargers (cont.)

Manufacturer	Model	Type	Function	Amperage	Voltage Output
Todd Engineering Sales, Inc.	Power Source Series	converter/ charger	high-frequency switching, tapered charging	30, 40, 45, 50, or 75 amps depending on model	13.2/14 volts dual voltage
Trace Engineering Corporation	812*	inverter/ charger	high-frequency switching, two-stage constant-current/ constant-voltage charging	50 amps	12.6–14.7 volts
	M1512*	inverter/ charger	high-frequency switching, multistage charging	70 amps	12.6–14.7 volts
	2512*	inverter/ charger	high-frequency switching, multistage charging	120 amps	12.8–14.7 volts
Vanner, Inc.	30-10 and 30-50	charger/ conditioner	linear charger with pulse-controlled tapered charging	10 or 50 amps depending on model	14 volts
	20-3600C*	inverter/ charger	high-frequency switching, multistage charging	120 amps	10–15 volts

NOTES:
Except for the portable chargers, all chargers can be used as converters.
*See Table 9-3 for inverter information on these models.

Voltage Adjustable	DC Distribution Panel	AC Distribution Panel	Comments
yes	no	no	true DC chargers, some models fan-cooled optional ADV-1 controller switches to float voltage after charging
fully	no	no	optional remote On/Off switch with LED indicator, 24-volt model available
fully	no	no	has battery temperature sensor, LED bar graph for voltage and current, optional remote On/Off LED monitor panel
fully	no	no	LED digital readout for voltage and current, optional remote On/Off LED digital monitor panel, 24-volt model available
no	no	no, but has AC outlet	unit is not a converter but will function as power supply with a fully charged battery in the system, uses SCRs for pulse charging, 24-volt model available
fully	no	no	LED lights show voltage and current, optional remote On/Off LED digital monitor panel, 24-volt model available

SIX

Solar Power for Battery Charging

Battery charging with solar panels has many advantages over other forms of charging. It is the safest form of battery charging because (1) there is only low amperage to deal with, not high amperage; (2) a solar charging system is not complicated; (3) no explosive fuels need to be handled as with portable generators; and (4) solar power is a renewable, free resource.

A Description of a Solar Panel

Solar panels are composed of *photovoltaic (PV) cells.* The first part of the word, "photo," comes from the Greek and means light; "voltaic" means producing electricity. Therefore, "photovoltaic" means electricity created by light, which is what a solar cell does: It absorbs light from the sun and creates electricity. A group of cells forms a *PV panel,* or module; two or more PV panels used together form an *array.*

How Photovoltaic Cells Are Made

Silicon dioxide is one of the most common minerals on earth, found in most rocks and sand. When it is in crystalline form, it is *quartz.* Quartz crystals are *piezoelectric,* meaning they have properties capable of generating electricity under mechanical stress (e.g., pressure). (Quartz crystals are used to control the AC frequency in inverters.) The crystals are also light-sensitive. As photons of light fall on a quartz crystal, some electrons are knocked out of their orbits, creating a flow of electricity.

Crystals are made by super-heating the silicon to a molten state and adding a small amount of boron. Then a seed crystal is inserted into the mix and rotated. As the crystal is slowly extracted from the mix, the molten silicon adheres to it, forming a single pure crystal. The new crystal is cooled by freezing as it is extracted. The crystal is formed into an ingot 3 feet long and 4 inches in diameter. Wafers 15-thousandths of an inch thick are cut off and etched with grooves to form microscopic pyramids that help absorb light. The wafers are treated on one side with a phosphorus compound, after which they are reheated.

A grid of 44 electrical contacts is printed on the surface of the cell. Leads are also printed on the cell to gather the current that will be produced. The front lead is the minus terminal; the back lead is the plus terminal. The completed cell is wired in series with other cells to produce the required voltage needed for a solar panel; one cell's output is between 0.45 and 0.50 volt.

The voltage of a cell remains constant, but the area determines the maximum amperage output. A typical 4-inch-diameter cell in bright sunlight produces about 2 amperes. Solar panels are rated in wattage. For example, the Siemens Solar Industries M-75 panel with 33 cells is rated at 48 watts at 16 volts, and delivers a maximum of 2.94 amperes.

The wired cells are sandwiched between sealant over a metal foil-covered layer of DuPont Tedlar, then mounted in an aluminum frame and covered with a special glass plate. A solar panel is composed of 30 to 36 cells.

How Solar Cells Work

The two surfaces of the wafer become either P-type or N-type silicon, depending on whether they contain boron or phosphorus. When the two surfaces combine, they form a PN junction, which functions like the PN junction in a diode. In fact, solar cells are light-sensitive diodes (Figure 6-1).

As a photon of light penetrates the P-type layer and strikes the PN junction, it causes negative charges to form in one layer and positive charges in the other. If metal contacts are placed on both sides of the two layers, a current flows, as in a battery. Once the electrical current is gathered, the cell works just like any other source of power.

Other Types of Solar Cells

In addition to single-crystal solar cells, there are square-shaped cells that contain many crystals. This type of cell is made by casting molten silicon into a rectangular ingot. Square-shaped cells are easier and cheaper to manufacture, but they are slightly less efficient than single-crystal cells.

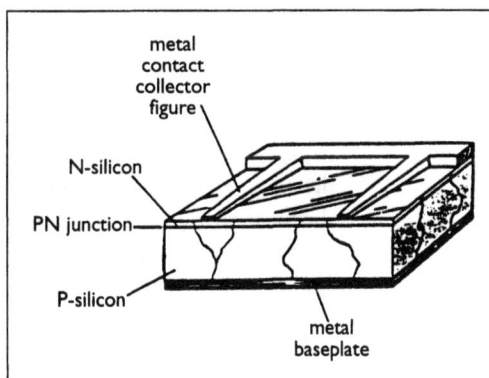

Figure 6-1. Cross section of a solar cell.
(Illustration courtesy of RV Solar Electric)

115

Another type is the recently developed amorphous, thin-film solar cell. This type of cell has no crystalline structure. It is made by placing a silicon-based alloy on a roll of flexible material, such as thin stainless steel, using an application method similar to printing. Manufacturing costs are low for this process because it can be automated, thereby eliminating some labor expenses. These solar panels are less efficient; about twice the surface area is needed to equal the output of other cell types.

The flexible panels can be installed in many places a rigid panel wouldn't fit—even over a curved surface.

Their lifespan can be only a few years, compared to 10 to 30 years for rigid panels. The flexible panels can be installed in many places a rigid panel wouldn't fit—even over a curved surface.

Panel Categories

Solar panels are available in three different categories: *high-voltage panels, self-regulated panels,* and *building-block panels* (Table 6-1). All but the self-regulated panels require a regulator (discussed later in this chapter).

A high-voltage panel contains two or more extra cells to compensate for voltage loss in a long run between the panel and the batteries or the load, as might occur in house installations. Solar panels also have some voltage loss when used in temperatures over 100°F (37.8°C); a high-voltage panel makes up this loss. High-voltage panels have a nominal voltage of 17 to 18 volts—1 to 2 volts higher in output than other panels. They can be used for RV installations, although they are costly compared to other panel types; however, in hot climates such panels might be of value. The Siemens M-55 panel with 53 watts, 36 cells, a voltage of 17.4, and an amperage of 3.05, is one example of a high-voltage panel (see Table 6-1). The highest-rated high-voltage panel (36 cells) is Siemen's ProCharger 4, rated at 75 watts with a 4.4-ampere output.

Self-regulated panels have fewer cells to provide the lower voltage that maintains a battery over long periods when it is not in use. These panels, with a maximum voltage of approximately 14.5, charge the battery only to that point. The batteries then refuse any further charge, thereby self-regulating the charge rate. While this is the theory behind self-regulating panels, variations in temperature can affect voltage output; therefore, the danger of overcharging exists. Of course, the charge voltage is applied only during daylight hours, since no charging can take place at night.

Self-regulated panels are available in inexpensive 2.5-, 5-, and 10-watt sizes, as well as the more costly 42-watt size. A self-regulated panel in the smaller 5- to 10-watt sizes may be practical for RVers who use their rigs only occasionally, but who wish to keep the batteries topped off between uses. Self-regulating panels cannot do serious battery charging, so their use is strictly limited to maintaining a charge in a

116

Table 6-1.

A Comparison of Solar Panels								
Mfr. Brand Model	Rated Watts	Rated Volts	Rated Amps	Open Circuit Volts	Short Circuit Amps	Size L&W	Type Cell Constr.	Panel Type
Siemens								
PC-4	75.0	17.0	4.40	22.0	4.8	48x21	Single	Hi-V
PC-2	35.0	17.0	2.10	22.0	2.4	25x21	Single	Hi-V
PC-1	17.0	17.0	1.00	22.0	1.2	25x11	Single	Hi-V
M-75	48.0	15.9	3.02	19.8	3.4	48x13	Single	BB
M-40	40+	15.7	2.55	19.5	3.0	48x13	Single	BB
M-55	53.0	17.4	3.05	21.7	3.4	50x13	Single	Hi-V
M-50	48.0	17.3	2.78	21.6	3.2	50x13	Single	Hi-V
M-65	43.0	14.6	2.95	18.0	3.3	42x13	Single	Self
M-35	37.0	14.5	2.56	18.1	3.0	42x13	Single	Self
M-20	22.0	14.6	1.50	18.2	1.65	22x13	Single	Self
Solarex								
MSX-56	56.0	16.8	3.35	20.8	3.6	44x20	Multi	BB
MSX-64	64.0	17.5	3.66	21.3	4.0	44x20	Multi	Hi-V
MSX-60	60.0	17.1	3.50	20.8	3.8	44x20	Multi	Hi-V
MSX-40	40.0	17.2	2.34	21.1	2.53	30x20	Multi	Hi-V
MSX-30	30.0	17.8	1.68	21.3	1.82	23x20	Multi	Hi-V
Kyocera								
LA-51	51.0	16.9	3.02	21.2	3.25	39x18	Multi	BB
LA-63	62.7	20.7	3.03	26.0	3.25	47x18	Multi	Hi-V
LA-45	45.3	15.0	3.02	18.9	3.25	35x18	Multi	Self
LT-34	34.0	15.0	2.26	N/A	N/A	27x18	Multi	Self

NOTE:
Watt, volt, and ampere ratings are based on a temperature of 77°F (25° C).
Lengths and widths are rounded off to the nearest inch.
BB = building-block panels, Hi-V = high-voltage panels, Self = self-regulated panels

battery or bank depleted by small phantom loads and the normal self-discharge of the battery. The lower-wattage models deliver less than 2 amperes.

To operate as designed, self-regulated panels should be connected to batteries of an ampere-hour capacity related to the size of the panel: smaller-wattage panels

Self-regulating panels cannot do serious battery charging, so their use is strictly limited to maintaining a charge in a battery or bank depleted by small phantom loads and the normal self-discharge of the battery.

paired with batteries of small capacity, and larger-wattage panels with batteries of larger capacity. Because these panels are self-regulating, no other regulation is needed.

Building-block panels are designed to be used singly or in combination to charge one battery or a bank of batteries. This type of panel is most often installed on RVs, especially those that may be lived in for long periods in campgrounds without electrical hookups. The Siemens M-75, rated at 48 watts, and the Solarex Corporation MSX-60, rated at 60 watts, are popular models. Building-block panels require some form of regulation.

Determining Panel Size

Panel size needed depends on the type and the intended use. Several years ago when we were staying in a primitive campground in Arizona, our neighbor was trying to recharge his battery with a solar panel after a night with no electrical hookup. He was using a small, self-regulated, 5-watt model, and was not having much success. He admitted he had just purchased the panel and was experimenting with it. He found that he did not have the right panel for the job he wanted it to do.

A rule of thumb is to pair a 50-watt panel with a 100-ampere-hour battery, a common Group 27 size. With a 200-ampere-hour battery bank, two 50-watt panels are needed; a 400-ampere-hour bank requires four 50-watt panels, and so forth.

A rule of thumb is to pair a 50-watt panel with a 100-ampere-hour battery, a common Group 27 size. With a 200-ampere-hour battery bank, two 50-watt panels are needed.

Another way to calculate panel size is by using a 1:2 ratio: 1 watt of solar power for every 2 ampere-hours of battery capacity. Because we are fulltimers and spend a lot of time in the Northwest—even in the winter—where there are many cloudy days, a ratio of 1.5:2 is more sensible: a 75-watt panel for each 100-ampere-hour battery, or three 50-watt panels for two 100-ampere-hour batteries. For those who spend time in more southerly climes, the 1:2 ratio is usually sufficient and is a good starting point for installing solar panels.

Two 50-watt panels deliver about 5 amperes in the direct, bright sunlight of a summer day. On average, the panels receive about 5 hours of sunshine per day, providing approximately 25 ampere-hours of charging per day. A 25-ampere-hour daily charge rate would handle most overnight camping needs with power to spare, including several hours of TV viewing and limited inverter use for other AC equipment. (In fact, two 50-watt panels can deliver a daily charge closer to 50 ampere-hours because the summer months average 10 or more hours of sunlight.)

Another way to select panel size is to calculate daily amperage usage (see Tables 2-6 and 2-7, pg. 24, 25). With a daily consumption of 30 ampere-hours, two panels capable of delivering 15 ampere-hours per day, even in the winter, would be suitable.

For self-regulated panels, figure the amount of daily discharge and select a panel that delivers that amount. For maintaining an SLI battery on a tow vehicle or motorhome, Siemens recommends its M-25, 22-watt panel for a 65-ampere-hour battery, and its M-65, 42-watt panel for a 135-ampere-hour battery. This is close to a ratio of 1 watt for every 3 ampere-hours of battery rating.

For systems with a phantom load of 1 ampere or more (24 ampere-hours daily), a self-regulating panel probably falls short of maintaining the batteries. A system of panels with a regulator is needed.

Most RV solar panel systems consist of two, three, or four panels that provide 5 to 11 amperes in perfect sunny conditions. A 4- or 5-ampere charge may not seem like much, but spread over 6 to 10 hours, it restores a lot of ampere-hours in the batteries.

A 25-ampere-hour daily charge rate would handle most overnight camping needs with power to spare, including several hours of TV viewing and limited inverter use for other AC equipment.

Most RV solar panel systems consist of two, three, or four panels that provide 5 to 11 amperes in perfect sunny conditions.

Panel Efficiency and Characteristics

As temperature rises, all solar panels lose efficiency because voltage output is reduced. At 80°F (26.6°C), the average cell produces about 0.49 volt; at this temperature, a panel of 33 cells produces 16.17 volts. On a hot day, it is entirely possible for the temperature of a panel mounted on the roof of an RV to reach 150°F (65.6°C). At this temperature, the output falls to 0.42 volt per cell, reducing the panel's output to 13.86 volts. This temperature-caused voltage drop of 2.31 volts results in reduced battery charging. Temperature susceptibility is one reason why high-voltage models are manufactured. Most solar panels are more efficient at 32°F (0°C) than at warmer temperatures.

Equalization-Stage Charging with Solar Panels

Solar panels have an advantage over some other methods of charging in that they automatically provide a mild equalization charge to the batteries every night. While this charge is not the high 16 volts provided in true multistage charging, it is a constant voltage ranging from 14.3 to 14.8, depending on the setting of the regulator. The voltage is held constant, but the amperage diminishes as daylight fades, thereby producing the mild equalization charge. This charge, which automatically occurs nightly, has an effect on batteries over time similar to the higher equalization charge applied once a month or so by multistage chargers.

Tracking the Sun

Certain factors affect the output of solar panels: the latitude of the location, the season in which they are used, and the position of the panels relative to the sun. While voltage remains constant if the temperature doesn't fluctuate, amperage varies proportionally to the angle of the panel and the amount of light falling on it. Ideally, the rays of the sun should fall perpendicularly on the surface of the panel; that is, 90 degrees to the panel's surface. From spring to autumn, with panels mounted flat on the RV's roof, sufficient sunlight reaches them to sustain a charge for most applications.

During the winter, however, it's another story. The relationship of sun to earth, illustrated in Figure 6-2, shows that the sun's position is much higher in summer than in winter. To catch the rays of the lower winter sun, there should be a way to tilt the panels upward. The sun circles the earth at a rate of 15 degrees of longitude per hour, which means it is moving 1 degree of longitude over the earth's surface every 4 minutes; therefore, the sun's angle to a solar panel varies constantly. Even if the panels were on some type of swivel, in addition to being tilted, they would need constant adjustment to keep receiving the maximum amount of sunlight, which is highly impractical. Positioning the panels about four times daily would be sufficient;

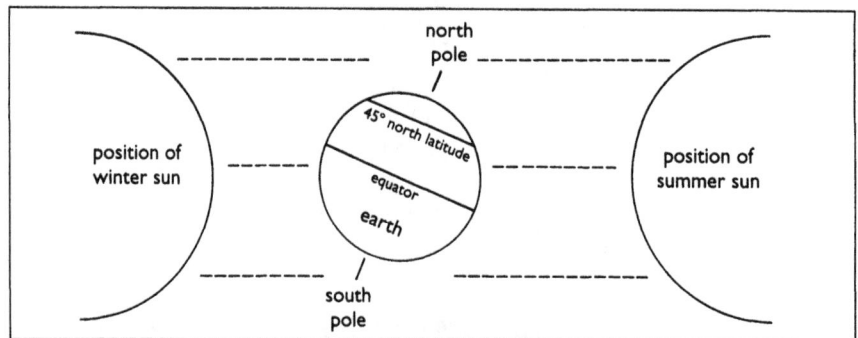

Figure 6-2. The sun's relation to earth in different seasons. Note how the sun's rays hit the earth at different angles in summer and winter.

Table 6-2.

Solar Panel Adjustment by Latitude		
Latitude (Degrees)	**Angle of Tilt (Degrees)**	**Approximate Locations**
15–25	15–25	Mexico
26	27	Lower Florida, South Texas
27	29	
28	31	Middle Florida
29	33	
30	35	Middle Texas
31	37	
32	39	Louisiana, Alabama, Georgia
33	41	
34	43	New Mexico, South Carolina
35	45	Arizona, Arkansas, North Carolina
36	47	
37	49	California, Tennessee
38	51	Kansas, Kentucky, Virginia
39	53	Nevada, Colorado, Illinois
40	55	Utah, Ohio, New Jersey
41	57	Pennsylvania
42	59	Nebraska, Iowa
43	61	Wyoming, Connecticut, Rhode Island
44	63	Oregon, Idaho, South Dakota
45	65	Wisconsin, Michigan, New York
Above 45 degrees latitude, add 20 degrees		Washington, Montana, North Dakota Maine, Alaska, Canada

NOTE:

These latitudes run approximately across the middle of the listed states or areas. Although the listed angles of tilt are within 2 degrees of accuracy, panels adjusted to within 4 or 5 degrees are satisfactory. If your state or area is not listed, use the angle of tilt for a neighboring state on or near your latitude.

in reality, most RVers wouldn't bother—we certainly wouldn't. Instead, we select campsites that provide the best and longest exposure to the sun, tilting the panels accordingly. Solar panels should face south for best results.

Table 6-2 shows the angle that panels should be tilted in the winter months in different parts of the country. Angles are measured from the flat surface of the panel to the roof, assuming the roof is parallel to the horizon. Tilting boosts the panel's amperage output during those winter months when daylight hours are few. It may be worth the effort, since tracking the sun for optimum charging is the equivalent of having the amperage output of an extra half panel.

The best way to measure tilt angle is using an angle-finder with a built-in level, found in most hardware stores. The angle-finder's plumb-like weighted needle points to a scale that shows the angle of the object and its relationship to the ground, automatically compensating for any unlevel condition of the RV.

Panels have maximum solar exposure in campsites with no trees or buildings that cast shadows on the panels. If sites are assigned, you may not be able to select the ideal site; if you have a choice, it is worthwhile to drive or walk around the campground and look at the sites. Think about how the RV will be positioned in the site: Which direction will it face? How will this affect the panel's exposure? Consider how the panels are mounted on the roof: Are they mounted parallel to the centerline of the RV or perpendicular to it? These factors affect output, especially if the panels have to be tilted. In campgrounds with lots of trees, look for open spaces between tree branches where light could reach the panels. Is it feasible to position the RV forward or backward in order for the panels to take advantage of the spaces?

If we are limited to maximum charging in either the morning or the afternoon, we prefer the sun to hit the panels in the morning so they begin charging as soon as possible after the previous night's usage of battery power. A little forethought in selecting a campsite can result in improved panel output and better battery charging.

Panel Protection

Because there is nothing mechanical in solar cells and nothing to deteriorate, solar panels may last as long as a half century or more if the glass covering the cells is protected from damage. Hailstorms and falling tree branches can be the most destructive to solar panels.

We try to avoid sites under large trees with dead branches. Solar-panel glass is sturdy, so pine cones and acorns don't usually cause damage.

Because there is nothing mechanical in solar cells and nothing to deteriorate, solar panels may last as long as a half century or more if the glass covering the cells is protected from damage.

Panels become hot when exposed to the sun, and ventilation is needed to dissipate the heat. They should be mounted slightly above the roof so air can circulate underneath, even when they are positioned flat on the roof. When maneuvering into campsites with low overhanging branches, take care to avoid a branch slipping into the space between the panels and the roof—a large-enough branch caught under a panel could rip it off. We make it a practice to inspect tree-shaded sites to be sure there are no branches that would interfere with the panels. Small branches can scratch the glass if they brush across the panels.

When panels are tilted, they are affected by high winds. A tilt of 40 to 70 degrees above the roof's surface can cause the panels to act like sails and "catch" the wind. If they are in the wrong direction in relation to the wind and the wind is strong enough, the mounting brackets can be wrenched from the roof. If the panels stay in place, wind pressure can loosen the mounting screws, perhaps causing leaks later. It may be a nuisance, but panels should be lowered as flat as possible in extremely high winds and, of course, always for traveling.

Regulators

All solar panels with voltages higher than those of the self-regulated panels must have some form of regulation (Figure 6-3). The purpose of a solar-panel regulator is the same as that of other types of regulators used in electrical production: to control the voltage produced by the panels and hold it to the desired levels for proper battery charging.

With solar panels, a regulator also prevents reverse flow. During the night, when no light falls on the panels and no voltage is produced, the voltage of the battery causes current to flow back into the panels, causing a slight battery discharge. In the opinion of some, this does not constitute a problem; they argue that the discharge during a single night is inconsequential. True, but what would happen over many winter nights when the panels might not be able to keep up with the discharge, or during several cloudy days, or when the RV is inside a repair facility for several days?

A simple way to correct reverse flow is to install a diode in the circuit; however, the voltage drop across the diode means the panels will produce slightly less voltage when the sun is shining. Regulators with either a built-in diode or a relay correct this problem.

Figure 6-3. Authors' Solar Guard regulator installation. *Below the regulator is the remote switch for the Trace 612 inverter.*

123

Two types of regulators are used with solar panels: the *series-pass regulator* and the *shunt-type regulator* (Figure 6-4). The series-pass regulator, or *charge controller*, is wired into the charge circuit on either the positive or negative lead, in series with the battery. It shuts off current flow from the solar panel to the battery when the voltage reaches a certain set point. When a load is applied and the voltage drops to a low set point, the charge controller again allows current to flow through the use of a relay that makes and breaks the connection. The relay disconnects the panels from the battery at night, serving the same purpose as a diode but without the voltage drop. Although series-pass regulators have some solid-state circuitry, the relays are mechanical and therefore subject to mechanical failures, such as spring breakage and contact pitting.

A variation of the series-pass regulator uses either MOSFETs or SCRs in its circuitry, which eliminates the relay but operates in the same manner. Diodes may be used, depending on the regulator's design. Multistage charging techniques are possible with this solid-state circuitry.

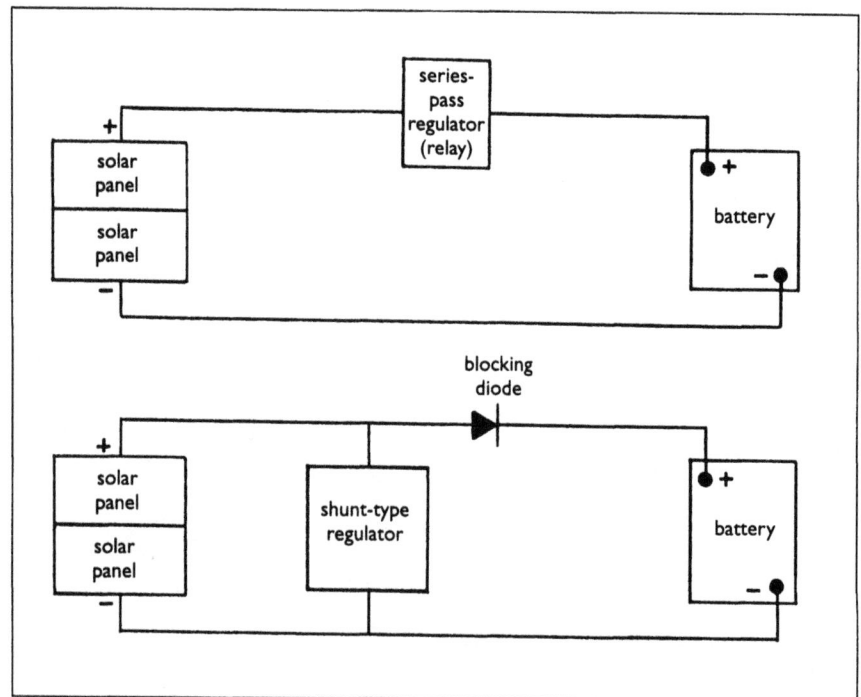

Figure 6-4. Circuits of a series-pass regulator (top) and a shunt-type regulator (bottom). There are many circuit variations other than this simplified version.

A shunt-type regulator is a solid-state device that regulates panel voltage by shunting current flow from the battery positive lead to the negative lead and back to the panels. This shuts off amperage flow to the batteries when voltage reaches a high set point. The current remains off until the battery voltage drops to a lower set point, at which point the current flows again. In addition to stopping reverse current flow at night, the regulator's diode also prevents reverse current flow when other forms of charging are used (e.g., an engine alternator, converter/charger, or portable charger). We think the tiny voltage drop across a diode is a small price to pay for the advantages it provides.

Diodes wired in the circuit of each panel can prevent a shaded panel from stealing output from a panel in full sun. If you have a regulator, do not use external diodes.

Depending on the unit, regulators can handle a variety of different amperages, from a few amperes to 30 amperes or more. Units that handle the higher amperage rates are designed for residential and commercial use where many solar panels, with a corresponding high-amperage output, are used. When selecting a regulator, make sure it is designed specifically for RV use. Regulator manufacturers are listed in Table 6-3 (pg. 126).

When selecting a regulator, make sure it is designed specifically for RV use.

Our Experience with Solar Panels

When we first became interested in solar charging in the 1970s, solar panels were expensive with low output, so it wasn't a cost-effective method of charging. It wasn't until just a few years ago, after solar panel output had improved and costs came down, that we decided solar power would be the answer to our battery-charging problems. Reading *RVers' Guide to Solar Battery Charging* by Noel and Barbara Kirkby reinforced our decision. (See Appendix A for ordering information.) Noel, president of RV Solar Electric Systems, suggested the company's package that included the RV Powerpac 2 solar kits containing two M-78 panels, the Solar Guard regulator, and the 600-watt Trace inverter with a built-in 25-ampere charger, which we purchased.

We selected the Solar Guard regulator because of its high-quality jeweled meter that indicates the charge voltage of the panels and, more importantly, the amperage charge rate to the batteries, and also because it has adjustable set points for both high and low voltages. This shunt-type regulator charges until the voltage rises to 14.3, when the battery is considered charged; then it shuts down until the voltage drops to 13.3, when the panels are again turned on. (The voltage set points may have to be adjusted slightly for battery type and personal preference.) The regulator can be recessed into a wall or mounted on a wall with a surface box.

125

Table 6-3.

Solar Regulators					
Manufacturer	**Model**	**Type**	**Function**	**Charge Voltage**	**Adjustable Set Points**
Ample Power Company	Smart Multi-Source Regulator (MSR)	shunt-parallel regulator	microprocessor, temperature-compensating, multistage charging	13.6–14.4 volts	no
RV Solar Electric	Solar Guard	shunt/diode regulator	transistor switching charging	14.3 volts	yes
Specialty Concepts, Inc.	SCI Automatic Sequencing Charger (ASC)	shunt/diode regulator	transistor switching charging	optional variable	two, high and low voltage
	SCI Mark III/15 Regulator	shunt/diode regulator	transistor switching charging	fixed	no
Sunlight Energy Systems	Sunlogic	series-pass regulator	high-frequency switching charging	14.3 volts	two
Trace Engineering Company	C-30A Charge Controller	series-pass regulator	relay controlled charging	variable	two, high and low voltage

NOTE:
These regulators represent only those practical for RV use; the list does not include units designed for residential use.

Solar Panel Installation

On our fifth-wheel trailer we installed the two solar panels on the sloping section of the roof, just behind the roof's highest point, over the bathroom below. Here the roof slopes downward from its high point at about a 15-degree angle. We hoped this placement would provide some measure of protection from low branches.

This location is opposite a holding-tank vent pipe, making the wiring run short. The wires enter the trailer through the vent pipe, and no holes—potential leak sources—needed to be drilled in the roof. (Wires can be routed through a refrigerator vent if holding-tank vents aren't convenient.) Inside the trailer, the vent pipe is routed through a closet. Just below the closet's ceiling, a small hole was drilled in the pipe. The wires exit the pipe there, run a short distance to the regulator, then back to the closet and down to the batteries in a compartment below at the front of the trailer, near where the vent pipe terminates. Caulking around the wires at the exit hole prevents odors from entering the trailer.

A single fuse block with a 25-ampere fuse was installed near the batteries on the positive wire from the regulator. The inverter was installed next to the batteries and

Maximum Amperage	Metering	Comments
20 amps	interfaces to and controlled by Energy Monitor II panel	unit will regulate several charging sources including unregulated and ferroresonant chargers up to 80 amps, optional battery temperature sensor; selectable battery type, LED charging indicator
12 amps	analog voltage and amperage	trickle charge connection for second battery (SLI), LED charging indicator
16 amps	no	optional temperature sensor, 24-volt model available, LED indicator, optional low voltage disconnect
15 amps	separate analog volt and amp meters	optional temperature sensor; 24-volt model available; LED indicator; optional low-voltage disconnect
6 amps	no	LED status indicators
30 amps	no	can be used with 24-volt systems

its remote switch put just below the regulator. (The switch and regulator are shown in Figure 6-3, pg. 123.) The entire installation took about a day to complete, including building a shelf to hold the inverter.

Some points to remember when installing solar panels: Because the panels are mounted on the roof, prevent leaks or water seepage by applying caulk under the mounting brackets. Before inserting the screws, generously coat the threads with caulk. If the RV's roof is plywood covered with rubber, the panels can be mounted firmly; however, if the roof is the aluminum-sheet type without a solid base, special care is needed. Because the sheet-metal screws have only thin metal to grip, make sure the screw holes are not too big. Alternatively, a plate of ¾-inch marine plywood or ⅛-inch aluminum can be fastened to the roof, and the mounting brackets attached to the plate. If plywood is used, seal it with paint or a waterproofing compound. Clean the roof to remove oxidation before installing the caulked mounting brackets or plates.

When installing the panel wiring, keep the panels covered—a heavy blanket or sheet of black plastic will suffice—to remove the voltage potential from the circuit.

As in other wiring, voltage drop in long wire runs occurs in solar-panel wiring, but, because lower amperage is involved, the drop is not as great as in high-amperage situations. Nevertheless, consider the length of the wire run and use the proper-gauge wire.

When we don't have an electrical hookup, we pay particular attention to how the trailer is parked. Because our panels are on a slope and not mounted parallel to the ground, we try to park with the back of the trailer facing either east or south so the panels receive full sun from morning through midday. This way, the batteries begin to recharge at the earliest possible time. Our second choice for parking is with the back of the trailer facing west to take maximum advantage of late afternoon sunlight.

Having the panels on a slope has been quite satisfactory. There are times when they would receive maximum sunlight if they were flat, but there are just as many times when they would need to be tilted for maximum sunlight. At these times, because the panels are already angled, we don't need to adjust them.

The solar-panel system has proven to be one of the best RVing equipment purchases we have ever made.

The solar-panel system has proven to be one of the best RVing equipment purchases we have ever made. It's difficult to evaluate the system's cost relative to its convenience and practicality, but we do know it has made primitive camping far more enjoyable than ever before because we no longer have to be concerned about discharged batteries. The system is silent, safe, and completely automatic in operation; the sun comes up, the panels turn on and do their job. The only maintenance required is to occasionally clean the glass with a window cleaner or water. All these advantages plus one more: Using solar panels is the best possible method of charging batteries.

Misconceptions About Solar Power

Many people have misconceptions about solar power. Some think it is used only for heating water or for heating a house in the winter. Even those who have solar panels sometimes don't quite know what they do. We recently read an article in which it was stated that using solar panels allowed storage of volts in the battery for future use. Volts are not stored in a battery—electrical energy, measured in ampere-hours, is what is stored. It was also stated that solar panels are designed to power equipment and appliances. In RV use, they are primarily intended for recharging deep-cycle batteries. To provide power for appliances, the solar panels would need an amperage output of 10 to 20 amperes or more, which could only be achieved with an array of at least six or eight panels. Panels should not be thought of as a power source for operating equipment; instead, they should be considered another method of battery charging, with the battery supplying the power.

Of course, on occasion, solar panels can be used to power equipment. We know of one RVer who used solar power to run the engine in his motorhome after an alternator belt broke. He did not have a replacement and was far from help, but he found his panels supplied enough amperage to handle the ignition system's requirements until he got home. He would have had a problem, however, if he had had to drive after dark.

We run 12-volt equipment, a roof vent fan for example, off the solar panels. The main point to remember is that when equipment is in operation, the batteries are not being charged, which is the primary purpose of the panels. If they handle the load, fine, but if not, the load will run off the batteries. Solar panels provide maximum charge when there is no load on the 12-volt system.

Panels should not be thought of as a power source for operating equipment; instead, they should be considered another method of battery charging, with the battery supplying the power.

The Perfect Charging System

We stumbled onto a technique for battery charging using solar panels that seems to be the ideal method. Shortly after we installed the panels, we just ignored them when we were in campsites with electrical hookups. The converter/charger handled the power supply and charging function, but the constant 14-volt output of the converter/charger was burning out lightbulbs much too quickly. We were replacing bulbs every two weeks or so in the light fixtures we used often. Our converter/charger doesn't have a user-adjustable voltage output, so there is no way of reducing the voltage. Since the voltage on the built-in battery charger on our inverter can be adjusted, we decided to use the inverter's charger. We thought that 13.7 volts would be a suitable setting. It worked insofar as lightbulb longevity was concerned, but using the inverter's charger created another problem. The SCRs in the inverter's circuitry create a great deal of RFI in our stereo system—not just in the AM radio band, but also in the cassette player. One day while listening to the radio and becoming annoyed by the hum, we decided to turn off the inverter and let the solar panels take over the battery charging, since panels do not create RFI.

We found ourselves with a perfect charging system. Now, the inverter/charger is turned off in the morning and the panels handle the charging and any loads during daylight hours. At night, when we are more likely to be watching TV than listening to the radio, the inverter is turned on so its charger can handle the nighttime 12-volt loads. With the accessible remote switch in the bedroom, it's easy to turn the inverter off and on whenever we wish.

Now, the inverter/charger is turned off in the morning and the panels handle the charging and any loads during daylight hours.

We make sure the inverter is off whenever we leave the trailer because of a problem that can occur with the refrigerator. When we have an electrical hookup, the refrigerator is on its automatic, or AC, setting, which switches to propane operation in the event of a power outage. With the inverter/charger on, if a power outage occurred while we were away, the 600-watt inverter would automatically switch to AC production and the refrigerator would continue to operate on AC. The inverter can handle the 300-watt load of the refrigerator, but there's no point in letting it draw power from the battery, since the refrigerator automatically switches over to propane operation in the absence of AC power.

Some time ago, we had to replace our trailer batteries and purchased the only ones available in the small town where we were: ordinary discount-store RV/marine deep-cycle batteries. Using our combination solar panel and inverter/charger system has kept these inexpensive batteries going for more than four years now without any problems.

What makes our system work so well is explained in Ample Power Company's catalog in a section called "Killing Batteries," written by David Smead, in which he lists many ways a battery should not be treated. Among them are two that account for the success we have had with our system: (1) Do not overcharge a battery by applying a voltage above 13.8 volts for extended periods; and (2) do not undercharge a battery by never charging it beyond 13.8 volts. At night, our inverter/charger puts out a steady 13.7 volts; during the sunny hours the batteries receive at least one charge of up to 14.3 volts from the solar panels.

The batteries are also allowed periods of rest in the daytime; the regulator turns off the solar panels when the batteries reach full charge. They rest until a load is applied that drops the voltage to the set point at which the panels turn on again. Batteries should rest between charging and use. Batteries that are constantly being charged and discharged are batteries that will have a shortened lifespan.

THE 120-VOLT
AC
ALTERNATING CURRENT
SYSTEM

SEVEN

Alternating Current Circuits

I n addition to the 12-volt direct current system, RVs also have a 120-volt alternating current system, which is identical to the type found in residences. The system is wired in the same manner, and the components, from the distribution panel to the wall receptacles, are usually the same. And, unlike much specialized RV equipment, AC electrical components are readily available at most hardware stores.

Today's RVs may have seven or more circuits because some of the installed equipment requires a considerable amount of power: microwave oven, up to 12 amperes; electric water heater, 5.5 amperes; compact washer/dryer, 16 amperes; dishwasher, 12 amperes; air conditioner, 13.6 amperes. To accommodate this equipment, the same type of distribution panel used in residences, although smaller, is often installed. If the residential type is not used, an RV might have a combination 12-volt

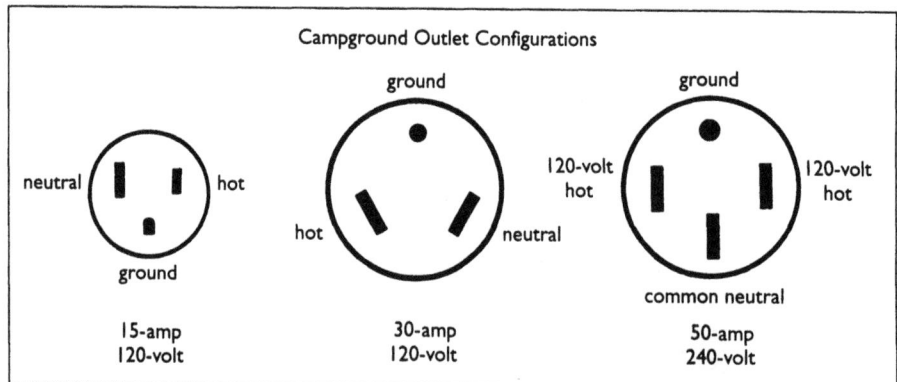

Figure 7-1. Standard campground outlet configurations. On the 50-ampere 240-volt outlet, each hot 120-volt blade represents one leg of the 240-volt supply.

DC/120-volt AC panel or, more commonly, a combination panel incorporated in the converter/charger (see Chapter 5).

Distribution Panels

The *power-supply assembly* supplies the 120-volt AC power to an RV and typically consists of the shore-power cable and a distribution panel for either 20- or 30-ampere service. The shore-power cable terminates in a plug that fits into one of the outlet configurations illustrated in Figure 7-1.

Current from the shore-power cable flows through the distribution panel's main 30-ampere disconnect master switch/breaker (20-ampere on older RVs). The other side of the switch/ breaker is connected to a bus bar, to which all the separate switch/breakers for the branch circuits are connected. These breakers are rated at 15 or 20 amperes, depending on the load the circuit will carry, and they are connected to the current-carrying, or hot, wires of each branch circuit. There may be two to seven branch circuits of 15 to 20 amperes each.

The distribution panel also contains another bus bar to which the return wires from the branch circuits are connected. The return wire from the shore-power cable is connected to the other end of this return bus bar (Figure 7-2).

The circuits go to various receptacles in different areas of the RV to provide power for a refrigerator, TV, and other appliances. Often a single air conditioner is wired into the

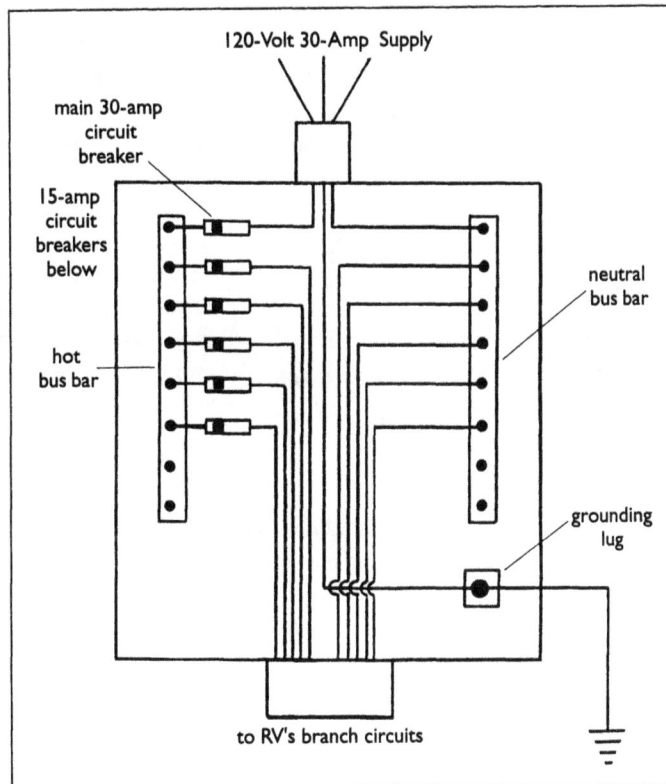

Figure 7-2. AC distribution panel system (most RVs have a simpler panel than illustrated).

133

same circuit as a microwave oven but, to prevent amperage overload, the two appliances are controlled by a SPDT switch so that both cannot be used at the same time.

Smaller RVs, tent trailers, pickup campers, and older RVs with just one wall receptacle may be set up for only 15- or 20-ampere service with a fused single switch or circuit breaker instead of a supply panel. Circuit breakers are used in most RVs nowadays; this is the best arrangement because screw-in AC fuses often become corroded, making removal difficult and dangerous.

When an RV's AC service is supplied by an AC generator or an inverter instead of the campground outlet, the input current reaches the distribution panel through either hard (i.e., permanent) wiring or the shore-power cable.

Wires

As in DC systems, all circuits and components of an RV's AC system are wired in parallel; however, AC wiring is different because three wires are involved instead of the two in a DC circuit. The *hot*, or *current-carrying, conductor* and the *neutral*, or *return, conductor* correspond to the positive and negative wires of the DC circuit. The return conductor is also a current-carrying conductor, but is grounded and does not normally have voltage potential. The third wire is the *grounding conductor*. (The neutral wire was once designated the ground conductor, but that became confusing when ground wires were incorporated; therefore, "neutral" is used instead of "ground.") The grounding conductor, which carries no current, is always at ground or earth potential—meaning there is no potential at all.

As in DC systems, all circuits and components of an RV's AC system are wired in parallel; however, AC wiring is different because three wires are involved instead of the two in a DC circuit.

The NEC stipulates that all AC systems be three-wire in order to make electrical equipment safer to use. Without a grounding conductor on electrical equipment with a metal housing, if a current-carrying part or wire shorted out to the housing, touching the metal could cause a shock severe enough to be fatal. Since electricity always seeks the path of least resistance, the grounding conductor provides this path—with a grounding to earth, which lessens or eliminates the shock hazard. The principle is the same as when lightning seeks the earth to neutralize or ground its electrical charge.

Floating Neutral

In residential wiring, the neutral conductor is always connected to the grounding conductor at the service entrance panel—the main panel controlling electrical service to the residence. This panel contains the master disconnect switch and the electric meter, and is where the neutral and grounding conductors are bonded together at the bus bar. *Bonding* is the term used to describe the metal-to-metal contact occurring whenever a circuit's conductors are attached to metal parts of a panel with metal fastenings such as screws, lugs, or bolts. The bus bar can be grounded to the earth using several methods, but it is usually done with a heavy wire clamped to a metal electrode grounding rod driven several feet into the earth. This bonding does not occur elsewhere in the AC electrical system in residential wiring.

An RV is said to be electrically "floating" because it is insulated from the earth, or ground, by its tires, which have the only contact with the earth (metal jacks do not provide an adequate ground). Therefore, the neutral conductor is also floated, or isolated, from all contact with the chassis or other metal parts of the RV. Only the grounding conductor is bonded to the RV. If the neutral conductor were connected to the chassis and metal parts, any metal on the RV would be electrically charged, shocking anyone who touched it while current was flowing through the system. This is why the neutral conductors must be floating throughout the RV (see Chapter 8).

Color Coding

According to the NEC's color-coding specifications, the insulating cover on the hot conductor should be either red or black, the neutral conductor white, and the grounding conductor green. The terminal screws on AC plugs or receptacles to which wires are connected are also usually color coded. The black hot wire is fastened to the brass screw, the white neutral wire to the silver screw, and the green grounding wire to the green screw. Solid copper cable, the type used in most residences, is also used in RVs. It is composed of three insulated solid copper wires in a PVC sheath. The hot and neutral wires are covered with a color-coded insulation—red or black for the hot wire, white for the neutral wire—but the grounding conductor is bare. (Romex is the brand name of a General Cable Company product, but is often used generically for any PVC-sheathed, solid copper cable.)

> *According to the NEC's color-coding specifications, the insulating cover on the hot conductor should be either red or black, the neutral conductor white, and the grounding conductor green.*

The Ground Connection

In an RV, the bare copper grounding wire is attached to a special connection, or bus bar, on the distribution panel, which grounds all circuit receptacles to the panel as well as the panel to the grounding conductor of the shore-power cable. Another single bare copper wire, which should be at least 8 gauge, connects and grounds the system to the chassis of the RV. An RV's system is not grounded to earth until its shore-power cable is connected to an AC power source outside the RV, such as a campground outlet; the grounding pin on the shore-power cable plug connects with the ground connection of the outlet. At either the outlet or the campground's service panel, the grounding and neutral conductors are bonded together.

When the RV is not connected to a campground outlet and some other AC power source (e.g., a generator) is used, the chassis ground provides some measure of protection, but—not being a true earth ground—it is not adequate for complete protection. It is the only ground source available, however, when not connected to shore power.

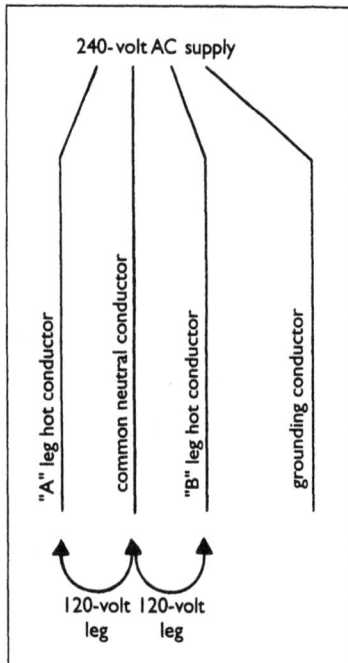

Figure 7-3. Basic wiring diagram of a 240-volt system.

240-Volt, 50-Ampere Systems

Bus conversions, large Class A motorhomes, and large fifth-wheel trailers are often wired for 240-volt, 50-ampere service. The 240-volt system is split into two 120-volt main circuits, or legs, to provide a usable voltage in the RV. (When using a voltmeter, the voltage across the two 120-volt hot conductors measures 240 volts.) This system requires a main disconnect fuse/circuit breaker and two subpanels, one for each 120-volt circuit. The subpanels, each with its own hot and neutral bus bar and breakers, split the heavier loads between them to balance the two circuits. Lesser circuit loads also are equally split between the panels.

A 240-volt system consists of three wires: two 120-volt current-carrying conductors and a single, common, neutral conductor used with both hot conductors to form the two legs. Added to these wires is a grounding conductor, which makes it a four-conductor system (Figure 7-3).

Campgrounds offering 240-volt service have outlets with the configuration shown in Figure 7-1, which is often referred to as a mobile home outlet because it is the type used in mobile home parks.

Some large RVs with just a 120-volt 30-ampere system may have a main panel and one subpanel. The main panel usually carries the circuits for heavy-amperage equipment, such as air conditioners; the subpanel contains the circuits for wall receptacles.

136

Alternating Current Wiring

In an AC system, amperage and wiring runs are determined by the same methods as for a DC system, except that the allowance for voltage drop should be 10 percent instead of 1 and 3 percent. Table 4-3 (pg. 70) can be used for the calculations. The ampacity of the wire must also be considered (see Table 4-2, pg. 69). In RV AC circuits, nothing smaller than 14-gauge wire should be used. This wire has an ampacity of 15 amperes, the amperage of typical circuits and fuses/breakers installed in RVs.

For RV AC circuits, the NEC sanctions the use of either solid copper wire with non-metallic (NM) sheathing (the Romex type commonly used in building construction) or stranded wire. Since keeping manufacturing costs down is a major consideration in RV construction, Romex-type wiring is often used because it can be strung without the conduit protection required for stranded wire. The NEC requires wire to be supported every 4½ feet with cable clamps, except near outlet boxes, where it must be supported within 8 inches of the box. These specifications are suitable for buildings but, in our opinion, they are not suitable for RVs. When the RV is moving, the unsupported lengths of wire vibrate and work against any tightly supported wire. The fatigue in these places eventually causes the wire to harden and fracture, creating open circuits and possible shorts. Romex-type wire is easy to use, crushproof, and covered with a good insulating PVC material; however, in the opinion of some in the RV industry, including us, solid wire should not be used because of the fatigue effect. The NEC is primarily concerned with electrical installations in buildings and other types of construction and often does not address specific RVing needs. When it does, it concerns itself with fire safety only.

Romex-type wire is easy to use, crushproof, and covered with a good insulating PVC material; however, in the opinion of some in the RV industry, including us, solid wire should not be used because of the fatigue effect.

For both DC and AC wiring, we prefer boat cable; we think it's the best wire available. It meets all UL specifications for use in boats, exceeds SAE specifications for DC automotive wiring, and meets U.S. Coast Guard standards for electrical systems. Boat cable has a rating of 600 volts at temperatures of 221°F (105°C) in dry locations and 167°F (75°C) in wet locations. Each wire is electro-tinned, providing excellent protection against corrosion, and covered with PVC insulating material. It's available in duplex (two conductors) and triplex (three conductors) types, which are covered with an oil-and-abrasion-resistant PVC outer jacket. Boat cable is easy to run, strip, and otherwise work with because it is flexible, multistranded copper wire.

For both DC and AC wiring, we prefer boat cable.

Boat cable does not carry the standard AWG markings. No letter code designates the insulation type; if a letter code appears, it designates the manufacturer. In addition to boat cable, we also like the easy-to-install, stranded, flexible wire types designated SO, SOW, ST, or STO (shore-power cables are made of STO), which are color-coded, three-conductor, hard-service cords suitable for indoor and outdoor installations as well as for portable cords (Table 7-1). (Boat cable and these wire types are not sanctioned by the NEC for installation by RV manufacturers.) Wire types that can be used for AC applications in RVs are listed in Table 7-1.

On its covering, wire is stamped or marked with gauge size and number of conductors; for example, 12/2 is 12-gauge wire with two conductors and 10/3 is 10-gauge wire with three conductors. When Romex-type wire is marked "14/2 with ground," there are two 14-gauge conductors with a separate ground wire. Wire also may be marked with a letter code indicating the type of insulation covering (Table 7-2, pg. 140).

Various types of conduit and sheathing can be used on stranded wire in RV installations, but the NEC specifies that metal boxes must be used for receptacle mounting with metal conduit, and plastic boxes for non-metallic sheathed cable in non-metallic PVC conduit.

If solid Romex-type wire is installed, plastic receptacle boxes with strain-relief clamps should be used, providing there is enough space to install a box of this depth. The wire should be supported with as many cable clamps as needed to prevent undue vibration. Standard duplex receptacles that accommodate two plugs are used with this type of box.

Because of the thin paneling on RV walls, most manufacturers use speed-wiring receptacles, which are units with the faceplate incorporated. They can be installed quickly by fishing the wire through the hole cut in the wall, stripping the wires and pushing them into their respective holes on the receptacle, installing the receptacle in the wall, and tightening the screws to hold it in place. Stranded wire cannot be used with a speed-wiring receptacle, and the stiff solid wire makes such installations difficult to repair or modify.

It usually takes some ingenuity to add an AC circuit or modify AC wiring in an RV.

Installation Practices

It usually takes some ingenuity to add an AC circuit or modify AC wiring in an RV. It's often necessary to route wires through walls using existing holes, such as those for furnace ducts. All wiring should be fastened down tight. Screw-type wire clamps are best; adhesive-backed clamps often come loose, especially if used on bare wood. Sometimes insulated staples can be used. When the wire goes through any material, place grommets or bushings around the wire at the hole. Wirenuts can be

Table 7-1.

Cable Types and Ratings			
Type	**Voltage**	**Wire**	**Specifications and Applications**
AC	120	Solid	Armor-Coated. Household AC 3-conductor with flexible metal tape. Does not require conduit.
Boat	12/120	Stranded	Marine Boat Cable. PVC-insulated. 2 or 3 conductors in outer jacket of PVC. Not for RV use, per NEC. Suitable for dry or wet locations, oil-resistant. Meets AWG and SAE standards and UL specifications.
AWM	12/120	S/S*	Appliance Wiring Material. Single wire. Same wire as MTW (below) and THHN (see Table 7-2). For charge lines or AC wiring in conduit and 12-volt interior wiring.
BX	120	Solid	Armored building wire. Same as AC wire.
GR	12	Stranded	Used for battery cables.
MC	120	Solid	Metal-Clad. Similar to AC cable. Three conductors. Meets UL specifications.
MI	120	S/S	One or more conductors in liquid- and gas-proof metal tubing or pipe. For AC wiring.
MTW	12/120	S/S	Machine Tool Wire. Thermoplastic building single conductor wire for 12- or 120-volt use. Suitable for charging cable.
NM	120	Solid	Non-Metallic sheathed cable with PVC covering (also known as Romex). Approved by NEC for RV use. Conduit not needed.
SJT	12/120	Stranded	Junior hard-service thermoplastic or rubber-coated. 2 or 3 conductors. NEC-approved for portable cords and cables only. SJTO is oil-resistant.
SO/SOW	12/120	Stranded	Similar to SJT. Water-resistant neoprene-jacketed portable cord. Not approved by NEC for permanent installation.
SP-2	12/120	Stranded	Rubber-coated extension cord. 2 or 3 conductors. For light to medium portable cords. SPT-1 has thermoplastic coating. Not approved by NEC for permanent installation.
ST/STO	120	Stranded	Hard-service cord NEC-approved for portable use. Used for RV shore-power cable. STO is oil-resistant.

NOTE:
*Available as either solid or stranded wire.

Table 7-2.

Insulation Covering of Common Electrical Cable Suitable for RV Use in 12- and 120-Volt Applications

Cable Designation*	Insulation Covering Types	Location Suitability	Heat Resistance Rating (in Degrees)
TW	Thermoplastic (PVC)	Wet	140°F/60°C
THW	Thermoplastic	Wet	167°F/75°C
THWN	Thermoplastic, nylon outer covering	Wet	140°F/60°C
THHW	Thermoplastic, nylon	Wet	194°F/90°C
THHN	Thermoplastic, nylon	Dry	194°F/90°C
RHH	Rubber (polyethylene)	Dry	194°F/90°C
RHW	Rubber	Wet	167°F/75°C
MTW**	Thermoplastic, oil-resistant	Wet	140°F/60°C
AWM**	Thermoplastic, nylon	Dry	194°F/90°C

NOTES:
*T = thermoplastic, W = wet locations, H = heat rating, HH = high heat rating, R = rubber or polyethylene covering, N = nylon covering
**See Table 7-1
All wire listed is usually single conductor and available in a wide range of wire gauges.

used to connect wires together, but crimp-type connectors are better because they are less likely to loosen from vibration. Use a proper connector; don't simply twist the wires and hold them together with electrician's tape. Tape can be used to hold the wirenut and wires tightly together, however. Use electrical junction boxes with cover plates whenever two wires are joined or several circuits are connected to a main circuit. If the box is metal, make sure a small jumper wire is connected between the grounding wire's connection and the box's lug to ground it. Any metal conduits or wire with a flexible metal covering also should be grounded. Never use aluminum wire of any type for electrical installations in an RV.

Never use aluminum wire of any type for electrical installations in an RV.

Ground Fault Circuit Interrupters

To eliminate shock hazards, the NEC prohibits the installation of standard receptacles near a water source. Instead, receptacles with a *ground fault circuit interrupter (GFCI)* must be used in RV bathrooms and galleys. An RV's exterior receptacles must also be GFCI-protected. A GFCI receptacle is often installed on a bathroom or galley circuit shared with an exterior receptacle, thereby protecting both.

GFCIs are available incorporated in a circuit breaker or, more commonly, in a receptacle, or as an adapter that is plugged into the campground outlet. When the shore-power cable is plugged into the adapter, the RV's entire AC electrical system is protected. The receptacle type is much less expensive than the other two.

GFCIs work on the principle that current flowing through an AC circuit is equal, or balanced, on both sides of the load. The amperage in a circuit flows through the hot conductor to the receptacle, or to an electrical device operated from the receptacle, and then returns through the neutral conductor with the amperage remaining the same throughout the circuit. If a change occurs in the current flow causing the amperage to become unequal, or out of balance, the GFCI senses the imbalance and trips, breaking the circuit. For example: If an electric drill with a metal case were being used and something shorted out to the drill's case, the current flow would become unbalanced since some of the current would be flowing through the grounding conductor; the GFCI would trip. A change in current flow of as little as 3 to 4 milliamperes (a thousandth of an ampere) activates the GFCI in milliseconds. It takes about 8 milliamperes to deliver a fatal current, so clearly a GFCI is a good protector.

The main component of a GFCI is a transformer in which both the hot and neutral wires are wound together around the primary side of the transformer. The opposing AC currents neutralize the magnetic effect in the primary winding so that no current flows in the secondary winding. The secondary side of the transformer goes to a double-pole, single-throw (DPST) relay with contacts that are normally closed. These contacts act as switches in the hot and neutral wires of the main circuit. An imbalance in current flow in the primary winding causes current to flow in the secondary winding, which, in turn, activates the relay, turning off the circuit. The campground outlet connection must have a good ground contact for a GFCI to function properly (see Chapter 8).

All GFCIs have a test circuit activated by a pushbutton. Pushing the button allows current to flow between the hot conductor and the grounding conductor through a resistor, which unbalances the current flow in the primary winding and trips the relay. A reset button restores the normal current flow.

We have experienced some minor problems with GFCIs. On our previous trailer, the GFCI in the bathroom also protected an exterior receptacle. Heavy rain would cause the GFCI to trip, so often when it was raining, we couldn't use the bathroom receptacle. The rain apparently created enough minor current leakage to activate the GFCI. Such inconveniences are worth putting up with, however, because of the protection a GFCI affords.

Alternating Current Circuits

EIGHT

Campground Hookups

The 120-volt AC power provided by a campground's electrical hookup is a great convenience and, at times, a necessity. With a little knowledge about this hookup and a few tools and accessories, this service can be used easily and safely.

One of the biggest problems many RVers have with campground hookups—the one we cited in the story that begins this book—is that loads larger than 15 amperes cannot be run on a 15-ampere circuit. Too many RVers seem to think that as long as an electrical outlet is available, anything can be run from that outlet.

Some years ago, we were in a campground during a severe cold snap. Our neighbor, who was living in an older trailer without an AC electrical system, was trying to heat the trailer with two 1,500-watt electric heaters. We were unaware of this until one morning we saw him inspecting the extension cord plugged into the campground's outlet. The cord was in several pieces with the insulation burned and split like wieners that had been roasted too long over a campfire. When we went over to see if we could help, the man told us he couldn't understand why his extension cords kept burning; this was the second one ruined. It was a cheap-quality, 16/3 extension cord—much too small a wire gauge to handle the load of two heaters. Table 4-1 shows that 16-gauge wire has an ampacity of 10, so our neighbor was trying to run two heaters, each drawing 12.5 amperes—a total of 25 amperes—on a cord rated to carry only 10 amperes, and all from a 15-ampere outlet.

To avoid overloading problems, RVers should learn to live within the amperage available from the campground outlet; with only 15 amperes available, electricity has to be used judiciously.

Electric heaters and air conditioners are responsible for most RVers' problems with 15-ampere campground hookups. The improper use of these appliances can cause an outlet's receptacle contacts to burn, which can cause a fire and overload the campground's circuits so much that voltage drops to unsafe levels.

Accessories for Campground Hookups

Campground hookups have several different amperages and voltages. The most common is the 30-ampere outlet with a receptacle that accepts a plug with two angled, flat blades and a round or U-shaped pin. Outlets in older campgrounds are the 15-ampere residential type, which accept a plug with two flat, parallel blades (smaller than those on the 30-ampere plugs) and a round or U-shaped pin. Some recently built campgrounds have 50-ampere, 240-volt service; these plugs have three large, flat, parallel blades and a round pin (see Figure 7-1).

RVers should carry various adapters to be prepared to use any type of campground outlet. The one we use most frequently is a 15-ampere male/30-ampere female adapter (Figure 8-1). With this adapter, our shore-power cable with its 30-ampere plug can be used in a 15-ampere outlet. With 15-ampere outlets, we also often use Innovative Marketing's Power Maximiser adapter, a small unit with two 15-ampere male plugs on one side and a 30-ampere female receptacle on the other (Figure 8-2). With the Maximiser, the RV's load is equally distributed between the receptacle's two 15-ampere female contacts. A full 30 amperes cannot be used, however, because the outlet is still breaker-protected for only 15 amperes. Using the Maximiser eliminates the tendency for the contacts to burn as they would when continually carrying high-amperage loads.

The next most frequently used adapter

Figure 8-1. Different types of 15-ampere male/30-ampere female adapters.

Figure 8-2. The Power Maximiser allows a 30-ampere plug to be used in a duplex 15-ampere receptacle.

143

Figure 8-3. A 30-ampere male/15-ampere female adapter.

Figure 8-4. Authors' 50-foot, 10/3 AWG extension cord with a 30-ampere receptacle on one end and a 15-ampere plug on the other.

is a 30-ampere male/15-ampere female, which allows a 15-ampere, 10/3 extension cord to be plugged into a 30-ampere receptacle (Figure 8-3). An extension cord is needed when the campground's outlet box cannot be reached by the regular shore-power cable, a situation we encounter frequently in certain public parks. A 10/3 extension cord with a 30-ampere plug and socket can be used; however, this type of cord is heavy and bulky, and may be difficult to store.

When using either the 15-ampere male/30-ampere female adapter or a 15-ampere extension cord, the rating of 15 amperes is the maximum load that should ever be carried. A circuit should never carry more amperes than that of the lowest rated component of the circuit, whether adapter, plug, cord, or outlet.

Purchasing good-quality extension cords pays off in years of service. We are still using a 50-foot 10/3 extension cord we purchased more than 20 years ago. We altered the cord by putting a good-quality 15-ampere male plug on one end and an outdoor-type box with a 30-ampere receptacle on the other so the trailer's shore-power cable can be plugged into it (Figure 8-4). Occasionally we also use a 50-ampere male/30-ampere female adapter (Figure 8-5). It's handy in mobile home parks where only 50-ampere, 240-volt service is available.

RVers who travel to many different campgrounds will find that a collection of various adapters comes in handy when they encounter outlet boxes mounted upside down with covers that prevent plugging in the standard, right-angle plug of the shore-power cable. For example, to be able to plug our 30-ampere shore-power cable

144

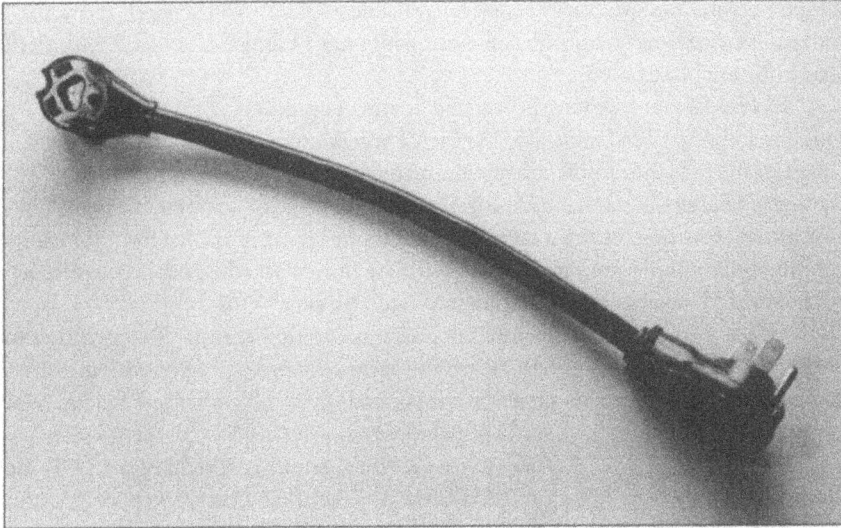

Figure 8-5. A 240-volt, 50-ampere male/30-ampere female adapter. This adapter uses one 120-volt leg of a 240-volt receptacle.

into an upside-down 30-ampere outlet, we would have to insert a 30-ampere male/15-ampere female adapter into the outlet. Plugged into this adapter would be a 15-ampere male/30-ampere female adapter (see Figure 8-1, pg. 143); the shore-power cable would plug into that.

If the RV is equipped for 50-ampere, 240-volt service, an adapter is needed to use the four-prong, 50-ampere plug on the shore-power cable in most campground outlets; 50-ampere service is not too common except in mobile home parks and luxury campgrounds. To use a 50-ampere plug in a 30- or 15-ampere outlet, a 30-ampere male/50-ampere female adapter or 15-ampere male/50-ampere female adapter is needed. These 50-ampere adapters allow full use of both 120-volt legs of the RV's 240-volt service: The adapter is wired so the two hot female contacts of the 240-volt side are connected together in parallel, making the two separate circuits into one. Remember that the entire 240-volt system is now limited to the amperage rating of the smallest side of the adapter—either 15 or 30 amperes.

Living Within Amperage Availability

To avoid overloading problems, RVers should learn to live within the amperage available from the campground outlet. This is usually not difficult with the 100 amperes (from the two 50-ampere legs) available with 240-volt service—even 30-ampere service is not too restrictive—but with only 15 amperes available, electricity has to be used judiciously.

It is important to know the wattage or amperage draw for all AC electrical equipment in the RV (Table 8-1). As for 12-volt equipment, look on the case or cover of the device or in the instruction manual for this information. Once the amperage ratings are known, add together the amperage of equipment that will be in use at the same time. If the total is higher than the service provided from the campground outlet, some equipment will have to be turned off while other items are in use to avoid blowing a fuse or tripping a circuit breaker.

Often overlooked in amperage calculations is equipment that is constantly running. A 6-cubic-foot absorption-type refrigerator operating on AC power uses 2.7 amperes, and a 40-ampere converter/charger consumes 5.5 amperes at full load, for a total of 8.2 amperes—more than half the amount available on a 15-ampere circuit. Adding a 13,500-Btu air conditioner that requires 13.6 amperes or a 1,500-watt heater that draws 12.5 amperes would push consumption over 20 amperes—far more than a 15-ampere circuit can safely carry continuously. This equipment cycles during operation and does not run at maximum amperage load constantly, so it might be possible to use these various appliances at the same time; however, repeated overloading hastens the burning of the shore-power cable contacts.

Adding a 13,500-Btu air conditioner that requires 13.6 amperes or a 1,500-watt heater that draws 12.5 amperes would push consumption over 20 amperes—far more than a 15-ampere circuit can safely carry continuously.

If we need to purchase a heater, we find one with a 1,250-watt rating (or a 1,250-watt switch setting) to lessen our overall amperage load. The heater would draw only 10.4 amperes instead of the 12.5 amperes of a 1,500-watt load. The difference in heat output is negligible, and an extra 2.1 amperes is available for other uses.

Phantom Loads and 15-Ampere Circuits

Phantom loads of AC TVs, VCRs, stereos, clocks, timers, microwave ovens, and other electronic appliances should be considered when operating on 15-ampere service. In a modern TV, which turns on instantly (instead of the slow startup of years ago), the circuitry is divided so part of it remains on constantly. VCRs and stereos have memory circuits that are active when the main switch is off. Many appliances have built-in timers wired into the circuit ahead of the power switch so they continue to function when the appliance is turned off; however, with this design, they

Table 8-1.

Wattage and Amperage of AC Appliances

Appliance	Watts	Amps
TV, color, 9-inch, AC or AC/DC	54	0.45
TV, color, 13-inch, AC or AC/DC	70	0.58
TV satellite and receiver	170	1.41
Videocassette recorder (VCR)	90	0.75
Videocassette player (VCP), AC/DC on AC	18	0.15
Refrigerator, 6-cubic-foot, AC/gas, on AC	300	2.70
Refrigerator, 8-cubic-foot, AC/gas, on AC	300	2.70
Refrigerator, portable, AC/DC, on AC	47	0.39
Converter/charger, 20-amp at maximum rating	420	3.50
Converter/charger, 30-amp at maximum rating	552	4.60
Converter/charger, 40-amp at maximum rating	660	5.50
Converter/charger, 75-amp at maximum rating	1,040	8.66
Air conditioner, 14,800-Btu/hr	1,920	16.00
Air conditioner, 13,500-Btu/hr	1,700	14.16
Air conditioner, 7,100-Btu/hr	1,200	10.00
Air conditioner, heat strip	1,920	16.00
Heater, electric	1,500	12.50
Heater, electric, on 1,250-watt setting	1,250	10.41
Microwave oven, small, 450-watt cooking rating	900	7.50
Microwave oven, large, 650-watt cooking rating	1,300	10.83
Washer/dryer, RV type	1,920	16.00
Coffeemaker	900	7.50
Iron	1,300	10.83
Hair dryer	1,200	10.00
Blender	300	2.50
Toaster	900	7.50
Vacuum cleaner, hand-held	240	2.00
Vacuum cleaner, canister	350	2.91
Sewing machine	150	1.25
Computer, desktop	100	0.83
Computer printer	240	2.00
Drill, ⅜-inch	350	2.90
Saber saw	300	2.50

NOTE: These ratings are approximate. Ratings may vary between manufacturers and from product to product.

are always drawing current. The only sure way to eliminate phantom loads is to unplug the appliance or switch off the outlet circuit.

AC-to-DC power adapters, the small black boxes that either charge batteries or supply power for all kinds of equipment—laptop computers, radios, cordless screwdrivers, to name a few—can be step-down transformers that convert 120 volts to whatever voltage is needed for operation. Even when the appliance is turned off or unplugged from the adapter, the primary-coil winding of the adapter's transformer is still consuming current as long as the adapter itself remains plugged in. Some adapters have solid-state circuitry to achieve the voltage reduction without a transformer, but they also draw current while plugged in. These adapters operate on mere milliamperes but, as we have shown, milliamperes can mount up to a phantom load that should be considered in amperage calculations. When an adapter is not needed to operate or charge the battery of an appliance, always unplug the adapter; don't "store" it in the receptacle. This eliminates unnecessary amperage draw and it's also a safety measure: Adapters get hot when they are plugged in all the time; eventually they short out, which might cause a fire.

In a converter/charger, current is consumed in the primary coil even when there is no load; this idle current, or phantom load, should be considered in amperage calculations.

Depending on the electrical equipment used, phantom loads may be an important factor when you are living on 15-ampere service from a campground hookup. Phantom loads are extremely important when the AC power comes from an inverter, and should always be considered in this circumstance (see Chapter 9).

Electrical Fire Prevention

Even if care is taken to avoid overloading circuits, the danger of fire still exists. As plugs and outlets age, constant loading to near-maximum amperage ratings eventually causes them to burn. The contacts in outlets and the metal blades on plugs are usually made of brass, which, in addition to the copper in wires, eventually crystallizes from the heat generated by high amperage loads; even constant use without overloading, over time, will cause plugs to burn. Crystallization raises the resistance of the blades or wires, causing them to heat up even more.

Routinely inspect the blades of all plugs; if the bright brass has changed to a pinkish color, it is time to replace the plug because crystallization is taking place and soon the blades will start to burn through. Unfortunately, replacement 30-ampere plugs will have a U-shaped grounding pin instead of the round pin of the original plug; the U-shape pin fits into a receptacle but does not fit into many adapters. The only way to make it fit is to file down the edges to make it round.

Outlets are harder to evaluate for crystallization. Usually burning appears around the edges of the hot or positive slot in the receptacle. If burning occurs on adapters made of molded plastic or rubber construction, the affected area shows signs of melting and may be raised in appearance.

When replacing plugs and outlets, check the condition of the copper wiring. If it has a dull pink color or is otherwise discolored or brittle, cut it back until bright copper shows before attaching it to a new plug.

In a campground, when we must use a duplex 15-ampere outlet with burned contacts in one of the receptacles, we use the Power Maximiser adapter, if possible. It makes contact with both receptacles in the box and probably provides a good connection between the two.

> *Routinely inspect the blades of all plugs; if the bright brass has changed to a pinkish color, it is time to replace the plug because crystallization is taking place and soon the blades will start to burn through.*

15-Ampere Receptacles Fused for 30 Amperes

Some 15-ampere duplex receptacles are fused for 30 amperes. We have found this condition more often in public campgrounds than private, and usually the campground has been in operation for years, still using the original wiring. Several outlet boxes, each containing a duplex 15-ampere receptacle, will be mounted on a few light poles, or even trees, scattered throughout the campground. The campground usually has no defined sites. It is expected that RVs will cluster near the outlet boxes and that two RVs will share one box—one plugged into the top receptacle, the other into the bottom, supposedly so each will have 15-ampere service. We don't like this type of hookup because we have no control over the amperage usage of the RVer who shares our outlet box.

These campgrounds are the most crowded in the summer when air conditioners are being used; running two air conditioners from the same duplex outlet presents problems. Even if it is fused for 30 amperes, the receptacle is rated at only 15 amperes and may be overloaded by the air conditioner alone, precluding use of any other electrical equipment. In such parks, we have found outlet boxes and plugs with a temperature so hot they cannot be touched.

> *It is expected that RVs will cluster near the outlet boxes and that two RVs will share one box—one plugged into the top receptacle, the other into the bottom, supposedly so each will have 15-ampere service.*

In situations like this, if the campground isn't too crowded, we use our Power Maximiser adapter. It allows us to have a full 30 amperes on a 15-ampere outlet because the load is split between the two receptacles. Trying to draw 30 amperes from either the top or bottom female connection alone, however, would severely overload the recepta-

149

cle. (We admit that this is selfish because it also prevents another RVer from plugging into the same outlet.)

When you encounter this type of outlet arrangement, assume that the wiring is old and undersized and, therefore, the voltage may be low; we have experienced voltage as low as 90 volts in some campgrounds.

Is the Wiring Correct?

Far too many campground outlets are improperly wired. Often a general maintenance person who may be skilled at lawnmowing or picking up trash, but who knows nothing about electricity, is the one who takes care of electrical repairs. Such a person may often connect wires incorrectly when replacing a burned-out receptacle or attending to other electrical problems.

Reversed polarity occurs if the hot and neutral wires are reversed, and using appliances on such a circuit can damage them.

Reversed polarity occurs if the hot and neutral wires are reversed, and using appliances on such a circuit can damage them. Years ago, polarity in AC circuits was not important because the current flowing both ways in the circuit did not affect most electric equipment in use. Now, however, with complex solid-state circuits in TVs, stereos, and other appliances, it's important to operate them only on circuits with the proper polarity. Equipment that would be damaged by reversed polarity has a plug with one blade wider than the other so the plug cannot be inserted in the receptacle the wrong way.

When the hot and ground wires are reversed, which makes the grounding wire a current-carrying conductor, a much more dangerous situation results. If you plugged into an outlet wired in this manner and then touched the metal skin or any metal part on the RV, you could receive a lethal electrical shock. We know of several RVers who have been killed this way. This same severe shock condition can result from wiring in an RV. When a receptacle in an RV is improperly wired with the hot and ground wires reversed, or even if a plug is replaced on an appliance and cross-wired this way, the shock potential exists. Furthermore, all other RVs on the same general circuit will be affected, so their occupants are also in danger. When making repairs or additions to an RV's electrical system or equipment, make doubly sure all wires are installed correctly.

Circuit Analyzers

The best and simplest method of detecting whether a circuit is wired properly is by using a *circuit analyzer*. These units can be purchased from hardware and RV supply stores. They are not expensive, usually costing about $6 to $10—a small price to pay for something that could save your life. No RVer should be without one.

A basic circuit analyzer has the usual 15-ampere, three-prong plug on one end and three small LEDs or neon lights on the other (Figure 8-6). For checking a 30-ampere outlet, a 30-ampere male/15-ampere female adapter is plugged into the outlet, and the circuit analyzer into the adapter.

We check every outlet we ever use. Our getting-underway routine includes plugging a circuit analyzer into an under-cabinet receptacle in the galley, where it is visible from the outside through the galley window. The galley is on the street side, as are most campground hookups, so when

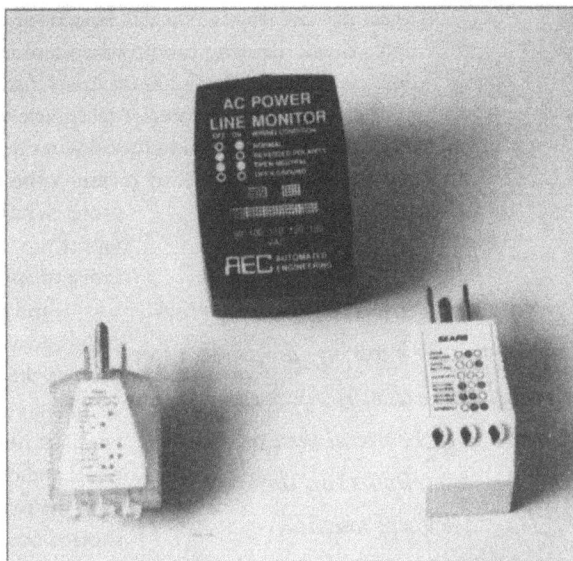

Figure 8-6. The two circuit analyzers on the bottom are three-light models. On the top is a two-light type with bar-graph voltage indicator.

we next plug in, a glance in the window lets us know the status of either a 15- or 30-ampere campground outlet's wiring. If an outlet looks old or burned or if we suspect there may be something wrong with it, before pulling into the site, we check it with another circuit analyzer we keep handy in the shore-power cable compartment.

Once the circuit analyzer is plugged in, the order in which the lights are lit or not lit indicates one of five wiring conditions in the outlet: correct or okay wiring, reversed polarity, open neutral, open ground, or hot and ground reversed. If no lights are lit, of course, the outlet has no power.

NOTE! If a circuit analyzer shows the hot and ground wires reversed, never under any circumstances use the electricity at such a site. To do so incurs the risk of a lethal shock.

When the light configuration of a circuit analyzer indicates an open neutral, there is power in the outlet but it is not usable since the circuit cannot be completed. A circuit analyzer does not indicate the quality of a ground—only if the ground contact has been made.

NOTE! If a circuit analyzer shows the hot and ground wires reversed, *never under any circumstances* use the electricity at such a site. To do so incurs the risk of a lethal shock. Be extra careful when removing the circuit analyzer from the outlet because the same shock hazard exists if the outlet's metal box is touched. If you plug your analyzer into an interior receptacle where it can be seen from outside, as we do, and it shows the hot and ground wires reversed when the shore-power cable is connected, avoid touching any metal on the RV or the outlet and carefully unplug the cable. Whenever a hot/ground reversal is encountered, report the condition to the campground manager and move to another site.

If the neutral and ground wires are reversed or shorted out in the RV's wiring, a dangerous condition exists: A shock can be received if the metal skin or other metal parts on the RV are touched.

If the ground and neutral wires are reversed, the circuit analyzer will probably show a correct circuit because the condition is not necessarily a problem if it occurs in a campground outlet; the neutral and ground wires are normally connected together at the service panel and do not affect the current in the RV. If, however, the neutral and ground wires are reversed or shorted out in the RV's wiring, a dangerous condition exists: A shock can be received if the metal skin or other metal parts on the RV are touched. This rarely encountered but potentially dangerous situation can be detected with a multimeter (see Chapter 11).

Other Types of Circuit Analyzers

More expensive circuit analyzers also show the AC voltage, but certain models have only two lights—instead of three—that indicate just four wiring conditions (see Figure 8-6). A two-light circuit analyzer does not show the dangerous condition of hot/ground reversal, so a three-light analyzer should be used for an initial outlet check.

The Line Alarm made by Power Alarm, Inc., has three indicator lights and also buzzes when a high- or low-voltage condition exists (Figure 8-7). This eliminates the need for regular voltage monitor-

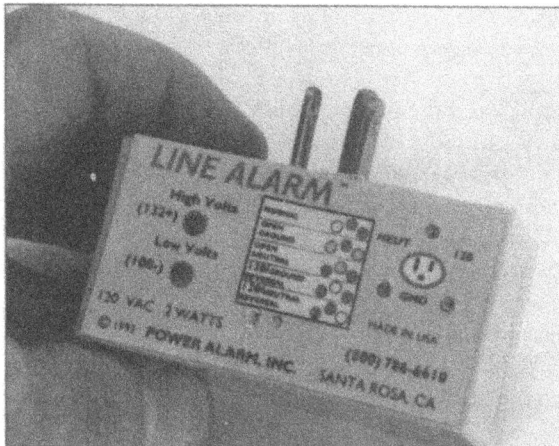

Figure 8-7. The Line Alarm circuit analyzer incorporates low- and high-voltage buzzer alarms.

ing since the Line Alarm audibly warns when a problem occurs.

A basic circuit analyzer can be removed once the outlet has been checked, but an analyzer with voltage readings or an alarm should be kept plugged into an interior receptacle where it can be easily monitored or heard.

Perhaps the most comprehensive circuit analyzer is the SureTest ST-1 Pro-Plus, distributed solely by Industrial Commercial Electronics, Inc. (Figure 8-8). When this analyzer is plugged into a campground outlet, it automatically performs several circuit tests, as well as giving the usual three-light readout. For a voltage-drop test, the SureTest applies a 15-ampere load and measures voltage drop as a percentage of total voltage. A digital display alternately shows the AC voltage and percentage of voltage drop. (The campground wiring may not be sufficient to safely carry a 15-ampere load if the voltage drop is greater than 5 percent.)

Resistance in the ground conductor (an indication of how safe the ground connection is) is shown by either a green light (safe), meaning the ground has less than 1 ohm of resistance, or a red light (unsafe), indicating a resistance of more than 1 ohm. The SureTest also shows if a false ground is present. This is the only circuit analyzer that evaluates the ground and neutral conductors for voltage potential. Less than a 4-volt potential is indicated by a green light; if more than a 4-volt potential exists, a problem is present, indicated by a red light. The unit is extremely sensitive: On our trailer it detected a leakage of only a few milliamperes between neutral and

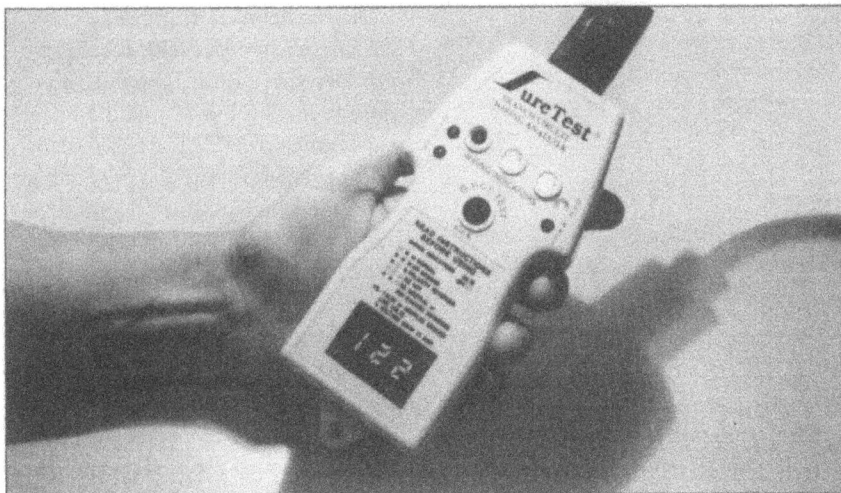

Figure 8-8. SureTest's multifunction circuit analyzer can perform many different tests on a campground's shore-power outlet.

ground (probably coming from our inverter). The SureTest also checks the performance of GFCIs. If every campground operator used a SureTest for initial and periodic checks, problems could be eliminated and outlets would be much safer to use.

Correcting Reversed Polarity

Reversed polarity, the most common of the improper wiring conditions in 15-ampere outlets, occurs when hot and neutral wires are reversed; it may be indicated on some circuit analyzers as "hot/neutral reversed." It's a condition that can be easily corrected.

A grounding or two- to three-prong adapter, found in any hardware store for less than a dollar, is needed. These adapters are designed so a three-prong plug can establish a ground connection when inserted into an older two-slot receptacle. Projecting from the top of the adapter is a metal tab with a hole in it. The tab is attached to the receptacle's face plate screw to make the ground connection; a 15-ampere three-prong male plug then can be inserted directly into the adapter. To correct reversed polarity, the grounding adapter must be modified (Figure 8-9).

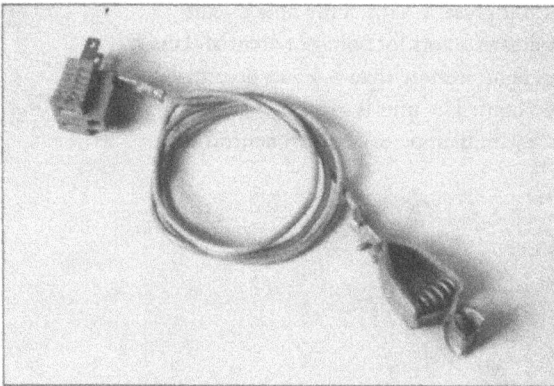

Figure 8-9. A 15-ampere reversed polarity/grounding adapter made by the authors. The wire with the alligator clip on the end is fastened to the adapter's ground tab with a solderless connector.

Since grounding adapters have polarized prongs, the first step is to file down the wide prong to the same width as the other prong. The plug then can be inserted into the campground outlet, turned around 180 degrees from the way it would be normally inserted. This reverses the hot and neutral blades of the plug and corrects the reversed polarity condition. Now, however, a good ground has to be established other than by using the tab in the normal way, so the next step is to make a grounding wire.

Attach a large alligator clip to one end of a 3-foot length of 14-gauge wire; this gauge has the needed 15-ampere ampacity. Attach the other end of the wire to the tab. The General Electric grounding adapter (Product No. GE 4391-S1D) has a tab the same width as a male, ¼-inch, quick-disconnect, solderless, crimp-on connector. It's a simple matter to attach the female counterpart of this connector to the tab: Attach it to the other end of the wire, and then slip it over the tab. The tabs on other brands of adapters are too wide for use with this connector so, if another brand is used, the wire has to be soldered to the tab. When the adapter is in place, turned around in the outlet, connect the alligator clip to a good metal ground, such as the metal pipe of the site's water hookup or even the metal of the outlet box.

After reversing the polarity and reestablishing the ground, do not assume that the circuit is now correct; always double-check it with the circuit analyzer. Since both prongs have been altered to the same width, there is always the chance the adapter may not have been inserted in the turned-around position. If the reversed polarity has been corrected but the circuit analyzer now indicates an open ground, wiggle the alligator clip until a good ground is achieved—sometimes the clip doesn't make a good connection because of paint or corrosion—or try a different ground source.

If reversed polarity exists in a 30-ampere outlet—a rare occurrence—use a 30-ampere male/15-ampere female adapter to reduce the connection to the 15-ampere size before plugging in the two- to three-prong adapter.

When the circuit analyzer verifies that the circuit is correct, the outlet is safe to use. Remember, a 15-ampere maximum load is all that can be applied when using a 15-ampere adapter to correct reversed polarity in either a 15- or 30-ampere outlet.

Correcting an Open-Ground Condition

A circuit with an *open ground* is another frequently encountered condition. Many campground outlets have poor grounds or none at all. When the circuit analyzer indicates an open ground, which means no ground, it can be corrected with the grounding wire on the two- to three-prong adapter used to correct reversed polarity. Plug in the adapter in the normal manner—not turned around—and fasten the alligator clip to a good ground. Once this is done, plug in the circuit analyzer again to make sure polarity hasn't been inadvertently reversed by the adapter being plugged in the wrong way.

An open-ground condition in a 30-ampere outlet requires a different means of correction. We have a special 3-foot-long, 10-gauge wire, which has 30-ampere ampacity. On one end is a solderless, crimp-on connector of the ring-tongue type with a ¼-inch opening; on the other end is an alligator clip. The ring connector is slipped over the grounding pin on the 30-ampere plug and the alligator clip is attached to a good ground (Figure 8-10, pg. 156). Because the ring connector doesn't make much surface contact with the plug's grounding pin, this isn't the most ideal ground, but it does provide some protection.

If you don't have an adapter for correcting reversed polarity or an open-ground condition, don't use the outlet: Damage to appliances can occur from reversed polarity

155

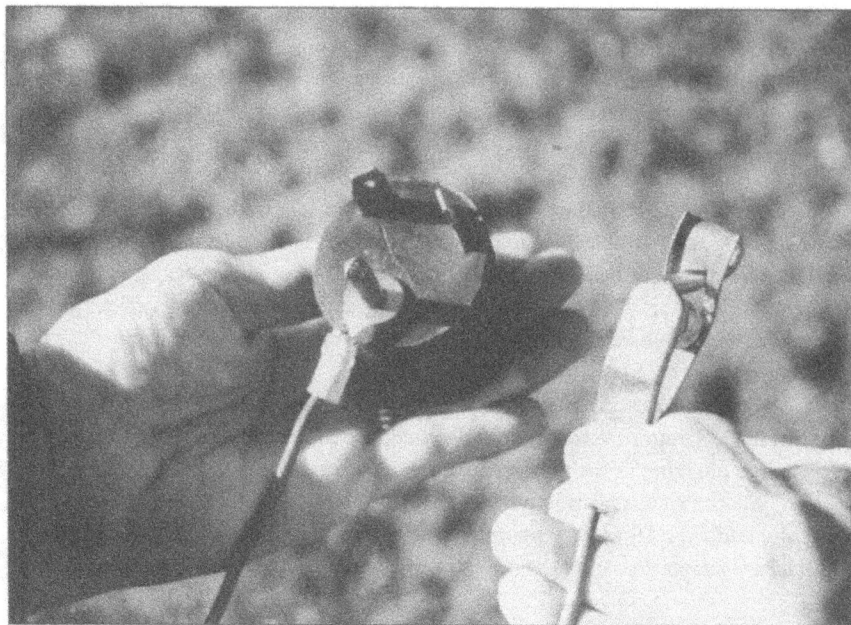

Figure 8-10. A wire with a ¼-inch ring connector on one end and an alligator clip on the other can be used to establish a ground on a 30-ampere outlet that is ungrounded. (For clarity, a 30-ampere adapter is shown instead of a 30-ampere plug.)

If you don't have an adapter for correcting reversed polarity or an open-ground condition, don't use the outlet: Damage to appliances can occur from reversed polarity and a shock hazard and lack of protection exists when the outlet is ungrounded.

and a shock hazard and lack of protection exists when the outlet is ungrounded. Report the condition to the campground management and move to another site. If GFCIs or surge protectors are to work as they are intended, there must be a good ground connection.

Surge Protectors

Just as in a residence, an RV should have a *surge protector,* or *surge suppressor,* to safeguard appliances and electrical equipment from voltage surges and spikes (Figure 8-11). A surge is a momentary voltage increase that lasts longer than one-tenth of a second; a spike lasts less than one-tenth of a second. Spikes and surges as high as 3,000 volts or more can occur in power lines when electrical equipment is shut off, causing a momentary increase in the supply voltage, or from static charges that build up on power lines during electrical storms.

Smaller spikes and surges can also occur in a campground's service lines. When an air conditioner or high-amperage electric heater is shut off in one RV, it can affect the voltage in the RVs next to it by causing a temporary rise. Wherever they come from, voltage increases can be damaging to TVs, VCRs, microwave ovens, computers, and other sophisticated electronic equipment. Even if the equipment is turned off, it is not safe; spikes and surges can jump over the small gap between the contacts in an on/off switch and severely damage electronic components.

The main components in a surge protector are metal oxide varistors (MOVs), dime-size disks that do not pass current in the normal manner. A good-quality surge protector has three MOVs: one wired between the hot and neutral wires, another between the hot and ground wires, and the third between the neutral and ground wires. The MOVs do not allow current to pass until the voltage rises to the MOV's preset rating—the clamping voltage; then the MOVs pass the harmful spike or surge to ground. Some surge protectors have only one MOV wired between the hot and ground wire, protecting only this part of the circuit.

A good-quality surge protector has an internal fast-blow fuse that blows and breaks the circuit if the current fluctuation is high enough. Other protectors use diodes instead of fuses for this protection. All surge protectors protect against

Figure 8-11. The surge protector on the left is for protection of the TV, including spikes coming through the antennna coaxial cable. The surge protector on the right is the Popular Mechanics brand, which has a high protection rating.

small voltage increases, but a large increase causes the protector to burn out like a fuse. If this happens, the surge protector is useless and has to be replaced. All surge protectors have a light to indicate that the unit has not burned out and is still working. If at any time the light is not lit when current is reaching the protector, replace the unit.

Some surge protectors have another light that indicates whether a good ground is present; a ground is essential for surge protectors to provide maximum protection. When a high-wattage appliance is powered by a generator or inverter, spikes and surges can occur when the appliance is turned on or off; a surge protector won't do its job when these auxiliary AC power sources are used. They are grounded only to the RV's chassis which, as was pointed out in Chapter 7, is not the best ground.

All surge protectors carry a clamping voltage rating, which can be anywhere from 130 to 600 volts. The lower the voltage rating, the better the protection.

When a high-wattage appliance is powered by a generator or inverter, spikes and surges can occur when the appliance is turned on or off; a surge protector won't do its job when these auxiliary AC power sources are used.

A surge protector with at least a 400-volt rating should be used for most appliances, including microwave ovens; however, for computers, the rating should be no higher than 140 volts. The Popular Mechanics brand surge protector (sold only by Wal-Mart), shown in Figure 8-11, is an excellent yet inexpensive unit. It has a clamping voltage of 130 rms and an electromagnetic/RFI noise filter, and costs about $5. The only drawback is that it is a one-female-receptacle unit, whereas other surge protectors have multiple receptacles.

We have several of the Popular Mechanics brand surge protectors and another brand made especially for TVs (see Figure 8-11). Because nearby lightning strikes and static charges can affect both the line voltage and signal strength, it grounds both the AC power line and the coaxial antenna cable. This surge protector is not a lightning arrester, however, so the TV is not protected against a direct or near strike. Before we installed a TV surge protector, we once had a picture tube burn out; on another occasion, an antenna amplifier burned out from static charges that came via the antenna. It's a good idea to install a switch on the hot wire to the TV amplifier so it can be turned off during electrical storms; otherwise, the amplifier may be destroyed because it will amplify any static charge picked up by the antenna.

Surge protectors can be installed on an AC distribution panel to protect the RV's entire electrical system. Some circuit breakers have a built-in surge protector, which can be used instead of the regular circuit breakers in some panels.

GFCIs and Campground Outlets

Sometimes a GFCI is installed in a campground outlet; we have had some problems with these installations. Being outdoors, they can be troublesome in rainy weather and when certain conditions exist on the RV. We remember one rainy day when we plugged into a GFCI outlet. About a minute after the shore-power cable had been connected, the GFCI breaker tripped. Thinking the weather caused the tripping, we reset the GFCI—but it tripped again. We began to think the outlet's GFCI was defective—we were fairly certain the problem was not in our 120-volt system—so we plugged into the adjacent site's outlet, and its breaker tripped. A long extension cord was run to other sites, with the same result. During one of the moments when we had current before the breaker tripped, we noticed the interior lights did not seem as bright as usual. This led us to think the converter/charger was at fault. It was unplugged and, sure enough, this time the breaker didn't trip. It wasn't actually a converter/charger problem, though. On its power cord, we had installed a plug-in filter to control the RFI coming from the converter/charger and affecting our stereo. Apparently the filter had enough leakage to ground to unbalance the circuit and cause the breaker to trip. Once the filter was unplugged, the problem was solved.

When a GFCI breaker repeatedly trips and it's not attributable to wet conditions, the best procedure for tracking down the problem is to eliminate various components in the RV's system until the offending one is found.

NINE

Inverters and Generators

Inverters and generators have much in common because of their ability to produce 120-volt AC power when campground hookups are not available. Their operation is entirely different, however: Inverters convert 12-volt DC battery power into 120-volt AC by means of a step-up transformer; generators produce AC power with an alternator.

Inverters are not efficient for big loads for long periods; they are best suited for smaller, short-duration loads. Conversely, generators are best for large loads for long periods and inefficient for small loads for short periods. Because a generator produces its full wattage potential regardless of whether the power is being used, this is an inefficient and expensive way to produce electricity if its capabilities are not fully utilized.

Inverters are best suited for smaller, short-duration loads. Generators are best for large loads for long periods.

As you can see, what might be a disadvantage with an inverter becomes an advantage with a generator. Because either can do the same job, but because their power characteristics are different, it is not unusual to find RVs equipped with both.

A generator is most often found in motorhomes because it is needed to run the air conditioner(s) during travel. If a motorhome isn't factory-equipped with a generator, it probably has a pre-wired space for one. *Genset* is the common name given to generators designed for permanent installation; they usually have an output of 2.5 kilowatts (kW) or more.

A generator, or even the necessary space for one, is rarely found in trailers. If a trailerist has a generator, usually it is a small portable model used outdoors and, most likely, stored in the tow vehicle.

A trailer's air conditioner is not used during travel, so many trailerists who want a built-in source of 120-volt power opt for an inverter. Inverters have much to recommend them. They are much smaller than even the smallest generator, so a large space is not needed for a permanent installation. They operate silently because they are powered by the RV's batteries, and there is no need for the smelly, potentially dangerous fuel required for generators. Inverters are maintenance-free except for an occasional dusting. The biggest disadvantage is that they can gobble up large amounts of ampere-hours from the battery bank's capacity; this is what makes inverters impractical for large loads and long-term operation.

Generators

Depending on the type of generator, it can produce either 120- or 240-volt AC electricity. Generators are powered by an internal-combustion engine, the shaft of which turns the rotor of an AC, self-excited, double-pole, single-phase alternator. The engine is designed to operate at a fixed rpm, either 1,800 or 3,600 revolutions per minute, to turn the alternator's rotor at the rate necessary to produce AC voltage of exactly 120 volts with a sine wave frequency of 60 Hz. The speed of the engine's governor-controlled crankshaft is the same as that of the alternator's rotor. The *governor* prevents voltage fluctuations, voltage surges, and brownouts that can damage appliances and electronic equipment. The governor is usually a mechanical device, although on some of the latest gensets an electronic governor controls engine speed. Generator-produced AC power is usually the same type—a true sine wave—provided by utility companies; however, some smaller generators have a sine wave that is not as true and distortion-free.

Most generators have a *four-stroke engine*, which means they have an oil reservoir similar to that on an automobile. Some of the smallest portable units have a

Figure 9-1. Coleman's 1,750-watt Powermate Pulse 1750 portable generator with a 15-ampere battery charging outlet. (Photo courtesy of Coleman Powermate, Inc.)

Figure 9-2. The popular Onan MicroLite 4-KW genset featuring a special sound-deadening cover for quiet operation. (Photo courtesy of Onan Corporation)

Inverters and Generators

two-stroke engine and use for fuel a gas/oil mixture of 50:1, as do many outboard motors.

Generators are available in all sizes, from small portables with an output of a few hundred watts to huge units with a 20,000-watt output or 20 kilowatts (Figures 9-1 and 9-2, pg. 161). The larger sizes produce 240-volt AC instead of 120 volts of the smaller units, and usually run on diesel fuel. One of these huge units can provide all the power for an average household.

Portable Generators

Small portable generators are usually gasoline-powered—a few small diesel models are on the market—and vary in output from 300 to 1,000 watts. The common operating speed is 3,600 rpm and they are governor-controlled to maintain the necessary speed.

Portable generators are lightweight, small, and compact; built-in handles make them easy to move. They are best suited for limited battery charging and powering small portable appliances and tools. Some small generators designed specifically for battery charging have an alternator output of as much as 150 amperes. These are available in both gasoline and diesel models, as well as 12- and 24-volt configurations.

Portable generators are best suited for limited battery charging and powering small portable appliances and tools.

The larger portable generators weigh 75 pounds, have outputs of more than 1,000 watts, and may be rated up to 8,500 watts (8.5 kilowatts). They are built into a tubular frame, which serves as protection and also provides a convenient handhold for transporting. They are suitable for running all tools, most appliances, and many battery chargers. A generator with a 2.5-kilowatt output or more can power an air conditioner and other large loads.

Both small and large portable generators have a built-in fuel tank and a means for manual starting. Some of the large units also have a battery and an electric starter. All portable generators have a simple control panel with a 15-ampere outlet, usually with a duplex receptacle and may include a voltmeter. Appliances and power tools can be plugged into the receptacle for use and, on larger units, the shore-power cable can be connected directly to the generator (to avoid initial overloading, turn off all loads in the RV before connecting).

Most portable generators also have a 12-volt DC outlet for battery charging and may even have studs for jumper-cable connections. The 12-volt power comes from a small separate winding in the stator that taps into the main winding and uses diode rectifiers to convert AC to DC. The battery charging capability is regulated to about an 8- to 15-ampere output and subject to the usual, but not especially efficient, tapered type of charging. Using an AC unregulated battery charger of approximately the same amperage may be faster and more efficient.

Portable units are not designed for permanent installation. Most are air-cooled and must be operated in the open to receive maximum ventilation. During operation and storage, generators must be protected from rain and other elements since vital parts can rust and corrode, shortening their life.

Portable generators are popular with trailerists because their power needs are usually less than those of motorhomers, and a smaller output is adequate. Some portable generators are small and lightweight enough to be stored in a trailer compartment or in the back of a tow vehicle, and can be a handy accessory. Storing a generator in the tow vehicle eliminates having flammable fuel in the trailer. Some motorhomers have a portable unit for the smaller jobs that their bigger generator can't handle efficiently (if they don't have an inverter for such jobs).

The biggest disadvantage of portable generators is that, being air-cooled, they have no sound insulation and are extremely noisy.

The biggest disadvantage of portable generators is that, being air-cooled, they have no sound insulation and are extremely noisy. Using one can make you very unpopular with your neighbors; in some parks they are prohibited. In national parks, generators that have a noise level higher than 60 decibels (dB) can't be used. Table 9-1 (pg. 164) is a partial list of portable generator manufacturers.

Gensets

Because gensets are designed for permanent installation, they have ventilation and exhaust systems needed for built-in mounting. Generator compartments have doors with ventilation openings and often the compartment will be open on the bottom, without a floor, in which case the generator is mounted on a rack. Some genset engines are like propulsion engines in that they are water-cooled; however, air-cooled units are most commonly used in RVs because the simpler design—with no water pump, radiator, or hoses—makes them easier to maintain and less costly to repair and service.

Gensets provide power either by being hard-wired into the main distribution panel of the RV's 120-volt AC system or by having a receptacle into which the shore-power cable can be plugged. In some cases, when shore power is available but not adequate for running two air conditioners, the genset can be used to operate one of them. Special wiring and switching at the distribution panel is necessary for this type of operation.

Most genset installations include electric starting that can be initiated by a remote switch in the RV. They have their own battery, starter, and circuitry for

Table 9-1.

Mfr.	Model	Engine Type	120-Volt Wattage Constant/ Surge	240-Volt Wattage Rating	12-Volt DC Charger Amperage	Flame Arrester
Coleman	Pulse 1000	Gas	800/1000	——	15 Amps	Standard
	Pulse 1750	Gas	1400/1750	——	15 Amps	Standard
	Vantage 3000	Gas	2600/3250	2600/3250	15 Amps	Optional
	Vantage 4600	Gas	4600/5750	4600/5750	——	Optional
	Vantage 7000*	Gas	7000/8400	7000/8400	——	Optional
Honda	EX350	Gas	150/350	——	6 Amps	Standard
	EX650	Gas	550/650	——	8.3 Amps	Standard
	EX1000	Gas	900/1000	——	8.3 Amps	Standard
	EX2200	Gas	2000/2200	——	8.3 Amps	Standard
Yamaha	EF600	Gas	500/600	——	10 Amps	Standard
	EF1000	Gas	850/1000	——	10 Amps	Standard
	EF1600	Gas	1400/1600	——	10 Amps	Standard
	EF3800E*	Gas	3300/3800	3300/3800	10 Amps	Standard
	EF6000E*	Gas	5000/6000	5000/6000	10 Amps	Standard
Kawasaki	GA550A	Gas	450/550	——	8.5 Amps	Standard
	GD700A	Gas	600/700	——	8.5 Amps	Standard
	GA1000A	Gas	850/1000	——	8.5 Amps	Standard
	GA1400A	Gas	1200/1400	——	8.5 Amps	Standard
	GE4300A	Gas	3800/4300	3800/4300	Optional	Standard
Balmar	PC100	Diesel	——	——	100 Amps**	N/A
	PC200	Diesel	——	——	150 Amps**	N/A
Epower	EPH1250	Gas	——	——	50 Amps	N/A
	EPH12100	Gas	——	——	100 Amps	N/A
	EPH12200KA	Gas	——	——	200 Amps	N/A
Porta-Gen	P1750	Gas	1750	——	——	N/A
	P3250	Gas	3250	3250	——	N/A
	P4000	Gas/Propane	4000	4000	——	N/A
	P5000	Gas/Propane	5000	5000	——	N/A
	P8500*	Gas/Propane	8500	8500	——	N/A

NOTES: * Electric start ** 24-volt models available

The list may not represent all of one manufacturer's products, and does not include all manufacturers of portable generators. Also not included are some portable generators designed for construction use because they are either excessively noisy or do not meet USDA flame-arrester requirements.

completely automatic operation. More sophisticated demand systems have automatic starting that can be initiated by merely turning on an appliance or air conditioner.

If the genset doesn't have an engine-hour meter, it's a good idea to install one to keep track of the hours an engine is run. Then it will be a simple matter to determine when maintenance is due.

Gensets are either gasoline-, diesel-, or propane-powered; usually the model chosen uses the same fuel as the motorhome's engine so two fuels don't have to be carried. Tapping into the main tank of the propulsion engine eliminates the need for a separate fuel tank for the genset.

A propane genset is ideally suited for trailer installation. Because propane is used for cooking and heating, there is a convenient built-in source of fuel. A genset can be mounted in a trailer's storage compartment—if it is large enough and has the necessary ventilation and exhaust provisions—or on a bumper extension at the rear of the trailer. On fifth-wheel trailers, a suitable location may be in the compartment under the gooseneck, which is often roomy and close to the propane supply.

A propane genset is ideally suited for trailer installation.

We have seen permanently mounted gensets in the beds of pickup trucks. It's a natural location if the truck fuel can be used to run the genset and if suitable protection from the weather is provided. It isn't too difficult to engineer a cover to fit over the genset to protect it. With this type of installation, the noise and vibration of the genset are isolated from the trailer. Table 9-2 (pg. 166) is a partial list of genset manufacturers.

Safety Procedures

A few simple rules for safe operation of generators and proper handling of fuel and equipment should be observed:

- Read the instruction manual and follow the manufacturer's recommendations for operation and service.

- To avoid unnecessary wear on a generator's engine and to avoid wasting fuel, never run a generator for any period without a load on the output.

- Never add gasoline to a generator's built-in fuel tank when the unit is hot; gas spilled on a hot exhaust manifold can catch fire.

- Store fuel for portable generators in a proper container, which should be mounted in accordance with local laws regarding the transportation of such fuel.

(safety procedures continued on page 167)

Table 9-2.

Genset Generators (Partial List)						
Manufacturer	**Model**	**Rated**	**Output**	**Voltage Regulated**	**Engine**	**Sound-proofing**
Generac Corporation	NP52G	5,200 watts	43.3 amps, 120 volts	yes	air-cooled, two-cylinder gasoline (propane optional)	yes
	NP66G	6,600 watts	55 amps 120 volts	yes	air-cooled, two-cylinder gasoline (propane optional)	yes
	NP80D	8,000 watts	66.6 amps, 120 volts and 33.3 amps, 240 volts	yes	water-cooled, three-cylinder diesel	no
Other models available: 7,200, 8,000, and 10,000 watts with gasoline engines						
Kohler Company	2.5CMZ21	2,500 watts	20.8 amps, 120 volts	yes	air-cooled, 6-hp, single-cylinder gasoline	no
	2.5CMZ22	2,300 watts	19.2 amps, 120 volts	yes	air-cooled, 6-hp, single-cylinder propane	no
	4.5CKM21	4,500 watts	37.5 amps, 120 volts	yes	air-cooled, two-cylinder gasoline	no
	4.5CKM22	4,000 watts	33.3 amps, 120 volts	yes	air-cooled, two-cylinder propane	no
	9CCO	9,000 watts	75 amps, 120 volts and 37.5 amps, 240 volts	yes	water-cooled, 16.5-hp, three-cylinder diesel	no
	14.5CCO	14,500 watts	120.8 amps, 120 volts and 60.4 amps, 240 volts	yes	water-cooled, 22-hp, four-cylinder diesel	no
Other models available: 7,000 watts gasoline, 6,200 watts propane, and 12,500 watts diesel						
Kwyatt Generators, Dometic Corporation	Kwyatt 4	4,000 watts	33.3 amps, 120 volts	yes	water-cooled, three-cylinder gasoline	yes
	Kwyatt 7	7,000 watts	58.3 amps, 120 volts	yes	water-cooled, three-cylinder gasoline	yes

Manufacturer	Model	Rated	Output	Voltage Regulated	Engine	Sound-proofing
Onan Corporation	MicroLite 2800	2,800 watts	23 amps, 120 volts	yes	air-cooled, 7-hp, single-cylinder gasoline	yes
	MicroLite 2500 LP	2,500 watts	18 amps, 120 volts	yes	air-cooled, 5.5-hp, single-cylinder propane	yes
	MicroLite 4000	4,000 watts	33.3 amps, 120 volts	yes	air-cooled, 9.5-hp, single-cylinder gasoline	yes
	MicroLite 3600 LP	3,600 watts	30 amps, 120 volts	yes	air-cooled, 8.6-hp, single-cylinder propane	yes
	Marquis I	5,000 watts	41.7 amps, 120 volts	yes	air-cooled, 10.3-hp, two-cylinder gasoline	yes
	Marquis III	7,000 watts	56.7 amps, 120 volts	yes	air-cooled, 14-hp, two-cylinder gasoline	yes
	Emerald Plus 4000 BGE	4,000 watts	33.3 amps, 120 volts	yes	air-cooled, 10.3-hp, two-cylinder gasoline optional 8.5-hp, propane	no
	Emerald Plus 6500 NHE	6,500 watts	54.2 amps, 120 volts	yes	air-cooled, 14-hp, two-cylinder gasoline	no
	Emerald Plus 6300 NHE	6,300 watts	52.5 amps, 120 volts	yes	air-cooled, 13.6-hp, two-cylinder propane	no
Power Technology Southeast, Inc.	CD 7000	7,000 watts	58.4 amps, 120 volts and 29.2 amps, 240 volts	yes	water-cooled, 10.9-hp, three-cylinder diesel	no

NOTE:
Only the leading manufacturers of gensets commonly used in RV applications are listed. All models of a manufacturer may not be included.

- When the engine is running, never check the oil level or add oil, and don't perform other maintenance except for certain adjustments that require the generator to be running (see the instruction manual).

- Check and clean the air filter as necessary and as specified in the instruction manual.

- When purchasing a portable generator, especially for boondock camping, make sure the muffler has a flame-arrester approved for forestry use by the U.S. Department of Agriculture.

- Since a generator suffers from lack of use, exercise it periodically, regardless of the type; many manufacturers recommend once a month, for at least 2 hours, at 50 percent or more of output capacity.

- During long periods when a gasoline-powered generator is not used, fuel becomes stale and a varnish-like substance forms in the carburetor. This plugs up narrow holes and adjustment screws, which have to be cleaned. To prevent this situation, use fresh fuel and regularly operate the generator.

- Make sure the carburetor is adjusted for the climate and altitude in which the generator will be used (see the instruction manual).

- Because exhaust gases are dangerous, frequently check all exhaust fittings for cracks and leaks. If the genset is installed in the rear of the RV, always make this check after the rear end has dragged over a curb or entrance ramp.

- Be sure that both a portable generator and a genset are used only in places where they receive a fresh supply of moving air. Do not use in a closed-in place where air circulation is poor—a condition that can exist when parked between buildings, or even among trees and in small canyons. Even though a portable generator is used outdoors, fumes and gases can still seep into the RV. A little carbon monoxide in the RV can cause headaches and watering of the eyes; a little more can kill.

- Because of the danger of carbon monoxide insidiously entering the RV, never run a generator while sleeping.

- To reduce the risk of fire, never store anything that can ignite quickly—oil- or gas-soaked rags and flammable liquids—in a generator compartment.

- Take care when handling electrical cords and connections when the generator is running. A shock from a generator can be as severe as from a power-company-supplied source.

- Monitor the generator's output with an AC voltmeter to check if the unit is delivering the right voltage under no load and if it is handling a heavy load without a serious voltage drop.

Noise Control for Gensets

In recent years some generator manufacturers have tackled the noise problem by designing sound-insulated units that are relatively quiet, such as the MicroLite and Marquis models manufactured by Onan Corporation. For those who have a noisy generator, the decibels can be reduced by lining the generator compartment with a special noise-abatement material. Watermaker RV Specialties, which developed the material, offers the Noise Magnet Kit. The material can drop the noise level by as much as 25 decibels (a drop of 10 decibels cuts noise in half). In one recent installation, the noise at a distance of 5 feet from the generator was only 62 decibels—considerably less than normal generator noise; in another installation, the noise level was 55 decibels, about the level of a Cadillac engine running 10 feet away.

The Power Factor in Generator Battery Charging

When using a portable generator to power a battery charger, certain considerations apply because of the charger's poor efficiency and its *power factor:* the difference between the actual power consumed and the rated power. In AC power, voltage and current each have an individual sine wave. Since AC power doesn't have a steady voltage and current as does DC power, the voltage and current can be out of phase with each other (Figure 9-3). This occurs when the reactive load of the charger's inductive transformer needs more energy to run the charger than its power rating. A power factor is expressed as a ratio: A power factor of 1 indicates no phase difference.

Because of their poor power factors, battery chargers draw much more current to operate than their DC output indicates. The normal poor efficiency, which might be only 75 percent, coupled with the power factor, can bring the total efficiency down to only 55 percent. Consider this information when selecting the output of a generator for use with a battery charger. Calculating a true power factor is complicated, but,

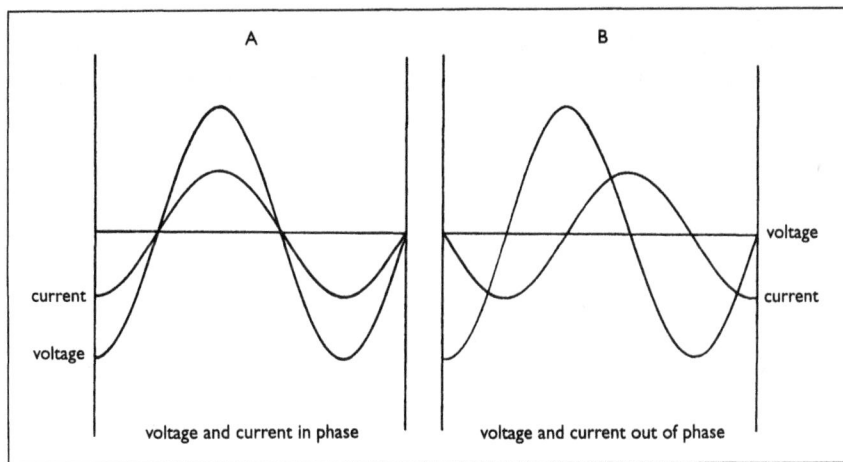

Figure 9-3. Power factor sine waves. In Figure A voltage and current are in phase—the normal condition of AC power. Figure B represents voltage and current out of phase, creating a power factor. This occurs with many converter/chargers and certain types of AC motors.

169

from data supplied by various manufacturers, we created a simple composite factor: 1.66; this is not the true power factor, but it can be used to calculate the needed generator size. This factor applies only to simple unregulated or regulated chargers, not phase-controlled or high-frequency types. Multiply the amperage of the charger by the voltage, and then by the factor; the result is the generator wattage size suitable for use with that particular charger. Using this formula, a 15-ampere charger can be used with a 300-watt generator. The 15 amperes of the charger multiplied by 12 volts equals 180; 180 multiplied by 1.66 equals 298.8; therefore, a 300-watt generator is suitable.

Because of their poor power factors, battery chargers draw much more current to operate than their DC output indicates.

Since a small portable generator requires very little fuel to operate, using one to power an unregulated charger is an efficient method of battery charging. To avoid overcharging, the battery voltage has to be monitored so it doesn't rise much above 14.5 volts.

Efficiency and the power factor also play a part in determining generator size for use with phase-controlled or high-frequency chargers, but a more important consideration is that smaller portable generators do not produce clean current—that is, free of spikes and surges. Often the sine wave is distorted and not true in its form. Phase-controlled or high-frequency chargers do not like this "dirty" current and simply will not run on it. They only operate on current with a pure, undistorted sine wave—the type produced by better-quality, higher-priced units, such as gensets, with a rating of at least 2,000 watts.

Power factors affect large *induction-type motors* (brushless), as well as transformers. When such a motor is powered by a generator, that factor may be as much as 2.68 because the generator must handle the large surge that occurs when the motor is started. If you intend to run an induction-type motor with a generator, check with the generator manufacturer to find out if it will do the job.

Generators Powered by Propulsion Engines

Add-on generators powered by the propulsion engine of a motorhome or tow vehicle are available. Anything that can be handled by a genset can be run from a propulsion-engine-powered generator, so this type might be considered instead of a large genset. There would be savings in space and weight—not to mention money (an extra motor with its own fuel system would not have to be maintained). Since the propulsion engine must be running to produce power, an add-on generator is not economical for small loads. One drawback to this type of generator is that when it is operating at full power, there is some loss of horsepower in the propulsion engine. When this type of generator is used and the RV is parked with the engine running, there is a danger of carbon monoxide seeping into the coach (see the safety rules listed previously in this chapter).

Mercantile Manufacturing Co.'s Auto-Gen M series is one brand of propulsion-engine-powered generators. A variable-speed drive system maintains a constant voltage at various engine speeds. Since these units produce a pure sine wave, they can be used to run all types of loads. The dimensions are 22 inches long, 19 inches wide, and 12 inches high, so the engine compartment has to be large enough to accommodate it. Outputs range from 2,500 to 6,500 watts; depending on the model, weights are 110, 130, or 140 pounds. While much lighter than a genset, the weight still has to be considered. Models with an output of 240 volts are available. Options include monitoring panels with voltage and frequency meters and voltage regulators.

A different concept in propulsion-engine generators is the Roadpower, manufactured by Power Technology, Inc., which is actually a special belt-driven alternator about the same size as a regular alternator (Figure 9-4). Instead of producing 12-volt power, the alternator has windings that produce 120-volt, three-phase current at a high amperage rate. The current is fed into a shoebox-size converter that produces a modified 60-Hz sine wave at any engine speed. As a matter of fact, at engine-idle speed, the 5,000-watt model produces 3,000 watts, enough to run a 13,500-Btu air conditioner with power to spare. Full wattage is developed at speeds above 4,000 rpm. A model that produces a true sine wave is also available.

Figure 9-4. The RoadPower propulsion-engine generator. Its high-wattage output can be used to run air conditioners and other high-amperage equipment.
(Photo courtesy of Power Technology, Inc.)

The AC power unit of the Roadpower, which converts the alternator's output to 120 volts AC, can be mounted anywhere; it does not need to be in the engine compartment. A remote panel that displays operational status and available power can be mounted near the driver's seat.

Roadpower alternators have outputs of either 2,500 or 5,000 watts; a two-alternator version produces a total of 10,000 watts at 230 volts AC. The combined alternator/AC power unit weight is under 50 pounds in the 2,500- and 5,000-watt models.

In a sailboat we once owned, we installed a propulsion-engine-powered, 3,000-

171

watt AC generator so we could run a compressor-type refrigerator while motoring or at anchor without shore power. A double-pole, double-throw switch on the output of the generator connected it to the boat's main AC system. It was turned on or off by a switch on the generator's positive field-current wire. When the engine was running, but the generator was off, it freewheeled.

Inverters

In recent years inverters have come into their own; their popularity is attested to by the large number of manufacturers now making them. The sophisticated solid-state designs are highly efficient. They may be installed in many RVs either as standard equipment or as an option. Many inverters have a built-in battery charger, making a compact double-duty unit (Figure 9-5). Inverters vary in size according to wattage output and may be one of three types for RV use: square wave, modified sine wave, or true sine wave.

Inverters have come into their own. They may be installed in many RVs either as standard equipment or as an option.

Figure 9-5. Heart's Freedom 10 inverter has a 1,000-watt output and 50-ampere multistage battery charging.
(Photo courtesy of Heart Interface Corporation)

Square-Wave Inverters

Square-wave inverters have been in use for many years. When we were in the motion picture business in the 1950s, we used this type of inverter, powered by a 6-volt battery, to run a portable, ¼-inch tape recorder for sound recording on location work. These inverters had an adjustable voltage output, and the correct voltage under load was obtained by reading a plug-in voltmeter. They were large, heavy, and awkward to use, but they did the job.

The square-wave inverters of today are much more sophisticated, but they do the same job—produce 120-volt current with voltage in the form of a square wave instead of the normal sine wave (Figure 9-6). Since there is no gradual rising to peak voltage or a diminishing of the voltage drop, a square wave develops its average voltage at peak voltage.

Square-wave inverters are suitable for powering many different items such as stereos and small hand tools, but they cannot be used for microwave ovens, which are sensitive to peak voltage. Computer video monitors do not run well on these inverters and, although they are suitable for some TVs, they may produce a shrunken image on some sets. Square-wave inverters cannot handle surges of more than 10 percent, so they are not suited for use with induction or capacitor-start motors with large current surge start-up needs. Heat is a by-product of all inverters; the square-wave type produces more heat than other types.

Most basic square-wave inverters lack voltage or frequency regulation, so voltage and frequency can vary considerably, particularly as battery voltage drops off. They are not very efficient, with some units operating at only 50-percent efficiency at full load. They may consume as much as 20 to 50 watts just to start up. They have no standby or idle mode, and must be turned on and off as power is needed. Although square-wave inverters have several disadvantages in certain applications, they do provide the least expensive method of AC production. They are available in sizes ranging from 125 to 1,000 watts. Tripp Lite is the leading manufacturer of square-wave inverters.

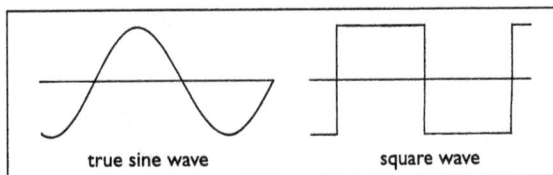

Figure 9-6. Square wave with true sine wave for comparison. The peak and average power of the square wave are the same, unlike the true sine wave (see Figure 3-4), and can adversely affect some appliances such as microwave ovens.

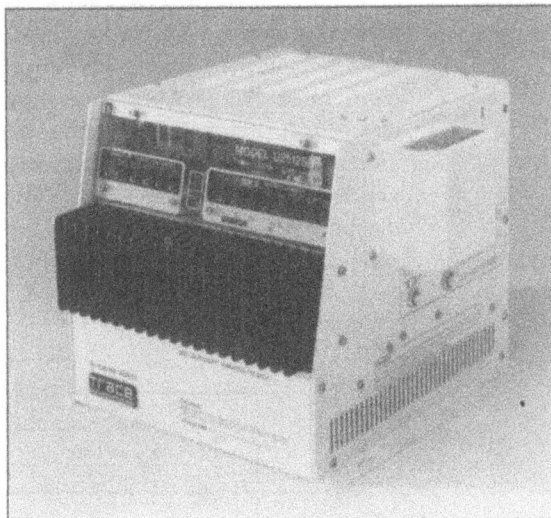

Figure 9-7. The Trace Model 2512 2,500-watt inverter with a 120-ampere multistage battery charger. Two units can be stacked to make a 5,000-watt-output version.
(Photo courtesy of Trace Engineering Corporation.)

Modified Sine-Wave Inverters

A *modified sine-wave inverter* is far more versatile than a square-wave inverter (Figure 9-7). It provides power for almost all electronic equipment, appliances, and all types of motors. Modified sine-wave inverters are available in sizes from 100 to 4,500 watts in either 120- or 240-volt versions that operate on either 12, 24, 36, or 48 volts.

173

True Sine-Wave Inverters

A *true sine-wave inverter* is manufactured by Exeltech, Inc. This inverter eliminates some of the problems encountered when running certain equipment on a modified sine-wave inverter. Exeltech's inverter has a special high-frequency switching circuit that produces the true sine wave. Units are available with outputs ranging from 250 to 6,000 watts.

How Inverters Work

Square-wave, modified sine-wave, and true sine-wave inverters work similarly, basically converting battery DC into AC, which may be either 120 or 240 volts, depending on the model. A step-up transformer with a split primary coil and a tap connection in the center of the primary winding makes the conversion. For the transformer to do its job, the direct current from the battery must first be changed into 12-volt alternating current by means of an *oscillator circuit* that operates two solid-state switches—usually either transistors or MOSFETs functioning as switches. The switches first shunt the current in pulses of energy through half of the split primary coil, then through the other half, thereby creating the two alternations of the sine wave (Figure 9-8). The pulses occur at least 120 times a second

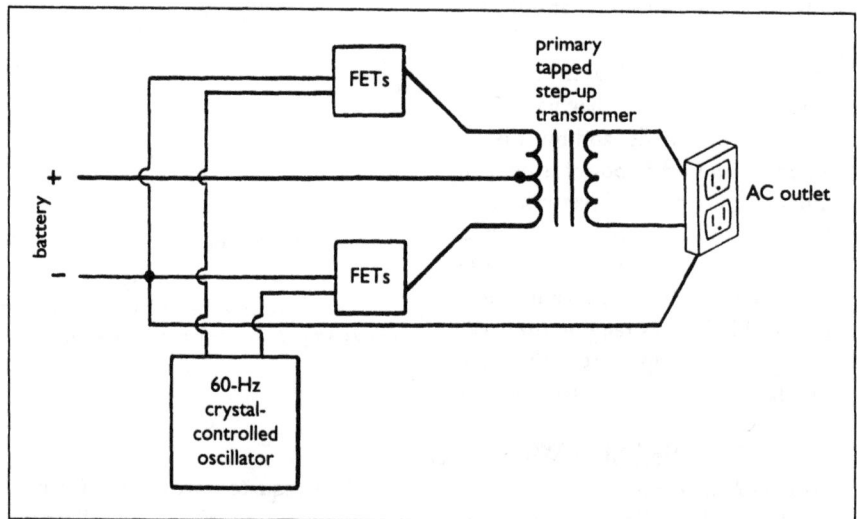

Figure 9-8. A simple diagram of how an inverter works. The crystal oscillator controls the switching of the FETs to create the two alternations of the AC output.

in square-wave inverters, and thousands of times per second in modified and true sine-wave inverters. The transformer then steps up the lower AC voltage to 120 volts through the secondary coil winding. The frequency, or how often the current reverses, is controlled by the oscillator circuit, and the end result must be a frequency of 60 Hz.

In Chapter 5 we discussed the resonant circuit used to maintain a constant voltage in ferroresonant converter/chargers. The oscillator circuit works similarly to a resonant circuit but, in this case, maintains the frequency at a constant 60 Hz rather than maintaining the voltage. The mechanical resonance of piezoelectric crystals is commonly used for this frequency control because the resonance is stable at various temperatures with a regulation of plus or minus 0.04 percent or better.

A Modified Sine Wave Versus a True Sine Wave

The voltage that produces a true sine wave develops power at less than peak voltage; in determining the voltage's true power, the power lost during the current-reversal process must be considered. The root mean square value of the sine wave, which is 0.707 times peak voltage of the alternation, is used to make the calculation. The voltage arrived at using this calculation may not be the average voltage of the sine wave involved, but it is the effective voltage. The peak voltage is 1.414 times the rms voltage. Rms power is the true power of AC electricity.

Rms power is the true power of AC electricity.

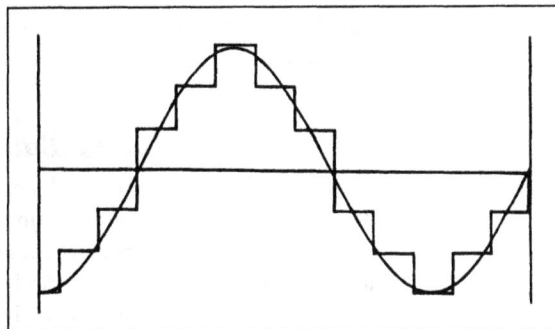

Figure 9-9. The "stairsteps" represent a modified sine wave. It is superimposed over a true sine wave for comparison. The steps of the modified wave average out to approximate the curve of the true sine wave. (An actual modified sine wave will have many more and smaller steps than illustrated.)

While a modified sine-wave inverter does not produce current using the same type of sine wave as the power company, campground hookups, or even a generator, the wave is a close approximation of the smooth curve of a true sine wave. The modified, or synthesized, sine wave produced is a series of short steps going up and down for each alternation of the wave (Figure 9-9). The modified sine-wave inverter can power almost all AC equipment because the pulses of the current it produces have an average voltage value very close to the rms of a true sine wave.

175

Inverter Efficiency

An inverter operating at 100-percent efficiency would produce 1 ampere of 120-volt power for every 10 amperes of 12-volt battery power, or 120 watts of 120-volt output for every 120 watts of battery power; however, no inverter operates at 100-percent efficiency.

Square-wave inverters reach a maximum of 55-percent efficiency at about 75 percent of full load. This translates to a 375-watt load for a 500-watt inverter and, to achieve the 375 watts, it draws about 45 amperes from a 12-volt battery bank. A 500-watt modified sine-wave inverter reaches as much as 95-percent efficiency at 25 percent of full load, 85-percent efficiency at full load, and draws 47 amperes for the full 500-watt load. Modified sine-wave inverters can handle a surge load three to four times the rated wattage of the inverter, whereas the square-wave inverter can handle only about 10 percent more than its wattage.

Determining Inverter Size

The total wattage of appliance use determines the size of inverter required. As with other similar calculations, total the wattages for all appliances that might be run at the same time. If none are used together, use the single highest wattage appliance for the total (see Table 8-1 for common wattages and amperages). At a minimum, the inverter size should equal the wattage of this total.

Calculating Battery Amperage Draw

You'll need to determine how much amperage from the battery will be consumed by appliances run from the inverter during an average period of use. Two simple formulas (from the Heart Interface Corporation instruction manual) that use either the equipment's amperage or wattage can be used to calculate the ampere-hours consumed. The formulas are based on an inverter efficiency of about 90 percent.

For wattage:

$$\left(\frac{AC\ watts}{12}\right) \times 1.1 \times hours\ of\ operation = DC\ ampere\text{-}hours$$

For amperage:

$$(AC\ amperes \times 10) \times 1.1 \times hours\ of\ operation = DC\ ampere\text{-}hours$$

The final figure obtained using either formula is the number of DC ampere-hours that will be consumed.

Calculating Battery Bank Size

Once the inverter size and the number of ampere-hours consumed have been calculated, the next step is to determine how large the battery bank should be. As discussed previously, batteries should never be charged at a rate higher than 25 percent of the total ampere-hours of the battery bank, and batteries should never have a load imposed on them greater than 25 percent of the total ampere-hours of the battery bank. Therefore, the size of the battery bank should be at least four times the maximum ampere load that will be applied to the bank.

Using this information and modifying the previous formulas, divide the inverter wattage by 12, then multiply this figure by 4 for the number of ampere-hours the battery bank should have. As examples, a 600-watt inverter would require a battery bank of 200 ampere-hours or two Group 27 batteries; a 2,000-watt inverter would need 667 ampere-hours or seven Group 27 batteries, or four 220-ampere-hour, 8D batteries. This calculation applies to all types of batteries, including gelled cells. Although gelled-cell batteries can tolerate discharges up to about 40 percent of battery capacity, the percentage does not apply to load size. As far as load is concerned, it is safer to calculate using the 25-percent load rate.

The size of the battery bank should be at least four times the maximum ampere load that will be applied to the bank.

Obstacles to a large battery bank may be space for installation and access for convenient servicing. Ideally, all batteries should be mounted on the sliding trays found on some large motorhomes (Figure 9-10). Adding the considerable weight of a number of batteries may be a problem, as well as the cost.

We installed a 600-watt Trace inverter several years ago and have found it to be adequate for our needs. The only appliances we can't use with it are the refrigerator (we run it on propane anyway when we don't have an electrical hookup), electric heater, and air conditioner. The inverter powers our two laptop computers and printer with very little amperage consumption. When boondocking, we usually use a small

Figure 9-10. An ideal installation is to have batteries on a slide-out tray, as are these two 8D wet-cell batteries on a Country Coach Class A motorhome.

177

black-and-white TV that runs on 12-volt DC. If we want to see something in color, the inverter can be used, on a limited basis, to power our color TV. We found we can even use the inverter for operating our 450-watt microwave oven for a minute or two; its surge output easily handles the short-time overload. (On inverter power, microwave ovens cook more slowly because they are affected by the modified sine wave's different peak voltage; cooking times must be adjusted accordingly.) We have been pleased to find how little the battery capacity diminishes with short-term, large AC loads.

We installed a 600-watt Trace inverter several years ago and have found it to be adequate for our needs. The only appliances we can't use with it are the refrigerator (we run it on propane anyway when we don't have an electrical hookup), electric heater, and air conditioner.

Other RVers with different needs can install larger inverters that easily handle the loads of higher-wattage equipment, as long as a large-enough battery bank is provided. A motorhomer friend of ours sometimes uses his 2,500-watt inverter for running the roof air conditioner while traveling. His 200-ampere alternator supplies the huge amount of amperage needed without depleting the battery capacity. All he needs to do is make sure the alternator belt is good and tight.

Inverter Ratings and Specifications

Once the wattage of an inverter has been determined, other unit specifications should be considered: the continuous wattage rating, the efficiency percentage (discussed previously), the power factor, and whether it has a reasonably low-amperage standby mode and a wide range of both input DC voltage and protective circuits.

The AC continuous wattage rating determines how large a load the inverter can safely carry. Do not confuse the surge rating with the continuous wattage rating. Often inverters have wattage ratings for different times of use (e.g., 15, 30, and 60 minutes) because as heat builds, the wattage output drops. Starting with a high rating at 15 minutes, the rating drops after 30 minutes of use, and drops further after 60 minutes.

Most high-quality, modified sine-wave inverters have a standby mode with a no-load or idle current draw. This consumption is very small; better units have current draws as low as 0.017 ampere while in a search mode and 0.4 ampere at full voltage. With such a unit, it is not necessary to turn off the inverter between jobs; it automatically trips to search mode where it idles until another load is applied. In some cases, the search-mode amperage is so low that the inverter can be left on all the time, but be aware that the search mode, no matter how low, is a phantom load. On many inverters, the load sensitivity can be adjusted so either small or large loads switch the inverter into full-voltage mode. On our inverter the load-sensing search setting is so low that turning on the TV does not trip the inverter to full voltage mode. It's necessary to first turn on another AC load—we use a nightlight—to activate the inverter. When the TV is turned on, the light can be turned off. This situation can exist with most inverters that have search modes.

The input DC voltage should have a large-enough range so the inverter maintains a regulated AC voltage output over the useful life of the battery. High-quality inverters have circuitry to compensate for dropping voltage as the battery's power is consumed. The inverter should hold this AC voltage output to a constant rms value of at least 3 percent.

Power-factor specifications indicate the inverter's capability for running various loads, especially motors. Power factors usually run from –1 to +1. In place of a power factor, the horsepower of a motor that the inverter can start may be given.

A good inverter should have a wide range of protective circuits that will shut down the inverter, through either automatic or manual reset circuit breakers, when conditions such as high or low battery voltage, high temperature, and over-current draw exist.

Inverter Features

Battery Chargers
Many sophisticated inverters have optional built-in battery chargers that provide either regulated constant voltage for charging or some form of multistage charging. Often these chargers are fully adjustable as to voltage set points. An inverter/charger can charge at rates from 25 to 120 amperes or more.

Remote Panels
Another option offered by many manufacturers is a remote panel that provides various means of monitoring and control, as well as an on/off switch. Some monitors have data such as amperage drawn from the battery, the amount of charging amperes, DC voltage input, and AC voltage output. Problems such as over-temperature or low battery voltage can also be indicated. With some inverters a remote panel is needed to adjust the various set points of the battery charger.

The remote panel we have is only a power switch with a blinking LED that indicates the charging status (see Figure 6-3, pg. 123). A remote panel is a necessity with any inverter, if for nothing more than for turning it on or off from inside the

RV; most inverters are installed in an outside compartment where they are not conveniently accessible.

Fan Cooling

Heat is the main enemy of consistent inverter output because it reduces output level over time. An option offered with many larger inverters is a cooling fan, which can extend the continuous output wattage range by many hundreds of watts. For instance, a Trace 2,000-watt inverter can increase its output to 2,500 watts with the fan option.

Stacking

Some of the larger inverters are designed so two units can be stacked together in parallel, doubling wattage output. The increased output can handle household-type loads if the RV's battery bank is large enough. A special electronic interface is needed for multiple inverter stacking.

Unsuitable Loads for Inverters

Some types of appliances and equipment are unsuitable loads for inverters. Electric clocks and clock radios are unsuitable because inverters are not normally used continuously. (If an electric clock is used on shore power, unplug it when using inverter power to avoid a phantom load.) Large AC loads such as heaters, air conditioners, electric ranges, water heaters, refrigerators, and large tools (e.g., table saws) are poor loads because of their high current demand.

Induction motors present problems for most inverters because they operate with the current out of phase with the voltage, and they need a surge wattage of four to six times the operating wattage to start the motor. Some inverters have circuits to correct this split-phase condition and can be used with such equipment.

Pocket Inverters

A great development in recent years is the pocket inverter. These small units range in size from 50 to 300 watts and can provide AC power for many appliances, including TVs and computers. They are equipped with a cigarette-lighter plug so they can be used wherever there is an appropriate socket. Like larger inverters, these small units have a high-frequency switching type of operation that produces a modified sine wave. Depending on the model, the surge wattage can be as high as 500 watts, and some units have the same protective features as the larger inverters, such as for overloading. Pocket inverters have a very small amperage draw when they are idling with no load, so they can usually be left on continuously. Over time, though, this phantom load can deplete the battery; therefore, when the RV is not being used, the inverter should be unplugged or its circuit turned off.

Pocket inverters are small enough to be used in the cab of a pickup truck or tucked away in a compartment where a TV is installed. In fact, many RV manufacturers equip units with TVs powered by these small inverters. The inverter is plugged into the socket on the 12-volt antenna amplifier and the TV's AC power cord is plugged into the inverter.

A pocket inverter can be a convenience even if a larger inverter is installed in the RV. It can be used for small loads and, being portable, can be used anywhere. Use small inverters with plenty of wattage to spare over the desired load, since their continuous output may not be as high as their rated wattage size. Table 9-3 (pg. 182) is a partial list of manufacturers of all types of inverters.

A pocket inverter can be a convenience even if a larger inverter is installed in the RV. It can be used for small loads and, being portable, can be used anywhere.

AC to DC Power Adapters and Inverter Use

Many of the AC to DC power adapters used to run some equipment may not be suitable for operating on an inverter. An inverter can affect how the equipment runs or the recharging of built-in batteries in some computers, hand tools, and other rechargeable equipment. Some adapters don't use transformers for the voltage reduction from 120-volt AC to whatever DC voltage the appliance requires, so the circuitry is not necessarily compatible with the modified sine wave of the inverter. This can cause burnout of either the equipment or its batteries. When the adapter is test run on the inverter, it heats up very quickly if it is not compatible; if it does not heat up beyond the normal amount, it probably can be safely operated with the inverter.

The NOTEpower pocket inverter made by Statpower Technologies Corporation is specially designed for operation of these adapters. It has an output of 50 watts and draws a maximum of 6 amperes of 12-volt power. The NOTEpower is suitable for computer operation and charging batteries for camcorders, cellular telephones, power tools, and other equipment.

An Efficiency Comparison

We wondered if it was more efficient to run an AC/DC color TV off a modified sine-wave inverter in the AC mode or to use the 12-volt DC mode using power directly from the battery. We calculated that on DC operation, our 9-inch TV consumed 19 ampere-hours for 4 hours of use. Using the Heart Interface formula for ampere-hour

181

Table 9-3.

Inverters						
Manufacturer	**Model**	**Input Voltage**	**Output Voltage**	**Continuous Wattage**	**Surge Wattage**	**Frequency Control**
Square-Wave Inverters						
Tripp-Lite	PV 400	12 volts	120 volts	400 watts	440 watts	no
	PV 550/PV 550B	12 volts	120 volts	550 watts	600 watts	no
	PV 600FC/PV 600FCB	12 volts	120 volts	600 watts	1,200 watts	60 Hz
	PV 1000FC/24	24 volts	120 volts	1,000 watts	1,100 watts	60 Hz
Modified Sine-Wave Inverters						
Heart Interface Corporation	HF600-12/ HF600-12M/ HF600-24	12 volts/ 24 volts	120 volts	600 watts	1,200 watts	60 Hz
	Freedom 10	12 volts	120 volts	1,000 watts	3,000 watts	60 Hz
	Freedom 25	12 volts	120 volts	2,500 watts	8,700 watts	60 Hz
PowerStar Products	UPG 400	12 volts	120 volts	400 watts	3,000 watts	60 Hz
	UPG 700	12 volts	120 volts	700 watts	3,000 watts	60 Hz
	UPG1300	12 volts	120 volts	1,300 watts	6,000 watts	60 Hz
Statpower Technologies Corporation	PROwatt 800	12 volts/ 24 volts	120 volts	800 watts	1,000 watts	60 Hz
	PROwatt 1500	12 volts/ 24 volts	120 volts	1,500 watts	2,000 watts	60 Hz
Trace Engineering Corporation	Model 812	12 volts	120 volts	575 watts	2,400 watts	60 Hz
	724	24 volts	120 volts	425 watts	2,400 watts	60 Hz
	M1512	12 volts	120 volts	1,500 watts	3,500 watts	60 Hz

(See table note on page 184.)

Idle Amperage Draw	Maximum Amperage Draw	Battery Charger (Amp Output)	Comments
3.5 amps	36 amps	no	
4 amps	45 amps	optional; charge rate: 8 amps	
1.2 amps	55 amps	optional; charge rate: 15 amps	
1.8 amps	43 amps	no	
0.06 amp	55 amps	no	transfer switch, optional; remote switch, optional
0.12 amp	92 amps	yes; charge rate: 50 amps; type of charge: multistage	transfer switch, yes; remote switch, optional; remote panel, optional; stacking, no
0.12 amp	230 amps	yes; charge rate: 130 amps; type of charge: multistage	transfer switch, yes; remote switch, optional; remote panel, optional; stacking, no
0.09 amp	36 amps	no	remote switch, optional; stacking, yes; Models UPG 700 and UPG 1300 can be stacked with this model for a total of 700 or 1,300 watts output
0.09 amp	65 amps	no	remote switch: optional; stacking: yes. This model and model UPG 400 can be stacked for a total of 700 watts
0.09 amp	120 amps	no	remote switch: optional; stacking: yes. This model and models UPG 400 and UPG 700 can all be stacked together for a total of 1,300 watts
0.3 amp	74 amps	no	transfer switch, no; remote switch, optional; remote panel, optional; 240 volts output, optional
0.6 amp	138 amps	no	transfer switch, no; remote switch, optional; remote panel, optional; 240 volts output, optional
0.022 amp	60 amps	optional; charge rate: 25 amps; type of charge: two stage, constant current/constant voltage	transfer switch, optional; remote switch, optional; remote panel, no
0.025 amp	20 amps	optional; charge rate: 12 amps; type of charge: two stage, constant current/constant voltage	transfer switch, optional; remote switch, optional; remote panel, no
0.035 amp	140 amps	yes; charge rate: 70 amps; type of charge: multistage	transfer switch, yes; remote switch, yes; remote panel, yes; stacking, no

(continued on next page)

183

Inverters and Generators

Manufacturer	Model	Input Voltage	Output Voltage	Continuous Wattage	Surge Wattage	Frequency Control
Modified Sine-Wave Inverters						
Trace Engineering Corporation (cont.)	2512	12 volts	120 volts	2,500 watts	8,000 watts	60 Hz
	2624	24 volts	120 volts	2,600 watts	8,000 watts	60 Hz
Tripp-Lite	PV 1200FC	12 volts	120 volts	1,200 watts	2,400 watts	60 Hz
Vanner, Inc.	20-800/ 20-800T	12 volts	120 volts	800 watts	1,400 watts	60 Hz
	20-2200TPF	12 volts	120 volts	2,200 watts	3,600 watts	60 Hz
	20-4400DPF	24 volts	120/ 240 volts dual	4,400 watts	8,500 watts	60 Hz
True Sine-Wave Inverters						
Exeltech, Inc.	SI-1000	12 volts	120 volts	1,000 watts	1,500 watts	60 Hz
	SI-2000	12 volts	120 volts	2,000 watts	3,000 watts	60 Hz
Pocket Inverters						
Fortron International Corporation	PC-150	12 volts	120 volts	150 watts	400 watts	60 Hz
PowerStar Products	PowerStar 200	12 volts	120 volts	200 watts	400 watts	60 Hz
Statpower Technologies Corporation	NOTEpower PW50	12 volts	120 volts	50 watts	75 watts	60 Hz
	PW125	12 volts	120 volts	125 watts	400 watts	60 Hz
	PW250	12 volts	120 volts	225 watts	500 watts	60 Hz

NOTE:
Only the leading manufacturers of inverters commonly used in RV applications are listed.
All models of a manufacturer may not be included;
models also have been selected for RV compatibility.

Idle Amperage Draw	Maximum Amperage Draw	Battery Charger Amp Output	Comments
0.03 amp	230 amps	optional; charge rate: 120 amps; type of charge: multistage	two units can be stacked with optional interface; 240 volts possible with optional step-up transformer; transfer switch, yes; remote switch, optional; remote panel, optional; stacking, yes
0.018 amp	120 amps	optional; charge rate: 60 amps; type of charge: multistage	transfer switch, yes; remote switch, optional; remote panel, optional; stacking: yes; two units can be stacked with optional interface; 240 volts possible with optional step-up transformer
2 amps	110 amps	no	transfer switch, no; remote switch, no; remote panel, no
0.7 amp	74 amps	no	transfer switch, optional; remote switch, optional; remote panel, optional
N/A	200 amps	no	transfer switch, yes; remote switch, optional; remote panel, optional; 240 volts, optional
N/A	200 amps	no	transfer switch, yes; remote switch, optional; remote panel, optional
N/A	133 amps	no	
N/A	267 amps	no	
N/A	15 amps		
0.25 amp	19 amps		
0.07 amp	4.5 amps		
0.07 amp	12 amps		
0.15 amp	22 amps		

consumption (mentioned previously in this chapter), and running the same TV on AC with an inverter, we calculated that it consumed the same amount: 19 ampere-hours. If you are contemplating the purchase of a TV for your RV and have an inverter to power it, consider a straight AC model and save yourself the extra cost of an AC/DC model; the efficiency of the two methods of operation is equal.

Interestingly, this equal efficiency does not apply to all appliances. Our video cassette player (VCP) is far more efficient on DC operation than on AC because it was designed as a DC unit. On AC inverter operation, it draws 7.75 amperes; on DC, only 3.3 amperes. AC/DC equipment should be checked for its most efficient operating mode.

Using Computers with Inverters

Inverters provide one of the best and most reliable power sources for computers and most printers because there is no danger from power line surges, spikes, and brownouts. Laser printers and fax machines that have SCRs or triacs as filters, however, do not operate well on power from modified sine-wave inverters. In fact, SCRs and triacs could be destroyed because they need a true sine wave to function properly. When in doubt, check with the manufacturer to determine if the equipment can be safely run by an inverter.

Installing Inverters

Inverters can be easily installed in just about any place that is dry and well ventilated, but they must be located as close as possible to the batteries (Figure 9-11). An inverter should not be installed in the battery compartment because of its corrosive atmosphere or in the compartment of a gasoline-powered generator because of the explosive nature of gasoline fumes. A diesel generator compartment is a suitable location, if the inverter can be kept clean.

Most problems with inverters— overheating and overloading—can be traced to excessively long cable runs or cable of inadequate size.

Inverters need to be close to the batteries because, due to the high amperages involved in their operation, large voltage drops would occur with long cable runs. Heavy cable, at least 4 gauge, is needed for inverters of around 600 watts; 3/0-gauge cable may be needed for larger inverters. The cable run from the inverter to the batteries should be no more than 10 feet long. Most problems with inverters—overloading and overheating—can be traced to excessively long cable runs or cable of inadequate size.

Be extra careful when connecting the inverter to the batteries. Most inverters are not protected from reverse DC polarity, and accidentally switching the cables will most likely burn out the transistors and FETs in the inverter's circuitry.

Twisting the positive and negative cables from the batteries to the inverter minimizes or eliminates hum and static in radios and TVs. When the wires are twisted, the magnetic fields surrounding the wires are neutralized and RFI is reduced. (For this reason, all DC power wires to radios and TVs should also be twisted.)

Once the inverter is mounted on a wall, floor, or shelf and connected to the batteries, it's ready for the AC wiring. All but the very largest inverters have a 15-ampere receptacle on the side, just as generators and gensets do. Using this receptacle is the easiest way of connecting the wiring to the inverter. This can be done with a 15-ampere plug with its wires connected to the distribution panel, or the shore-power cable can be used, if it reaches. If a 30-ampere shore-power cable is used, an adapter is necessary; the Power Maximiser is a good choice (see Chapter 8). When inverter power is needed, simply insert the plug, unplugging it when the job is finished.

Most large inverters need to be hard-wired directly into the AC distribution panel because they don't have built-in receptacles. The wiring from the inverter must be separated from that of the incoming shore-power cable, either by a relay or switch, to prevent the two sources from supplying current to the RV's circuits at the same time. Such backfeeding of current can damage the inverter and other equipment, and the massive overload that would occur could cause a fire.

Figure 9-11. Authors' inverter installation in the compartment under the gooseneck on their fifth-wheel trailer. To the left of the Trace 612 inverter is a Todd Power Source PC-45 converter/charger. The battery compartment is to the left of the converter/charger. The receptacle to the right of the inverter is used for the inverter's battery charger; the receptacle under the inverter is for the converter/charger. In each receptacle is a circuit-breaker surge protector. (Figures 9-16 and 9-17 are wiring diagrams of this installation.)

Twisting the positive and negative cables from the batteries to the inverter minimizes or eliminates hum and static in radios and TVs.

Transfer Switches and Relays

Many inverters, especially the large ones, are intended more for residential use than for RVs. These inverters have a built-in automatic transfer switch, or relay, the purpose of which is to protect the entire AC system and isolate different power supplies from each other (Figure 9-12). Transfer switches, as the name implies, transfer the AC supply from one power source to another. They can switch between shore power and an inverter or generator, and can also be used between a generator and an inverter.

An inverter's built-in transfer switch works automatically and allows the power

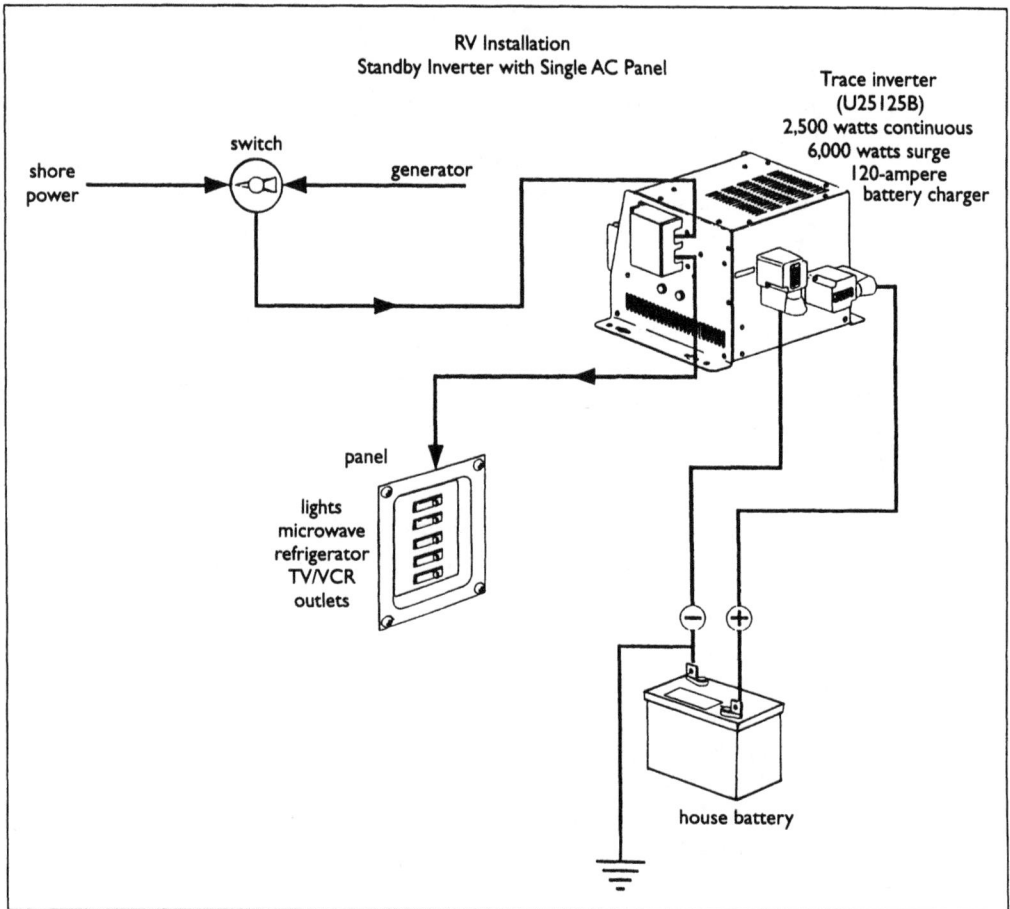

Figure 9-12. Diagram of an RV's AC system including an inverter with a built-in transfer switch, which controls the main circuit panel. The inverter remains in standby mode and activates if the AC power supply is interrupted. (Illustration courtesy of Trace Engineering Corporation)

RV Electrical Systems

from the campground hookup to be transferred to the inverter whenever the shore-power cable is unplugged or the shore power is turned off. Some inverters effect this transfer so quickly—15-thousandths of a second—that appliances do not even go off. Some models switch fast enough to prevent computers from crashing.

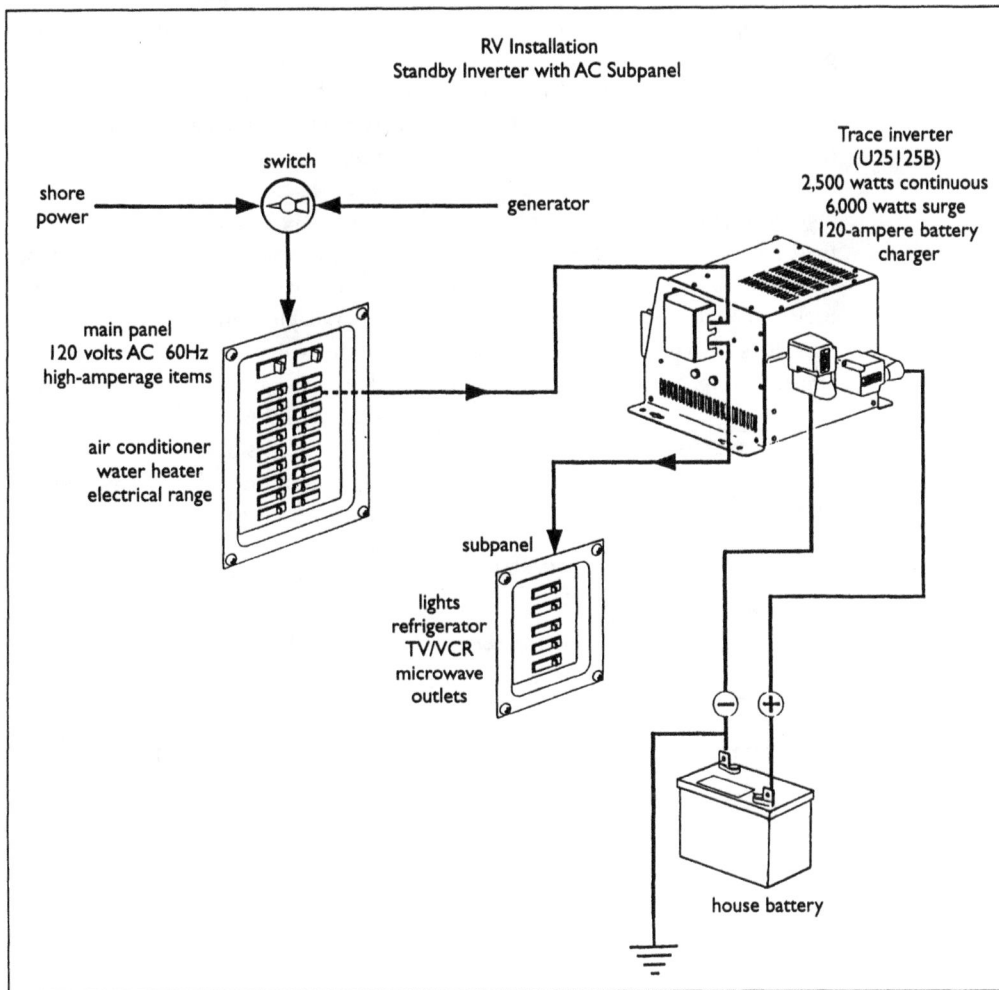

Figure 9-13. Diagram of an RV's AC system showing how an inverter's built-in transfer switch is wired between the main panel and subpanel to provide automatic switch-over when AC power is interrupted. (Illustration courtesy of Trace Engineering Corporation)

A problem with most built-in transfer switches is that they must be wired ahead of the AC distribution panel so all AC shore power coming into the RV from the shore-power cable must go through the inverter first. This can involve considerable rewiring of the RV, especially if the inverter is in the 600- to 1,000-watt range. For wiring these small units, the AC distribution panel must be split into a main panel and a subpanel (see Chapter 7). In RVs with a main panel and a subpanel, the main panel typically carries the heavy loads, such as the air conditioner and electric water heater; the subpanel is for the smaller loads. Since the small inverter can only handle the loads of the subpanel, it must be wired between the main panel and the subpanel (Figure 9-13, pg. 189). Most RVs do not have separate main panels and subpanels—they usually have only one small panel with five or six circuits, including those of high-amperage equipment. Rather than doing extensive and expensive rewiring, there are two ways the inverter can be wired to bypass the built-in transfer switch.

One way is to use a double-pole, double-throw manual switch for changing back and forth between shore power—when it's available—and the inverter. Since most RVs are wired for 30-ampere shore power, the switch should have at least a 30-ampere rating. Such a switch can also be used between a generator and an inverter, or between shore power and a generator. These switches have a three-position toggle lever: one side movement of the lever connects to one circuit, the opposite side movement to the other circuit, and when the lever is in the middle position, the switch is off.

DPDT switches, such as those made by Hubbell, Inc. (Model No. 3032A), are wall switches and can be installed in a wall or any other location by using a standard, single-gang switch box and a cover plate.

The second method is to use a DPDT power relay instead of a switch (Figure 9-14). This is the same type of relay incorporated in the built-in transfer switch in inverters and it can be wired to function the same way.

Essentially, relays are switches that are automatic in operation. Double-pole relays have two coils—one for each pole-side of the relay—that move a spring-loaded double arm between two sets of electri-

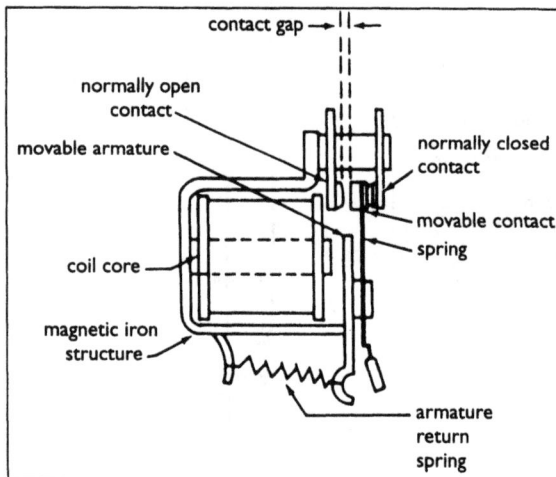

Figure 9-14. Single-pole double-throw relay. One half of a double-pole relay is shown.
(Illustration courtesy of Dayton Electric Manufacturing Company)

cal contacts on the relay, a separate set for each pole. The spring normally keeps the contacts between those of the arm and one terminal closed so that current can flow through both poles of that circuit. The terminals of the other set are normally open. As a control current activates the electromagnetic coils, they magnetically pull the arm against the power of the spring and away from the closed position to connect with the other set of double contacts. When this contact is made, it allows the current to flow through both poles of the other circuit.

A relay can be likened to a railroad track switch. The track switch moves between two different tracks, and makes it possible for trains from either track to move onto the main track. A relay switches back and forth between the shore power and the inverter, routing the current through its center terminals to the distribution panel. As for the wiring, the control current comes from the shore-power side, and it activates the relay causing the contacts to switch from the inverter side to the shore-power side whenever the shore-power cable is plugged in. When shore power is absent, the relay's spring-loaded contacts are normally closed to the inverter's connections. The control current of relays can be either AC or DC and can have various voltages.

We prefer to use double-pole rather than single-pole switches or power relays because they completely isolate each power supply's circuit from the other; we believe this is a safer installation. If a single-pole unit is used, the hot wires are connected to the switch or relay, and the neutral wires have to be joined together at a common junction. When neutral conductors are joined together, there is always the danger of stray current finding its way to the ground chassis connection and creating a shock hazard.

We prefer to use double-pole rather than single-pole switches or power relays because they completely isolate each power supply's circuit from the other; we believe this is a safer installation.

Two relays, or a relay and a switch, can be used to link together shore power, a generator, and an inverter so they switch from one another either manually or automatically. Either a relay or a switch is between the shore power and the generator; another relay is between this combined source and the inverter. If shore power were not available and the generator were turned on, it would supply the power; if neither were on, the inverter would take over.

Our Inverter Wiring

In our installation, the inverter's built-in transfer switch was bypassed with a separate relay (Figure 9-15, pg. 192). We used a Dayton Electric Manufacturing Company DPDT power relay (Model No. 5X847). Although we made our own

191

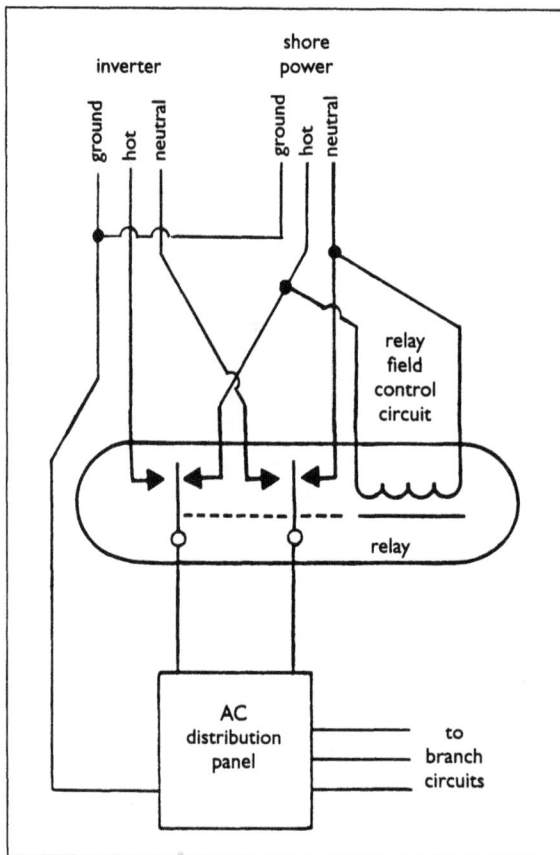

Figure 9-15. Schematic of authors' relay wiring.

The battery charger or the converter/charger will try to supply the DC power to the inverter, thus feeding back into itself. If this is allowed to happen, the result will be a disaster: All the FETs in the inverter will burn out.

cover, Dayton offers a dust cover for this relay (Model No. 4A079). The Dayton SPDT power relay could be also be used (Model No. 3X745). The lead wires from our shore-power cable were attached to the normally open circuit terminals of the relay, and short jumper wires were run to the control current terminals. This allows the shore-power current to be the controlling current for the relay operation. The terminals of the other poles are connected to a 10/3 cable coming from the inverter. The center terminals are connected to the distribution panel terminals through two other short 10-gauge wires. The green (grounded) wires of all three devices are joined together, providing a good ground. These wires are also connected to the chassis via the grounded wire from the distribution panel.

One problem with wiring an inverter with a built-in battery charger and a separate relay into the entire AC system of the RV is that when shore power is off and the inverter is activated, the battery-charger power cord of the inverter will still be plugged into the AC system. If a converter/charger is used instead of an inverter with a built-in battery charger, the converter/charger will also still be plugged into an AC outlet. The battery charger or the converter/ charger will try to supply the DC power to the inverter, thus feeding back into itself. If this is allowed to happen, the result will be a disaster: All the FETs in the inverter will burn out. There is no problem if the inverter's built-in transfer switch is used because it automatically disconnects the charger circuit when the inverter is on.

RV Electrical Systems

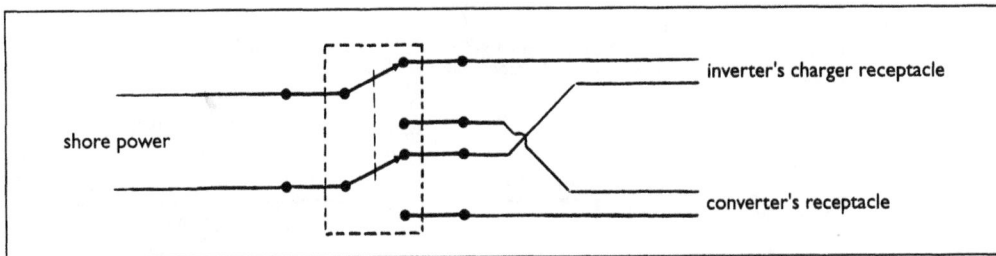

Figure 9-16. Wiring of double-pole double-throw switch. The grounding conductors are not shown; they would be similar to those shown in Figure 9-15.

Since we bypassed the switch, in order to eliminate this feedback problem, a 12/3 cable was run from the shore-power conductors to a DPDT switch (Figure 9-16). The connections with the shore-power cable are made at the relay, but on its upstream side toward the shore-power cable. With this arrangement, whenever the shore-power cable is plugged in, the special circuit is hot; when the shore power is off, the circuit is dead.

Two separate, three-wire cables are attached to the DPDT switch, each terminating in a 15-ampere, circuit-breaker-protected, duplex-receptacle outlet box. Our converter/charger is plugged into one outlet and the power cord of the inverter/charger into the other. This arrangement allows us to select whichever battery-charging device we want to use simply by switching to it. With a special circuit that does not run through the distribution panel, the inverter is protected from DC feeding back to power the inverter from either its built-in charger or the converter/charger (Figure 9-17, pg. 194).

Power relays are much less expensive than DPDT switches. They may be stocked in large electrical supply stores or can be ordered.

Manufactured transfer switches are available from MagneTek. They are designed to be used with generators but can be used with inverters. It might be more desirable to use a ready-made switch rather than a do-it-yourself transfer switch made from a relay. The MagneTek switch has a DC coil to avoid line voltage dropout, relay chatter, and reduced hum. A time delay of 60 seconds is included to allow generators to get up to speed before the AC load is applied. This delay feature does not allow for instantaneous changeover from shore power to inverter use, which is an important consideration. These switches are available in 120-volt AC 30-ampere or 240-volt AC 50-ampere models. Todd Engineering Sales, Inc., also makes a 30-ampere switch in both 120- and 240-volt versions with a generator time-delay.

193

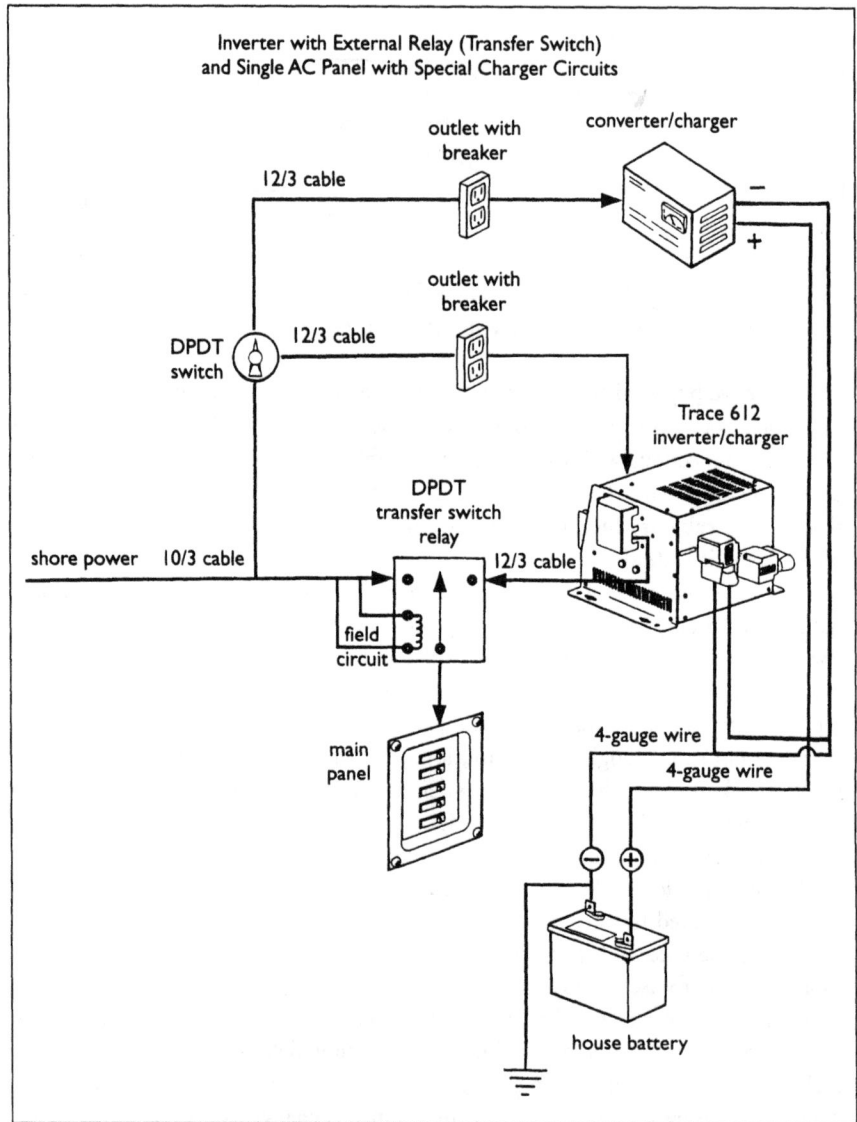

Figure 9-17. *Authors' wiring layout. For simplicity, all AC wiring, which is three-wire conductors, is shown as a single line instead of three lines, which are normally used to represent the three-wire conductors.*

(Basic illustration courtesy of Trace Engineering; modified to show authors' installation)

TEN

Monitoring AC and DC Systems

I t makes little sense to install elaborate equipment such as inverters, generators,
high-capacity alternators on propulsion engines, solar panels, and upgraded con-
verter/chargers unless there is a way to monitor various conditions in the system to
know whether the equipment is functioning properly. Even if an RV is equipped
with just the basic electrical equipment, some monitoring is necessary to avoid finding out after the fact that the batteries are dead or why the air conditioner's compressor burned out. Most problems need not occur if the various electrical systems are
monitored regularly.

The monitors may be combination panels, meters hard-wired into the system,
or various portable plug-in and hand-held meters. Monitoring devices run the
gamut from simple—some far too simple to be useful—to elaborate panels that
might include such nonelectrical functions as outside temperature and water level in
the tank. Only five basic functions need to be monitored: AC voltage, AC amperage,
DC voltage, DC amperage, and battery ampere-hours. (See Table 10-1, pg. 196, for
a selection of monitoring meters.)

AC Voltage Monitoring

When using an electrical hookup, RVers should know
what the AC voltage is, since this is the most important
AC measurement. Monitoring is easy; voltage can be
read from a simple *plug-in voltmeter, panel-mount voltmeter,* or *multimeter.*

*When using an electrical hookup,
RVers should know what the AC
voltage is, since this is the most
important AC measurement.*

Analog voltmeters are available from electronics supply stores. Radio Shack has
a small plug-in voltmeter (Catalog No. 22-104) that can be left in a receptacle in the
RV to provide a constant voltage check. Panel-mount voltmeters are available small
enough to be installed in various wall or cabinet locations in an RV. Such a meter

195

Table 10-1.

Individual Monitoring Meters			
Manufacturer	**Model**	**Type**	**Range**
Ample Power Company		alternator ammeter shunt-type	−200–0–200+ amps
Automated Engineering Company	660 P	DC voltmeter	9–25 volts
	661 P	AC voltmeter	90–135 volts
	666	DC ammeter shunt-type	0–30 amps
	9070	AC ammeter shunt-type	0–30 amps
Modutec, Inc./Emico	55DVV-015	DC voltmeter	0–15 volts
(Electro-Mechanical	55DVV-030	DC voltmeter	0–30 volts
Instrument Co.)	55DAA030	DC ammeter series-type	0–30 amps
	55DAA-100	DC ammeter series-type	0–100 amps
Equus Products, Inc.	6618	DC voltmeter to one decimal place	8–18 volts
	6148	DC voltmeter	9–17 volts
	6140	DC ammeter series-type	−60–0–60+ amps
Weems & Plath	25200	DC voltmeter to one decimal place	8–18 volts
	25198	DC voltmeter	9–16 volts
	26198	DC voltmeter showing battery state of charge as percentage	0–100 percent
	25900	AC voltmeter	99–150 volts
	20161	DC ammeter series-type	0–50 amps
	20171	DC ammeter shunt-type	0–100 amps
	20176	DC ammeter shunt-type	0–150 amps

NOTE:
Autoparts stores offer a selection of both DC voltmeters and DC series-type ammeters.
   Meters listed are a selection of special-purpose meters, mainly digital, or battery-condition meters.
Ah = ampere hour(s)

can be connected by using a length of two-wire lamp cord with a plug on the end—the wires attached to the meter, the plug placed in any convenient AC receptacle. A simple analog voltmeter is inexpensive; more costly meters have a digital LED or *liquid crystal display (LCD)*. Digital models are either the panel-mount or plug-in type (see Chapter 8). Many expensive meters also provide a true rms voltage.

Readout	Mount	Comments
analog dial	panel-mounted circular, 2 inches	
LED digital	panel-mounted rectangular, 2 x 4 inches	
LED digital	panel-mounted rectangular, 2 x 4 inches	
LED digital	panel-mounted rectangular, 2 x 4 inches	50-amp or 200-amp shunts available
LED digital	panel-mounted rectangular, 2 x 4 inches	50-amp or 200-amp shunts available
analog dial	panel-mounted square, $2\frac{3}{8}$ x $2\frac{3}{8}$ inches	
analog dial	panel-mounted square, $2\frac{3}{8}$ x $2\frac{3}{8}$ inches	
analog dial	panel-mounted square, $2\frac{3}{8}$ x $2\frac{3}{8}$ inches	
analog dial	panel-mounted square, $2\frac{3}{8}$ x $2\frac{3}{8}$ inches	
LED digital	panel-mounted circular, 2 inches	LED bar-graph display showing battery charge state; adjustable high/low voltage setting flashes bargraph as warning
analog dial	panel-mounted circular, 2 inches	expanded color-coded scale showing state of battery charge
analog dial	panel-mounted circular, 2 inches	
LCD backlighted digital	panel-mounted circular, $2\frac{1}{4}$ inches	user adjustable high/low voltage flashing visual alarm; bar graph shows battery state of charge in percentages
analog dial	panel-mounted square, $2\frac{1}{4}$ x $2\frac{1}{4}$ inches	expanded-scale color-coded shows battery state of charge
analog dial	panel-mounted square, $2\frac{1}{4}$ x 2 $2\frac{1}{4}$ inches	expanded-scale measures 11–13 volts
analog dial	panel-mounted square, $2\frac{1}{4}$ x $2\frac{1}{4}$ inches	expanded-scale
analog dial	panel-mounted square, $2\frac{1}{4}$ x $2\frac{1}{4}$ inches	
analog dial	panel-mounted square, $2\frac{1}{4}$ x $2\frac{1}{4}$ inches	
analog dial	panel-mounted square, $2\frac{1}{4}$ x $2\frac{1}{4}$ inches	

The accuracy of the meter isn't too important, because only an approximate voltage reading is needed. Inexpensive meters, which may have an inaccuracy as high as 10 percent, still indicate if the voltage is too high or too low. Low voltage can cause damage to air conditioner compressors and other appliances, high voltage can hurt microwave ovens and computers; motors are adversely affected by both high and low voltages. For checking inverter and generator voltage output, a more precise measurement is needed, and this can be obtained only from a highly accurate analog meter, digital meter, or meter that reads true rms voltage.

After a voltmeter is installed and regularly monitored, you develop an awareness of how it reads in different situations—for instance, the reading before and after an air conditioner or heater is turned on or when a brownout occurs—and can take appropriate measures. A voltmeter also indicates whether the voltage is fluctuating or steady.

Another simple means of AC monitoring is to install a nightlight in a receptacle visible from most locations in the RV. Since most of the lights and other equipment are 12-volt, it is sometimes not immediately obvious that the AC power has gone off; a glance at the nightlight will let you know. We use a General Electric neon unit called a guidelight (Model No. GE3960-02D). The light is molded into the plug casing. It's the smallest nightlight available and lasts longer and uses less current than units with replaceable bulbs. (This is not the nightlight mentioned in Chapter 9 that we use to trip the inverter—that one has a bulb.) Another reason we like the neon nightlight is that it flickers instead of emitting a steady glow when the inverter comes on line—another indication of an external power failure. Being alerted to the situation, we turn off certain AC appliances that we do not want to run off the inverter.

AC Amperage Monitoring

It is sometimes useful to be able to monitor AC amperage, but installing a panel *ammeter* for this can be expensive and, for most RVers, not necessary. The main advantages of monitoring AC amperage are to determine whether the incoming service is being overloaded and enough amperage is available from the power supply to operate the appliances you want to use. Ammeters are useful for monitoring a generator outlet and its load, as well as for evaluating amperage consumption of a single appliance by eliminating all loads except the one being measured.

Panel-mounted ammeters are connected in series on one side of the circuit, requiring the entire current load to pass through the meter. Another type of ammeter uses an auxiliary shunt, which is placed in series in the circuit instead of the meter. With the shunt-type ammeter, the meter itself can be located where desired and connected to the shunt with smaller-gauge wire than a series-type meter (Figure 10-1). A *shunt* is a device with a known resistance that causes a voltage drop across itself as current flows through it. By measuring the voltage drop, it is possible to determine current flow. To illustrate: If the shunt has 1 ohm of resistance and the measured voltage drop is 1 volt, the current flow is 1 ampere. A shunt-type ammeter is actually an extremely sensitive voltmeter. The scale on the face of the meter is calibrated to read in amperes instead of volts. This type of ammeter is usually expensive and not normally needed for measuring AC unless there is a special need for very accurate amperage measurements.

An easy method of checking AC amperage is with a portable, clamp-on ammeter (Amprobe is the brand name of a common ammeter sold in electrical supply stores). These units have jaws, similar to those on a pair of pliers, that are opened and then closed around a single conductor of the circuit to be measured. The meter measures the magnetic field produced around the wire and, because the field is proportional to the amount of current flow, the amperage is given. These devices also may have features that provide AC and DC voltage readings.

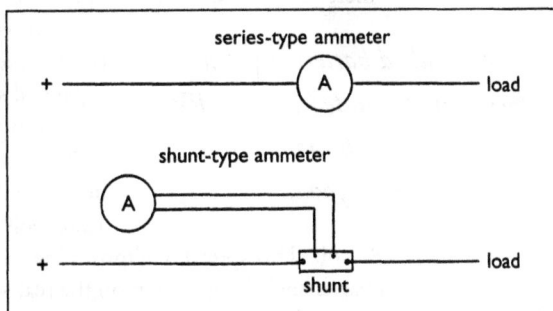

Figure 10-1. Wiring for series-type and shunt-type ammeters. (An A in a circle is the schematic symbol for an ammeter.)

DC Voltage Monitoring

Monitoring DC systems is even more important than monitoring AC systems. Because of the ever-changing, fluctuating state of charge in the batteries, a way to continually monitor both voltage and amperage is needed. Voltage indicates the state of charge in a battery and whether it is receiving a charge. Amperage provides information about the rate of charging or discharging taking place. This data is important to properly maintain and operate the DC system to prevent early battery failure.

Monitoring DC systems is even more important than monitoring AC systems.

As discussed in Chapter 2, the most accurate way to determine a battery's state of charge is by measuring the specific gravity of the electrolyte with a hydrometer. Because this method is neither convenient nor practical for daily or hourly checks, another way to check the state of charge is needed; a voltmeter provides the needed information.

Battery-Condition Meters

A good *battery-condition meter* gives a readout of actual battery voltage. The so-called battery-condition meters incorporated in most RV monitor panels are far from being good. On many, an LED indicates the state of charge in the battery as low, fair, good, or charging. Because this information is inaccurate and meaningless, this type of meter is worthless. No better are the meters on which a needle moves over red, green, or yellow areas to represent the state of charge.

The so-called battery-condition meters incorporated in most RV monitor panels are far from being good.

Most *analog voltmeters*—the needle type—have an expanded scale from 9 to 16 volts; however, even they are not suitable as battery-condition meters because the scale is not expanded enough for accurate voltage readings. The difference between a fully charged battery at 12.63 volts and a discharged battery at 11.82 is only 0.81 volt. This spread of almost nine-tenths of a volt is usually represented by about a quarter-inch-long section on the scale—hardly enough for determining the exact battery voltage. Compounding the problem is that some meters have a percentage of error greater than the difference between a fully charged and discharged battery.

Only one battery-condition meter of this type is worthwhile: it's made by Weems & Plath and is an analog meter that reads in percentage of charge instead of voltage (Figure 10-2). The scale is quite large, with markings from zero to 100 percent. Beneath this scale is another scale that shows the useful charge range of the battery.

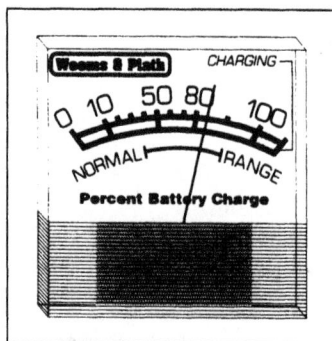

Figure 10-2. Weems & Plath battery-condition meter with a readout in percent of charge.
(Illustration courtesy of Weems & Plath.)

To be truly useful as a battery-condition meter, a voltmeter should be a digital type that gives readings to two decimal places, showing not tenths but hundredths of a volt. A reading of this accuracy covers the range of the useful life of a battery (11.82 to 12.63 volts) in a total of 81 increments, and also accurately shows the readings above or below this range. A single-decimal-place meter has only nine increments over the same range.

A reading above 12.63 volts indicates that the battery is either being charged or maintained by a float charge. When the charge rate is 14.5 volts or higher, the charging device is doing its job efficiently and the wiring in the system is adequate. An equalization-stage voltage shows as 15 to 16 volts; a float-charge reading is around 13.65 volts. If it is known that no charging is taking place, then a high reading indicates the surface charge remaining across the battery terminals from recent charging.

We stated previously that it is not possible to accurately measure true voltage until a battery has rested for at least 24 hours; however, without waiting this long, it's possible to get a reasonably clear picture of what is happening within the battery.

When a load is placed on the battery, the voltmeter shows the extent of the voltage drop caused by the load. Heavy loads may drop the voltage to 12.30 or lower; light loads may cause a drop to only about 12.50 or so. As the load is removed from the batteries, the voltage should bounce back to a high level. The extent of the bounce-back indicates general status of the batteries. For example, say an appliance is turned on and is running off the inverter, which is drawing a 25-ampere load for 1 minute. A well-charged battery should be able to withstand this load without any appreciable drop in voltage—maybe a couple of hundredths of a volt at most. If the batteries are accepting a charge well, with a minimum amount of sulfate clumping on the plates, the voltage should return to a high reading near the full-charge level or even higher. If the voltage does not return to a reading much above the load level, the batteries have not accepted the last charge readily. An equalization charge may be needed to restore them, or one of the batteries may have gone bad and needs to be replaced.

Studying the voltmeter as various loads are applied, coupled with ammeter readings taken at the same time, provides a clear picture of the 12-volt system's performance.

It's easy to see why a meter that reads to only one decimal place doesn't provide a truly accurate representation of battery voltage. Such a meter provides useful information about the voltage changes occurring, but not as accurately as the two-decimal-place models. Studying the voltmeter as various loads are applied, coupled with ammeter readings taken at the same time, provides a clear picture of the 12-volt system's performance.

SLI Batteries and Monitoring

Many monitors have been designed to check the condition of house batteries, especially while camping without an electrical hookup when they receive the greatest discharge. Little equipment exists, however, for monitoring what could be the most important battery in the 12-volt system: the engine-starting, or SLI, battery in motorhomes and tow vehicles. Most motorhomes and tow vehicles have an ammeter or voltmeter deemed by the chassis manufacturer as adequate to tell you all you need to know about the battery system. Usually it's a voltmeter with few or no markings on the dial.

The voltmeter in our pickup truck, for example, has an expanded-scale with an 8 at the bottom and an 18 at the top. In between are a series of varying-distance incremental markings, but no indication of what they mean. The meter can only give an approximate needle reading of voltage. The needle moves to a lower position when the air conditioner is on, and that's about all the meter tells us: The voltage is

lower when the air conditioner is on. Years ago vehicles were equipped with ammeters, but as amperage output of alternators increased to meet the higher requirements of modern vehicles, manufacturers found it was cheaper and simpler to install
voltmeters because the heavy run of cable an ammeter requires was
eliminated.

*Figure 10-3. Equus Model
6618 digital voltmeter. Bar
graph at left of LED shows
battery voltage.*
(Illustration courtesy of Equus Products, Inc.)

RVers interested in the condition of their SLI battery should
install an accurate voltmeter. It shows if the battery is holding its
capacity from charge to charge and, since the SLI battery gets a
rest (usually overnight when the engine is not running), it provides
a reading of the rested-battery voltage. If after a reasonable rest the
voltage is below 12.6 volts, it's time to replace the battery. As with
most meters, a digital-readout type provides the most detailed
information. Equus Products, Inc., is the only manufacturer of a
digital voltmeter with a 2-inch dial that fits in the standard, automotive, add-on meter panels available at auto parts stores (Figure
10-3). The meter has a single-decimal-place readout with a voltage
bar graph that flashes if battery voltage is low.

DC Amperage

A means to measure amperage provides the data needed to complete the full picture
of the 12-volt DC system. Since an ammeter measures current flow in a circuit, it
can be used to obtain information about the power being consumed by various loads
in the circuit or to measure the amperes flowing into the battery during recharging.
This data can help evaluate the 12-volt DC system at any time. Depending on how
the ammeter is connected to the system, it is possible to measure all loads and charging rates at the same time. Many ammeters give plus readings for charging amperage
and minus readings for discharging amperage (Figure 10-4). With a glance at this
type of meter, it is immediately apparent whether the amperage is charging or discharging, which helps in fast troubleshooting of the charging devices.

In evaluating battery condition, using the ampere readings along with the voltage readings helps determine what effect a particular load has on the voltage. Most
constant loads on batteries are from using lights at night, so the accumulated loads
of an evening's usage can be monitored to conserve battery energy. Since batteries
shouldn't be regularly discharged more than 25 percent of capacity and never more
than 50 percent, amperage consumption can be adjusted so the batteries won't discharge too much.

You can decide on a specific rate of amperage consumption for an evening that
allows you to live within the 25- to 50-percent ampere-hour discharge. You might

Figure 10-4. Ammeter installed in tow vehicle for monitoring charging amperage.

select 10 amperes as the amperage consumption that should not be exceeded at any one time during the evening. Periodic monitoring of the ammeter, every hour or so, indicates when too much amperage is being consumed. Any time the load is too high, simply turn off some of the lights or other 12-volt equipment. If the consumption rate was held to 10 amperes or less over a period of 5 hours, the batteries would be depleted by no more than 50 ampere-hours.

When recharging, a comparison of ampere and voltage readings is necessary to know what is happening in the system. The ammeter shows the amount of charge going into the battery and, according to how quickly amperage drops and voltage rises, indicates how fast the batteries are accepting the charge. From this, the approximate length of time needed for recharging can be determined. If the ammeter drops rapidly, the batteries are accepting the charge readily and weren't discharged too much. If the charge rate drops slowly, the batteries have been discharged extensively and a long time is needed for recharging. Knowing the amount of ampere-hour discharge the night before also provides an idea of how long the recharging should take. If there is any problem in understanding the amperage/voltage relationship, keep an hourly log of ammeter and voltmeter readings for a few days; on paper the relationship will be evident.

A series- or shunt-type ammeter is used for DC monitoring. A *shunt-type ammeter* is more accurate and also more expensive. A *series-type ammeter* is placed in series in the battery circuit, usually on the positive wire, and carries the full-amperage load.

In one of our trailers, a –20–0–20+ series-type ammeter was installed between the converter/charger's fuse panel and battery. This ammeter was satisfactory because the charger in the converter had only an 8-ampere output, and we rarely had a discharge greater than 20 amperes. Twelve-gauge wire was sufficient for the short run to the wiring between the batteries and the converter/charger.

When recharging, a comparison of ampere and voltage readings is necessary to know what is happening in the system.

If monitoring is required for higher amperages, heavier wire is necessary. If the charging or discharging amperage rate were 50 amperes, 6-, 4-, or even 2-gauge wire would be needed to connect the ammeter to the circuit. To prevent a serious voltage drop in a long wire run in spite of using heavy-gauge wire, the ammeter should be located close to the charging source or batteries (see Table 4-3, pg. 70).

With a shunt-type DC ammeter, which is similar in operation to its AC counterpart, the shunt is placed in the battery circuit in series; however, the heavy cable has to run only to the shunt, which can be placed anywhere in the existing circuit. Light-gauge wire can then be run from the shunt to the ammeter, which can be placed wherever desired. This is a far better arrangement than having the long run of heavy cable that a series-type ammeter would require.

In one of our trucks we once used a series-type analog ammeter for monitoring only the charge to the house batteries in the trailer—nothing else. The truck had an alternator with a small amperage output, so 8-gauge wire was heavy enough for the run between the alternator and the batteries. Running the wires to the ammeter, which was mounted under the dashboard, was easy because of the flexibility of the small wire. The installation would not have been so easy if the wire had been the 4, 2, or aught gauge needed for larger alternators. Wire in these gauges is too large, stiff, heavy, and hard to route conveniently.

The ammeter we used was a –60–0–60+ analog type (see Figure 10-4). It was adequate for our monitoring needs since it indicated whether all connectors in the charging circuit were making good contact and whether the batteries were charging.

On our ammeter, the needle registered very little deflection for a 5-ampere charge on the 0–60+ half of the dial. An ammeter with the smallest amperage range that can handle the load should be used. A lower-range meter has more incremental markings or greater spaces between them so the smaller ampere readings are easier to see. There are no 2-inch digital shunt-type ammeters available for this kind of monitoring. In fact, it is very difficult to find any suitable monitoring equipment for tow-vehicle installations; even if such equipment could be found, the tow vehicle usually has little room for additional meters on or under the dashboard.

204

Ampere-Hour Meters

The ultimate in DC monitoring is a meter that measures the ampere-hour capacity of the batteries—a very useful instrument to have (Figure 10-5). Such a meter shows how many ampere-hours have been removed from the batteries during discharging and how many have been restored during recharging.

The ultimate in DC monitoring is a meter that measures the ampere-hour capacity of the batteries—a very useful instrument to have.

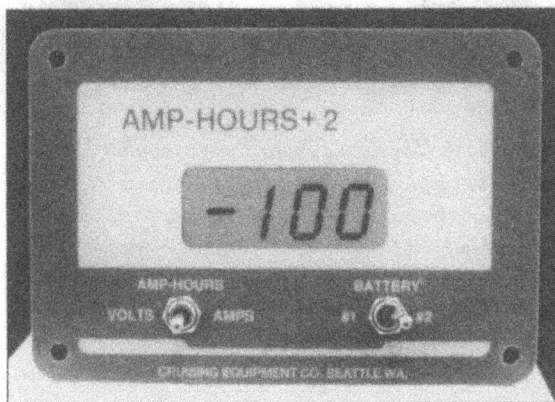

After installation, the meter must be adjusted to read zero ampere-hours when the batteries are fully charged. Then, as power is used, the readout shows the accumulated ampere-hours removed from the battery. As the batteries are recharged, the meter shows a diminishing reading until the batteries are charged, when the meter again reads zero.

An ampere-hour meter is the only instrument that gives an instantaneous readout of ampere-hour capacity in a battery bank. Deluxe ampere-hour meters have three-way switches to read amperage and voltage in addition to ampere-hours.

Linear and Exponential Ampere-Hour Meters

To better understand the difference between a linear and an exponential ampere-hour meter, let's briefly review what ampere-hours are and the factors involved in their computation. Amperage multiplied by time is the definition of an ampere-hour. For example, 10 amperes for 2 hours or 2 amperes for 10 hours would equal 20 ampere-hours. Remember, for each ampere removed from the battery, 1.2 amperes must be replaced, due to the inefficiency of the charging process. Other factors to be considered include battery temperature, size of the amperage load, and recovery rate after the battery has rested.

Linear ampere-hour meters total the amperes removed from a battery during

Figure 10-5. CECO's Amp-Hour+2, one of the company's three ampere-hour meters. The panel provides a readout of battery voltage, amperage discharge and charge rates of various systems, and the accumulated discharge in ampere-hours of two battery banks. The panel interfaces with CECO's Ideal alternator regulator and can be used in conjunction with the Alpha regulator (shown in Figure 3-14). One of the panel's functions is to measure the Charge Efficiency Factor of batteries, which indicates battery lifespan. (Photo courtesy of Cruising Equipment Company)

205

Figure 10-6. The Ample Power Energy Monitor II is one of the most sophisticated monitoring panels. It measures voltage, amperage, and battery temperature; provides an exponential computation of ampere-hours remaining; and includes an English-language battery charge state (shown as ⅞ FULL in the photo). It interfaces with the Next Step alternator regulator (shown in Figure 3-13) and also with solar panels with an optional relay. A PC computer interface is available for recording all data. It has an alarm system for high and low voltage and high temperature, and also calculates the accumulated lifetime ampere-hours for two battery banks. (Photo courtesy of Ample Power Company)

discharge and then count the amperes being returned, with an extra amount added to compensate for charging inefficiency.

Exponential ampere-hour meters consider the factors of temperature, load size, and battery recovery rate, and make further corrections accordingly. The corrections are arrived at through several complicated mathematical formulas; therefore, exponential meters have more complex circuitry and are more expensive than linear meters. Both types of ampere-hour meters provide valuable information unavailable from other types of meters.

Combination Monitoring Panels

A variety of monitoring panels are available, so RVers can find panels with features suited to their individual needs. Combination panels may include voltmeters, ammeters, and ampere-hour meters for one, two, or three battery banks. More elaborate versions provide an alphanumeric readout of the remaining battery capacity in ampere-hours or in simple fractional readings with capacity expressed as seven-eighths full, one-half full, and so on. Panels may also have temperature measurement and high and low voltage alarms. They are available for 24-volt systems and multiple battery banks. The more sophisticated panels provide readouts of accumulated lifetime ampere-hours per battery bank and have a computer interface. With appropriate software programming, all data can be logged and evaluated. Table 10-2 (see page 208) lists several manufacturers' panels, two of which are illustrated in Figures 10-6 and 10-7.

The least expensive panels have analog meters; more costly panels provide highly

A variety of monitoring panels are available, so RVers can find panels with features suited to their individual needs.

accurate LED or LCD digital readouts. Generally, LED displays are easier to read at night, but LCDs are more visible in the daytime. LEDs use much more power than LCDs, so to prevent a constant phantom load, an LED model should have an on-off switch.

With this wide selection of panels, which equipment should you have to monitor your RV's 12-volt system? At a minimum, metering should include a voltmeter and an ammeter that takes readings from as close to the battery as possible. If these meters are wired into the system between the batteries and the DC fuse panel, they will provide readings of battery voltage, amperes in, and amperes out (see Table 10-1). In motorhomes it is convenient to be able to monitor both the house and SLI batteries, so a meter with a two-battery-bank capability should be used. Separate monitoring panels or meters are needed for both the tow vehicle and the trailer. This is the minimal monitoring equipment needed for proper system evaluation. Monitoring can be done with individual meters or the metering functions can be incorporated into a combination panel.

The next most desirable meter is an ampere-hour meter. The more elaborate panels with an ampere-hour meter also include an ammeter and voltmeter, and may have other features. Although ampere-hour meters are expensive, they pay for themselves because they help maintain a properly operating and efficient DC system.

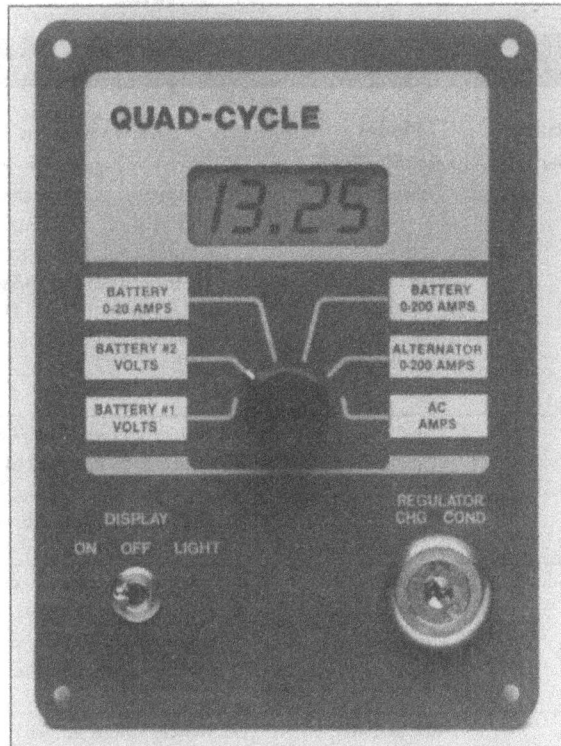

Figure 10-7. The CECO Quad-Cycle metering panel is actually a multistage alternator regulator with monitoring capabilities. It measures amperage in two different ranges and voltage for two battery banks. Optional features include monitoring of AC voltage, AC current, alternator amperage output, and water and fuel tank capacity.
(Photo courtesy of Cruising Equipment Company)

Our Monitoring Installation

Over the years, after trying many different ammeters and voltmeters, we now have a good setup with the SCI Mark III Battery Monitor from Photocomm, Inc.

(text continued on page 210)

Table 10-2.

Manufacturer	Model	Functions	Range
Ample Power Company	Energy Monitor II (EMON II)	DC battery voltage to two decimal places; DC amperage shunt-type charge/discharge; exponential Ah consumed/remaining; fractional English language display of remaining battery capacity; battery temperature	0–50 volts; 0–400 amps, 0–200 amps auxiliary, 50–3,267 Ah, 0–212°F
	ESP Monitor	DC battery Voltage to two decimal places; DC amperage shunt-type charge/discharge; exponential Ah consumed/remaining; fractional English-language display of remaining battery capacity; battery temperature	0–50 volts; 0–400 amps, 0–200 amps auxiliary, 50–3,267 Ah, 0–212°F
Balmar Products, Inc	DCM 2000 Monitor	DC battery voltage to two decimal places; DC amperage shunt-type charge/discharge; linear Ah consumed/remaining; Percent Ah remaining; battery temperature	6–48 volts; 0–200 amps; 0–9,999 Ah; 0–212°F
	DCM 8000 Monitor	DC battery voltage to two decimal places; DC amperage shunt-type charge/discharge; linear Ah consumed/remaining; Percent Ah remaining; battery temperature	6–48 volts; 0–200 amps; 0–9,999 Ah; 0–212°F
Bogart Engineering/ Real Goods Trading Corp	The Tri-Metric	DC voltage to one decimal place; DC Amperage shunt-type charge/discharge; linear Ah consumed	8–35 volts, 0–999 amps, –999–0–999+ Ah
Cruising Equipment Company	Amp-Hour Meter	DC battery linear Ah consumed	0–1,999 Ah
	Amp-Hour+ Meter	DC battery voltage to two decimal places; DC amperage shunt-type charged/discharged; linear Ah consumed	9.5–18 volts, –255–255+ amps, 0–9,999 Ah

NOTE: This list of panel meters covers most of the known manufacturers' products but may not be all-inclusive. Ah = ampere-hour(s)

Readout	Mount	Comments
LCD backlighted, digital alphanumeric, membrane keypad entry	panel-mounted, 4½ x 5½ inches	monitors two battery banks with two sense lines; battery temperature compensating; interfaces with Smart and Next Step regulator series; programmable audible alarms for temperature, over/under voltage, 50% or 80% Ah depth of discharge; shows accumulated lifetime battery Ah one/two banks; optional regulator for solar panels; optional computer interface with software for logging data; 12- or 24-volt operation
LCD backlighted, digital alphanumeric, membrane keypad entry	panel-mounted, 4½ x 5½ inches	all of the features of the EMON II panel plus monitors three battery banks for voltage and amperage from three charging sources; auxiliary generator control, control of security alarm system, control of alternator regulator output
LCD backlighted digital, membrane keypad entry	bracket-mounted, 3 x 4½ x ¾ inches	monitors two battery banks with two sense lines; programmable audible alarms for temperature, over/under voltage; optional provisions for monitoring charging output of alternator, charger, and solar panels
LCD backlighted digital, membrane keypad entry	bracket-mounted, 3 x 4½ x ¾ inches	same features as DCM 2000 plus monitoring of up to eight battery banks; English-language alphanumeric readout of many displays
LED digital	panel-mounted, 4¾ x 3⅛ inches	available with either 500- or 100-amp shunts; user-adjustable for efficiency factor; 12- or 24-volt operation; light indicates when battery is fully charged
LCD backlighted digital	panel-mounted, 3 x 4½ inches	compensates for Charge Efficiency Factor in Ah readings; monitors one battery bank
LCD backlighted digital	panel-mounted 3 x 4½ inches	compensates for Charge Efficiency Factor in Ah readings; monitors one battery bank; designed to operate with CECO's Ideal alternator regulator; 24 volts available

(continued on next page)

Manufacturer	Model	Functions	Range
Cruising Equipment Company (cont.)	Amp-Hour+2 Meter	DC battery voltage to two decimal places; DC amperage shunt-type charge/discharge; linear Ah consumed	9.5–18 volts, –255–255+ amps, 0–9,999 Ah
	Quad-Cycle Regulator/Monitor	DC voltage to two decimal places; DC amperage shunt-type charge/discharge	9.5–18 volts, 0–20 amps, 0–200 amps
Heart Interface Corporation and CECO	Link 2000 Monitoring and Inverter Control	DC voltage to two decimal places; DC amperage shunt-type charge/discharge; linear Ah consumed	8.5–50 volts, –500–500+ amps, 20–2,000 Ah
Jemtech Enterprises	Batterywatch BW1A	DC voltage to one decimal piece	7–15 volts
Specialty Concepts, Inc.	SCI Mark III Monitor	DC voltage to one decimal place; DC amperage shunt-type charge/discharge	0–35 volts, 0–100 amps, 0–30 amps
Weems & Plath	45161 Monitor	DC voltage expanded scale; DC amperage series-type	9–16 volts, 0–50 amps
	40161 Monitor	DC voltage percentage of charge; DC amperage series-type	0–100 percent, 0–50 amps
	45976 Monitor	AC voltage; AC amperage series-type	90–150 volts, 0–50 amps

NOTE: This list of panel meters covers most of the known manufacturers' products but may not be all-inclusive. Ah = ampere-hour(s).

(Figure 10-8, pg. 212). This unit was designed primarily for monitoring solar panel output, but it was easily adapted to our system. It is available with either one or two 100-ampere shunts or optional 500-ampere shunts. The panel's rotary switch has positions for Current A, DC Voltage, Current B, and Off. The Mark III LED digital

Readout	Mount	Comments
LCD backlighted digital	panel-mounted, 3 x 4½ inches	compensates for and displays Charge Efficiency Factor as a percentage; monitors one/two battery banks; designed to operate with CECO's Ideal alternator regulator for control of charging both SLI and house battery banks; 24 volts available
LCD backlighted digital	panel-mounted, 6 x 4½ inches	combination alternator regulator and monitor for two battery banks; multistage-type regulator; also monitors alternator output, AC voltage, AC current, and water-tank level; suitable for motorhome installation; 24 volts available
LCD backlighted digital with LED indicator lights	panel-mounted, 3¾ x 5¾ inches	designed to monitor and control Heart's Freedom series inverters and up to two battery banks; multiple push-button switches for inverter, charger, setup, equalize charge mode, volt reading, amp reading, Ah reading; 12-/24-volt operation; panel will interface with CECO's Ideal alternator regulators
LED digital	panel-mounted, 2¾ x 5¼ inches	monitors one battery bank; has adjustable audible low voltage alarm; optional model for two battery banks, toggles between readings for each bank; optional model for one bank without alarm; 24-volt available
LED digital	panel-mounted, 5¼ x 8½ inches	monitors one battery bank; four-position rotary switch operation (off, current #1, volts, current #2); High- and low-voltage warning lights; 12-/24-volt operation; optional 100- and 500-amp shunts
analog meters	panel-mounted, 7½ x 5¼ inches	three pushbuttons select between three battery banks
analog meters	panel-mounted, 7½ x 5¼ inches	three pushbuttons select between three battery banks
analog meters	panel-mounted, 7½ x 5¼ inches	for monitoring AC shore power

readout is to one decimal place. Two other LEDs warn of low and high voltage; the settings are adjustable.

Panels can be connected and wired in various ways. If we had a motorhome, the Mark III would be wired with the house batteries hooked up to Current A and the

Monitoring AC and DC Systems

Figure 10-8. The authors' Specialty Concepts, Inc., Mark III monitoring panel (see Figure 10-9 for schematic). In the photo, the display shows the solar panel charging rate. Below the panel is an AC voltmeter. The switch on the left is for selecting either the inverter's battery charger or the converter/charger.

SLI battery to Current B in order to monitor current flow in the two different battery banks. Since we have a fifth-wheel trailer, we are interested in monitoring only the house batteries.

Because the panel's readout does not show plus or minus current, it's not possible to know whether a current reading is a discharge or a charge value, so our installation is wired in an unusual way (Figure 10-9). The shunts for both Currents A and B were hooked up so the A shunt is placed between the batteries and the load, on the ground side of the battery. This way, Current A reads only discharge current from the batteries. The B shunt was placed on the negative wires from the various charging devices, between the batteries and the devices. The negative wires from the converter/charger, inverter/charger, and solar panels, and the negative charging cable from the tow vehicle's alternator are connected directly to the shunt. The Current B reading shows only charging amperage from the charging device in use, with one exception: When the inverter is on and functioning as an inverter instead of a battery charger, the Current B reading is the discharge amperage consumed by the inverter. By switching between the two current settings, we can gather a range of

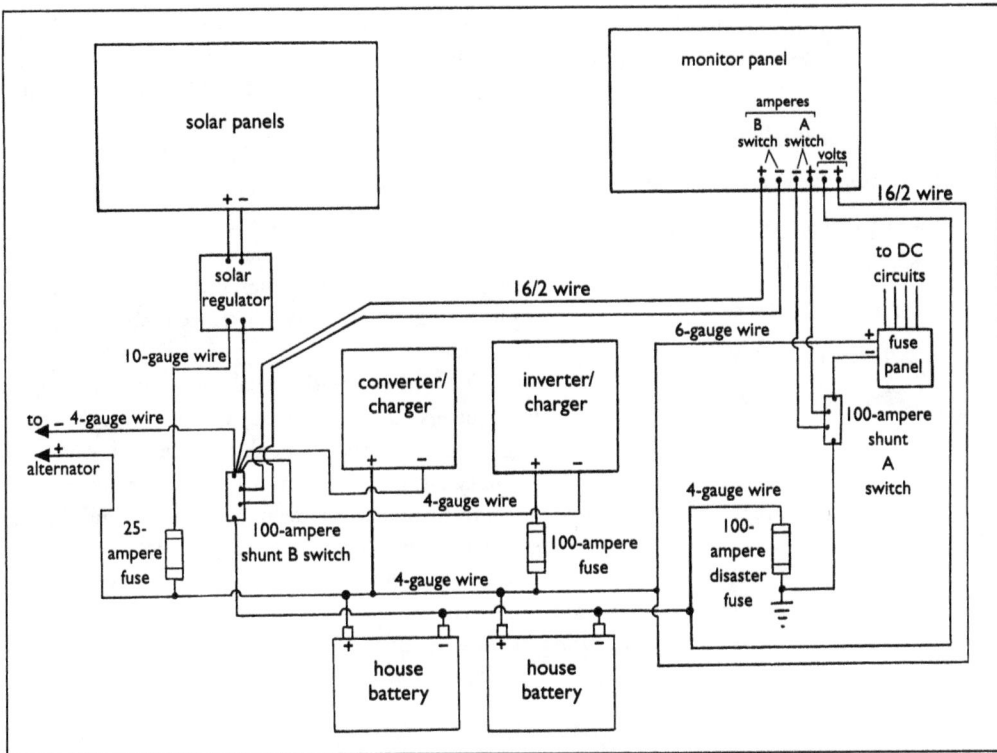

Figure 10-9. Schematic of authors' monitoring panel and DC system.

information about the 12-volt system. Since our electrical needs are modest and our inverter is small, we elected to use 100-ampere rather than 500-ampere shunts.

The voltage setting on the rotary switch is connected to the batteries so the battery voltage can be checked directly. When we want measurements more accurate than the tenths (one decimal place) the monitor provides, we use a multimeter that reads in hundredths (two decimal places). Although this monitoring system has been satisfactory, we eventually intend to add an ampere-hour meter or, perhaps, replace the panel we have with a multipurpose panel.

Multimeters

A multimeter, or multitester, measures many electrical functions and tests various electrical equipment and circuits (Figure 10-10, pg. 214). (In years past, this instrument was called a *volt/ohm/milliampere meter* or *VOM.*) Since a multimeter is invaluable for general electrical system troubleshooting and can perform myriad tests and measurements, this portable hand-held device should be included in every RVer's tool kit. Multimeters are available in many versions. They can be as small as a pocket calculator or slightly larger than a cordless telephone, costing as little as $10 or as much as several hundred dollars. Multimeters have many functions or just the basic functions, which provide readings for both AC and DC voltage, resistance (ohms), and DC milliamperes.

Since a multimeter is invaluable for general electrical system troubleshooting and can perform myriad tests and measurements, this portable hand-held device should be included in every RVer's tool kit.

The readout is either analog or digital. Analog multimeters range in accuracy from 0.5 to 1.0 percent. Digital multimeters are much more precise, with an accuracy rating range from 0.1 to 0.5 percent. A digital multimeter usually has many more features than an analog multimeter, and the digital display, which can be to either one or two decimal places, provides a far more accurate reading than a needle on a scale. Some digital multimeters measure up to 20 amperes for both AC and DC circuits.

For testing or measuring a device or circuit, the multimeter's two metal-tipped probes are used. The wire lead of the positive probe is red, the negative probe is

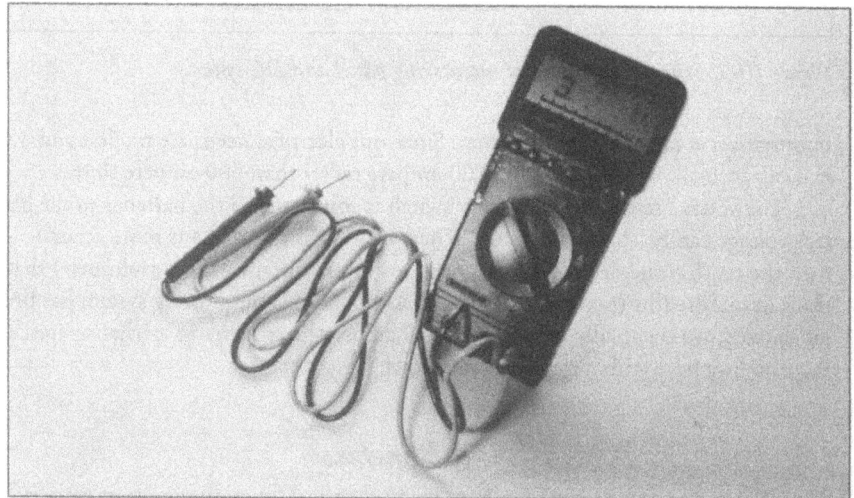

Figure 10-10. Radio Shack rms autoranging multimeter.

black. Each lead is plugged into its respective positive or negative jack on the meter, and the probe ends are placed into or against the device or circuit to be checked.

RVers find that a multimeter is of greatest value for reading voltage and resistance and checking continuity. The voltage settings are used for troubleshooting and electrical tests such as checking batteries, DC circuitry, and campground AC outlets. The resistance setting (on some multimeters this is also the continuity setting) is used for measuring resistance and checking the continuity of circuits, resistors, diodes, and other devices. Using the multimeter for these tests is described in Chapter 11.

On multimeters, a rotary selector switch is used for the function settings; for each function, there are usually several range positions. For example, there may be three ranges for both AC and DC voltages: zero to 15, zero to 150, and zero to 1,000 volts. On an analog multimeter, after the switch is placed at the desired setting, the needle position on the corresponding scale on the face of the meter provides the reading. Some digital multimeters have an auto-ranging feature: Once the basic function is set, the meter automatically gives the correct reading without having to set the range with the rotary switch.

The resistance or continuity setting on an analog meter is usually marked RX1KΩ. This setting signifies that the resistance is the reading on the scale multiplied by 1,000 ohms. A reading of 3 translates to 3,000 ohms; a reading of 10 is 10,000 ohms. Elaborate multimeters may have several resistance ranges, with settings of RX1, RX10, RX100, and maybe even RX10K. Usually only analog multimeters have these settings for resistance, but they can be found on some digital models. A beeping continuity check is a feature of some digital multimeters.

Depending on the model, there may be a separate milliampere setting for AC and DC, or just a DC milliampere setting. Most analog multimeters don't have the necessary circuitry for providing readings of full amperes, which would be valuable to RVers.

Selecting a Suitable Multimeter

A simple, inexpensive—under $20—multimeter is suitable for RV use as long as it has the features desired and its limitations are understood. It's much easier to get the hang of using a simple multimeter than a complex instrument. A problem for first-time multimeter users is finding a good instruction manual. The manuals that come with meters are often badly written, sometimes to the point of being unintelligible. For a good explanation of how multimeters work and how to use them, we recommend *Using Your Meter* by Alvis J. Evans, available from Radio Shack (Catalog No. 62-2039). Included in the book are instructions for several tests that apply to RV systems.

Radio Shack is one manufacturer of quality multimeters. Their Micronta multimeters are offered in a wide range of models and prices. Fluke and Simpson are other excellent brands, but it may be difficult to locate a dealer. We recently purchased a Micronta digital multimeter from Radio Shack (Catalog No. 22-174), selected partly because it has so many features useful for checking RV systems. In addition to the highly accurate two-decimal-place readout and auto-ranging features, it reads AC voltage as rms voltage and indicates the frequency of that voltage; this is handy for checking generator or inverter output. It also measures and checks resistors, diodes, transistors, capacitors, and both AC and DC amperages of up to 10 amperes—convenient for measuring small loads and appliances. A great feature is the temperature probe, with readouts in either Fahrenheit or Celsius, which can be used to evaluate the performance of air conditioners, refrigerators, water heaters, and furnaces. Probably it could even be used to check battery temperature, but we'll never know; we aren't about to insert the probe of such an expensive item into sulfuric acid.

ELEVEN

Maintenance, Troubleshooting, and Repairs

S afety is discussed in other chapters, but a more detailed overview of safe practices to be followed when doing maintenance, troubleshooting, or repairs is in order. Forgive us if we repeat ourselves; electrical safety can't be emphasized too much. Too many people have a blasé attitude about this force that can kill, maim, and burn if it isn't dealt with properly. Electrical safety involves good working habits and a respect for the power of electricity. Reading the following sections carefully could save your life.

How Electricity Can Kill and Cause Damage

Both AC and DC have the potential to deliver lethal shocks, but low-voltage DC systems are considered relatively safe to work with, particularly if the voltage is 24 volts or less. An AC system, because it involves 120 volts or more (10 times the voltage of a 12-volt system) is a different story. Contact with this voltage causes the muscles of the hand to contract, with the often unavoidable result of the hand clutching the wire or contact more tightly. Obviously, this is an extremely dangerous situation because you can't let go of what may be killing you. DC requires five times more current than AC to cause the same muscle contractions. One milliampere of current can be felt, 12 milliamperes causes muscle contraction, 25 milliamperes can kill, and more than 100 milliamperes is definitely lethal.

How electrical current passes through the body determines how the heart and other vital organs are affected and how much damage occurs. The body's resistance ranges from 1,000 to 500,000 ohms for dry skin and much less for moist, wet, or broken skin. When current enters the body, the body becomes part of the circuit and, just as in any other circuit, good connections are important for the completion of the circuit. If current enters the body through one of the hands and a good ground contact is established through the other hand or the feet, the pathway of the current creates a circuit that will most likely pass directly through the heart, which is in an almost straight line from entry point to exit point. The current causes the heart muscle to fibrillate and the pumping action stops.

It is very important to avoid electrical contact through both hands at the same time. Because of this danger, there is an adage about electricity that should be kept in mind: Old electricians always keep one hand in their pocket when making high-voltage tests; that is why they become old electricians. This is a good rule to follow, particularly when using a multimeter to check AC voltage. A good method is to manipulate the two probes with only one hand when they are inserted in an outlet receptacle—much as you might handle a pair of chopsticks. If a shock is experienced, the current passes through only one hand; far better to have the current go from thumb to index finger than from hand to hand. Always avoid touching any metal parts of the probes.

Old electricians always keep one hand in their pocket when making high-voltage tests; that is why they become old electricians.

In addition to the potential to kill, electrical contact can also cause severe burns. Even 12-volt DC contacts can cause damage; considerable arcing occurs when a wrench shorts out between the two terminals of a battery. We once had an accident in which a wrench slipped during removal of a battery cable; the resultant arc instantly burned a quarter-inch hole in one end of the wrench. Never touch the two terminals of a battery with your hands. You probably won't get a shock, but don't take the chance.

Never touch the two terminals of a battery with your hands. You probably won't get a shock, but don't take the chance.

Safety Rules

For personal protection, follow these safety rules religiously when working with electrical circuits and equipment; they apply to both AC and DC power:

1. Always turn off or disconnect the power from circuits before working on them. Also unplug or turn off equipment before attempting repairs or troubleshooting.

2. When it is necessary to make tests or adjustments to circuits and equipment with the power on, always make sure another person is standing by to turn off the power if something goes wrong.

3. Whenever working with electricity, wear shoes with rubber or composite soles so your feet won't be grounded. If this is not possible, stand on a rubber mat, a

piece of dry wood, a rug, or layers of nonconducting material such as corrugated cardboard.

4. Use only one hand for handling test equipment probes. Even go to the extent of keeping the other hand in your pocket or behind your back to eliminate the possibility of creating a ground. If you are apprehensive about working with live AC circuits when testing, wear rubber or latex gloves, but still observe the one-hand rule.

5. If you suspect that any electrical device, receptacle, outlet box, or conductor presents a shock hazard, first touch it very lightly with the back of the hand or a single finger. Muscle contraction there automatically breaks the circuit.

6. Never do any electrical work in wet, snowy, or damp locations. Do not plug shore-power cables into a campground outlet in such conditions, and don't plug into an outlet if the post it's mounted on is sitting in a puddle. Do not turn on equipment or switches when they are wet. Make sure clothing is dry and not damp or wet; wet clothing increases the danger from shock.

7. If possible, insert plugs into campground receptacles with fingers only—don't hold them with the whole hand.

8. Always work with adequate lighting. Don't ever attempt to reset a tripped circuit breaker on a campground outlet in the dark. Always look inside the outlet box with a bright flashlight before putting your hand into it.

9. For maximum protection, make sure all AC circuits have a good ground connection at the outlet.

10. Another danger exists with electricity: fire. To prevent fire, don't overload circuits. Overloaded circuits can melt wire insulation and burn switch and receptacle contacts. Burned or melted insulation results in bare wires, which creates more problems. Avoid touching melted insulation; it's hot enough to cause severe burns.

To prevent fire, don't overload circuits.

Battery Maintenance and Safety

In a 12-volt system, the potential for the greatest dangers stems from the battery itself and the compartment in which it is kept. Most problems occur during battery installation or maintenance. Improper battery handling can result in fire, personal injuries such as burns, and even blindness. Batteries must be maintained, but in the process, safety considerations must be uppermost.

Maintenance is important for prolonging the life of RV batteries (unless they are the sealed or gelled-cell type, which need no maintenance). It involves proper recharging, as well as maintaining the fluid level of the electrolyte.

The tools and supplies needed for battery maintenance include a hydrometer, post and clamp cleaner, wire brush, distilled water, lubricating spray such as WD-40, dielectric grease, pump pliers, two half-inch open-end wrenches, baking soda, water, and paper towels.

Keep the battery case clean. Dirt contributes to rapid corrosion of battery cable fittings. Remove dirt from around the cell caps by wiping with a damp paper towel; if it's greasy dirt, use a dry towel. A wire brush removes stubborn accumulations. Keep the vent caps on when cleaning the top of the case. If dirt, oil, or grease gets into the cells, it will contaminate the electrolyte and shorten the life of the battery. If any metal chips or shavings fall in, the plates short out, destroying the cell.

Regular cleaning is especially necessary for batteries mounted on the tongue of conventional trailers. Even batteries in plastic battery boxes collect a lot of dirt. Removing soot that accumulates on tongue-mounted batteries when a diesel-powered tow vehicle is used is a time-consuming job. Don't allow this soot to get inside the battery; it is a particularly bad contaminant for electrolyte. Motorhome batteries located in an engine compartment, or on an open framework where they may not be in battery boxes, are also exposed to considerable road grime.

Once the batteries are cleaned, remove the caps to check the electrolyte level. On most batteries there are two caps, each covering three cells; remove them one at a time. Do not expose yourself to any more open cells of sulfuric acid than necessary.

Add only distilled water to the electrolyte. Never use tap water.

Check and fill the cells regularly, as needed. Never allow the electrolyte level to get below the top of the plates. When the plates are exposed to air, sulfate forms on the exposed parts and serious damage can occur.

Add only distilled water to the electrolyte. The bottled water available in grocery stores is suitable only if it is labeled distilled water, not spring water. Never use tap water. Most tap water has impurities, including minerals, that can damage the plates and interrupt the charging process.

For pouring water into the cells, we use a 3-ounce paper cup, bending the rim into a V-shaped spout. The cell should be filled just to the level of the ridge, or bull's eye, around the bottom of the fill-pipe tube. Too much water does not allow space for gassing to occur and, consequently, the electrolyte may boil out of the cell.

In our trailer's battery compartment there isn't much room above the batteries, so when we check the water level we must use a mirror and a flashlight. The flashlight beam is directed into the cell by bouncing it off the mirror, thus providing a clear view of the electrolyte level in the neck of the opening relative to the bull's eye. Rather than an inconvenience, we consider this indirect view to be a safety feature: The eyes of the person checking the cells are not directly over the cell opening and are therefore protected from sulfuric acid that might bubble out of the cell—which can happen if the battery is in the process of being charged. Although the sulfuric acid in the electrolyte is diluted, it is still dangerous; if it gets into your eyes it can blind you. If this happens, flush the eye repeatedly with many changes of fresh water and then immediately see an ophthalmologist.

A small amount of sulfuric acid on your skin can cause severe burns. The best way to stop the burning is to sprinkle baking soda on the affected area (it neutralizes the acid) and then flush well with water. If acid gets on clothes, rinsing the spot with water won't stop the cloth from rotting; if baking soda is applied before rinsing, the item might be salvaged.

Many people wear eyeglasses or goggles for protection when working around batteries; it's a good idea, as is wearing rubber gloves and a rubber or plastic apron. If you don't take these precautions, at least wear old clothes and shoes when doing battery maintenance and be extra careful not to expose your eyes and skin to acid.

Hydrometers

A hydrometer is used to check a battery's specific gravity—its state of charge (Figure 11-1). A hydrometer is a glass tube with a rubber bulb on one end and a rubber hose, or tube, on the other. Inside the tube is a weighted float with a scale on its side with markings for specific gravity readings. The reading is taken from the float's position in solution relative to the scale. Some hydrometers have corrections for ambient temperature. (Some inexpensive hydrometers have four small, different-colored, weighted balls, each representing one-

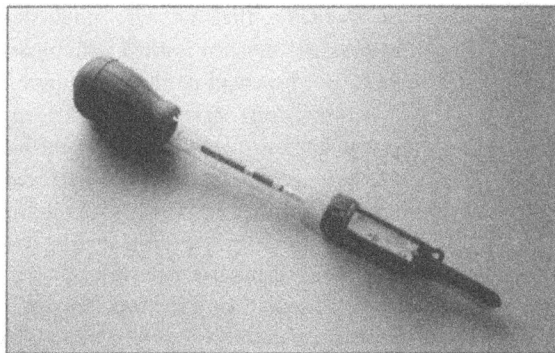

Figure 11-1. Edelmann's Model 40B-VP hydrometer with thermometer so readings can be adjusted for ambient temperature.

quarter of the battery's charge. The number of balls floating shows only whether the battery is charged or not. This type of hydrometer should not be used when an accurate check is needed.)

To obtain a reading, squeeze the bulb and place the hose in the electrolyte solution of a cell. Releasing the bulb sucks enough of the solution into the tube to cause

221

the float to rise with the liquid. How deeply the float rides in the fluid determines the reading; the level of the solution will be at one of the scale markings, which is the specific gravity of the electrolyte. If the hydrometer has a correction for ambient temperature, make this adjustment to the reading just obtained. Repeat the test for each cell in the battery. The specific gravity of all cells should be almost uniform—the reading of a fully charged battery is 12.65. A 50-point difference in any cell's reading from the others indicates that the cell is bad and the battery needs to be replaced.

While taking the reading, the float may stick to the tube's side; tapping the tube jars it loose. Always return liquid to the same cell from which it was removed to prevent contaminating a cell from which a reading hasn't yet been taken. If the liquid in the cells is below the proper level, water has to be added and the battery has to be recharged and allowed to stabilize for 24 hours or so before another accurate reading can be made.

The innocuous-looking hydrometer can turn into a dangerous instrument when it is filled with sulfuric acid; as a precaution before performing hydrometer tests, place a bucket of water nearby. During hydrometer tests, sulfuric acid is siphoned back and forth from the cells into the hydrometer. If an accident occurs, the water can be used to flush out eyes and wash the acid from skin and clothing. The hydrometer must be flushed with plenty of fresh water after each use and stored in a location where acid residue isn't a problem.

If there isn't enough room above the batteries to insert the hydrometer, as is the case in our battery compartment, the batteries must be removed, one at a time, and set on the ground to make the readings. To avoid creating sparks when removing batteries, always disconnect the negative cable first, then the positive one. When the cables are reattached, reverse the order: the positive cable first, then the negative cable.

When using wrenches to remove battery cables, be careful not to touch both battery posts at the same time. Doing so causes much arcing and sparking—a hazardous situation. Eyes and hands can be severely burned from arcing. To prevent arcing and sparking, we use half-inch open-end wrenches to remove battery cables; this size wrench is shorter than the distance between the two battery posts.

The greatest danger in working with batteries is explosion, which can be caused when the hydrogen gas and oxygen always present around the vent caps ignite. A battery explosion can cover you with acid, even kill you, and burn up your RV to boot, so take great care to guard against this occurrence.

Never install any electrical equipment such as battery chargers or converter/chargers in the battery compartment. Electrical devices have switches or relays that can arc during use, which can ignite explosive gases in the compartment, no matter how well ventilated it is. For the same reason, never smoke or use lighted candles or anything else with a flame while working around batteries.

While we are on the subject of disasters, here's another important safety precaution: Remove all rings from your fingers—including a wedding ring— before working on batteries or anything electrical, for that matter. If a metal ring shorts out between a battery post and a wrench, it can either melt or become red-hot, causing the loss of your finger. It's a good idea to also remove a watch—one with a metal band could cause problems, but any watch might be damaged by sulfuric acid.

Working with and around batteries can be dangerous, but it should not dissuade anyone from performing important maintenance. We have been doing it for years without any problems. If the proper safety precautions are observed, no difficulties should arise. Just don't ever become lax about precautions and don't be careless. Always keep in mind the dangerous potential of batteries. If you would rather not be bothered with maintenance, perhaps you should have sealed or gelled-cell batteries, which need none.

If you would rather not be bothered with maintenance, perhaps you should have sealed or gelled-cell batteries, which need none.

Corrosion and Battery Cables

When a battery is removed from its compartment or box and before it is hooked up again, the posts and cable clamps should be cleaned. For this maintenance job, use a post and clamp cleaner—a two-in-one tool that is separated into individual tools by twisting it apart. On one end is the clamp cleaner, a cone-shaped brush that is twisted back and forth inside the cable clamps to remove corrosion and grease accumulation. The post cleaner is a short tube with a circular metal brush around the inside. It is placed over the post and twisted back and forth to clean off the corrosion.

After the clamps and posts are bright and shiny, spray them with WD-40 or another lubricating spray—better still, coat them with a dab of dielectric grease (available at auto supply stores).

Corrosion, but not grease, can also be removed by using a weak mixture of baking soda and water—about a half teaspoon of soda to about 3 ounces of water. We use a small paper cup to pour a small amount of the mixture on the post. The mixture foams up and dissolves the corrosion instantly. Before pouring the mixture, make sure the battery's vent caps are tightly closed to prevent the soda solution from entering any of the cells. Blot up any excess with paper towels. After using baking soda, wash the top of the battery at least twice with water and blot dry. Residue from the baking soda/sulfuric acid reaction is a good conductor; if not removed, it can slowly drain the battery.

Batteries in engine compartments seem to develop corrosion more readily than in other locations, perhaps because an engine compartment is such a dirty environment. One way to prevent corrosion is with a chemically saturated pad that fits under the post connections of the battery. These inexpensive pads are readily available at auto supply stores and mass merchandisers. Pads should be replaced when they show signs of disintegration, about every six months or so.

To avoid damaging the posts, a tool that lifts the cable clamps off the posts is available. Pump pliers can also be used. For extra protection, the clamp lifter or pliers should have insulated handles.

It's much safer to remove just one battery cable than a bunch of cables and wires that flop around and create sparks.

Don't overload battery posts with a lot of clamps and other connections—every one is a potential arc hazard when it's removed or replaced. Most deep-cycle batteries have marine-type posts that can accommodate a battery cable clamp on the thick, lower part and several smaller wires, with crimp-on ring connectors that slip over the threaded bolt on the upper part. A wing nut secures them all. A marine-type post is convenient when several connections must be made to the battery, but it's not the best or safest way to make the connections. It is better to use a separate distribution post or bus bar instead (see Chapter 4) because it's much safer to remove just one battery cable than a bunch of cables and wires that flop around and create sparks.

Battery Compartments

Because batteries give off an explosive gas, all battery compartments must be ventilated to the outside, so don't block or cover any vent holes in the compartment or on its door. Even though openings are places where dirt, road dust, and diesel soot can enter, don't cover them. If extra batteries are added to the system and there is no room in the existing compartment, use battery cases with vent tubes in the bottom. When such a case is used, drill a hole in the floor of the compartment where it is to be installed and insert the vent tube. The tube extends below the RV and provides the needed ventilation.

Multimeters

For electrical troubleshooting, a multimeter can be the most valuable item in the tool kit. Using a multimeter is virtually the same with either analog or digital readouts. Analog meters are not as accurate as digital meters and their scales are hard to interpret and read, which adds to their inaccuracy. The scale has a mirrored strip across the face of the dial to aid in reading the needle movement more accurately. To take a reading, align the needle with its reflection so the needle appears as a single image. This puts your eye in the correct position for a proper reading. When your eye is focused off to the side and not aligned properly with the needle, a faulty reading results.

To make full use of our multimeter, we have made several different leads, adapters, and gadgets (Figure 11-2). One two-wire lead has our special 12-volt plug on one end (see Figure 4-9, pg. 93). On the other end, the two wires have been separated and a banana plug put on each wire. With this lead, 12-volt battery voltage can be monitored simply by inserting the plug into one of the DC receptacles located throughout our trailer. Since our digital multimeter has a two-decimal-place readout, very accurate battery voltage readings can be obtained.

Another set of leads has a regular two-prong polarized AC plug on one end and banana plugs on the other. The AC rms voltage of the inverter, campground outlets, and frequency of the AC supply can be checked with this lead. Working with this adapter can be dangerous if it is not used properly. If you make a similar adapter, heed this warning when using it: ALWAYS INSERT THE PLUGS ON THE END OF THE LEADS INTO THE JACKS ON THE METER FIRST, THEN INSERT THE AC PLUG INTO THE RECEPTACLE. This is extremely important; to do otherwise means handling live lead plugs charged with 120 volts as they are inserted into the meter.

The box accessory shown in Figure 11-2 is used with the multimeter to measure the amperage draw of DC appliances equipped with the 12-volt plug we use—not the cigarette-lighter type of plug. The box has a male 12-volt plug on a cord on one end and a female chassis socket on the other. Inside the box, the positive wire from the male plug is connected to a fuse holder and then goes to a red *tipjack* (a smaller jack that accommodates the tip of a probe). A black

Figure 11-2. Accessories for use with authors' various multimeters. Left: test leads with plug for AC voltage readings. Bottom: test lead with 12-volt polarized plug for checking battery voltage from RV's 12-volt outlets. Right: accessory for measuring DC draw of equipment with a 12-volt plug on power cord. Box is fused and has provision for plugging in the multimeter's leads for taking readings.

Always insert the plugs on the end of the leads into the jacks on the meter first, then insert the AC plug into the receptacle.

225

tipjack is mounted next to the red one and connected to the positive wire of the female socket. The negative wire is wired directly from the male plug to the female socket. In use, the multimeter probes are plugged into the two tipjacks in the box and the male plug is inserted into a 12-volt receptacle. The appliance to be checked, perhaps a stereo, is plugged into the female socket and the reading is taken. This accessory was created for convenience since we have several pieces of equipment with 12-volt plugs. It is a nuisance to take measurements when it is necessary to first break connections in a circuit, which may require unsoldering a connection in order to place test equipment in series for the measurement. The box makes it easy to measure any 12-volt appliance up to the multimeter's maximum of 10 amperes. To avoid damage to the multimeter, a fuse holder for a 10-ampere fuse was installed because the ampere measurement function of the multimeter is unfused and, therefore, unprotected.

Other accessories can make various measurements much easier. Radio Shack offers several accessories that can be attached to the probe ends: alligator-clip adapters, wire-piercing adapters that permit attaching a lead to any wire, and several sizes of spring-loaded, hook-type adapters for making connections to bare wires and other metal components.

Leads are available with 90-degree, right-angle jack plugs, which make for easier lead handling for some measurements; coiled leads are also available. Any lead can be altered to accept the accessories described previously.

Two other useful multimeter accessories can be made from two 3-foot lengths of 14-gauge stranded wire. On one wire are insulated alligator clips on each end; on one end of the other wire is a quarter-inch, female, spade-type solderless connector with a male connector of the same type on the other end. Applications for these accessories are explained later in this chapter.

Tools Needed for Troubleshooting

In addition to the multimeter and its accessories, other tools should be in the RVer's electrical tool kit:

- Cable Cutters. The type with curved jaws that cut through heavy-gauge and lightweight wire.

- Crimping Tool. For crimping solderless connectors. A crimping tool may incorporate wire cutters and strippers.

- Wire Strippers. For removing insulation from wires. Wires should always be stripped so the copper strands are not nicked or cut. Simple wire strippers just strip the wire; other strippers hold and measure the wire as the stripping is done. Strippers of several sizes and types may be needed.

- Diagonal Cutters. For cutting protruding copper strand ends after soldering; also for cutting wire. This tool comes in several sizes.

- Regular Pliers. One of the best tools around.

- Electrician's Pliers. For shaping and bending heavy wire; also has wire-cutting jaws.

- Long-nose Pliers. For working in hard-to-reach places and for picking up small electronic parts. (Tweezers are also useful for this.)

- Soldering Iron. Pencil or gun type. A soldering iron of about 25 watts is best for electronic work. The heat output from high-wattage, gun-type soldering irons can damage some electronic components, such as transistors. Soldering irons can be either a 120- or 12-volt model; we have one of each.

- Coil of resin-core solder of 0.062-inch diameter.

- Desoldering Bulb. For removing old solder from a joint.

- Screwdrivers of different sizes with both flat and Phillips tips or, better, a multitip screwdriver with an assortment of tips, including the all-important square tip that fits the most common type of screw used in RVs. Also a set of mini or jeweler's screwdrivers.

- Pocketknife. For cutting off wire and cable insulation too large for wire strippers.

- Small set of socket wrenches.

- Set of open-end and box wrenches.

- Solderless Connectors. An assortment of all kinds and sizes.

- Roll of plastic electrician's tape.

- Heat-shrink Tubing. Keep several sizes on hand.

The items in a tool kit vary according to individual preferences. Tools that one person thinks are essential may not be considered so by someone else. Some think a test light is a valuable tool, yet we have never used one; we prefer the multimeter instead. A test light shows only the presence of voltage; we want to know its actual value. For those who want a test light, Radio Shack has a good neon model that works on both AC and DC and sells for a couple of dollars (Catalog No. 22-102).

Another tool we use occasionally is a *voltage sensor*, a wand-like device with an LED that lights if an AC voltage is nearby. (Radio Shack is the only place we have ever found this tool; Catalog No. 22-103.) It does not need to be plugged in, just placed near a wire or wall where AC wires may be present. Merely holding a voltage sensor near an outlet causes the LED to light, so it can be used to trace an AC circuit by running it along a wall.

Although not specifically electrical tools, the following tools are useful when tackling electrical projects: cordless electric drill, saber saw, Dremel tool (which we have used for jobs larger than it was ever intended to handle), and a full set of mechanic's socket wrenches.

Troubleshooting with a Multimeter

Checking AC and DC Voltage

To obtain either an AC or DC voltage reading, simply insert the plugs on the ends of the leads into their respective holes on the multimeter; the red positive lead plugs into the plus jack and the black negative lead plugs into the minus, or ground, jack. Make sure the right jack hole is used since some meters have several holes for different kinds of readings. Again—we can't emphasize this enough: ALWAYS CONNECT THE LEADS TO THE MULTIMETER FIRST BEFORE CONNECTING THEM TO THE DEVICE BEING TESTED. Place the selector switch on the desired setting and turn on the multimeter. Then connect the two leads across the circuit to get the voltage reading. Insert the probes into the slots of a receptacle or touch the probes to the two wires on a light fixture or anywhere else in a circuit (Figure 11-3).

When checking DC voltage, if the probes are accidentally connected in reversed polarity, the needle dips off the scale on analog meters and shows a minus reading on digital models. Polarity is not a factor for AC readings.

When measuring voltage on certain devices, the safest and easiest method is to fasten the negative probe to a convenient ground source (e.g., the housing of a furnace or refrigerator) with an alligator clip. Then use the positive probe to touch other various contacts on the device to measure the voltage. The function of a switch can be checked in this manner. First, measure the voltage at one contact of the switch, then measure the other contact. If the switch is closed, a reading appears on both sides. If the switch is open, there is no reading on one side. You might wonder why this simple check might be necessary. Wouldn't it be known if a switch was on or off? Not if the switch

Most troubleshooting involves simple voltage checking.

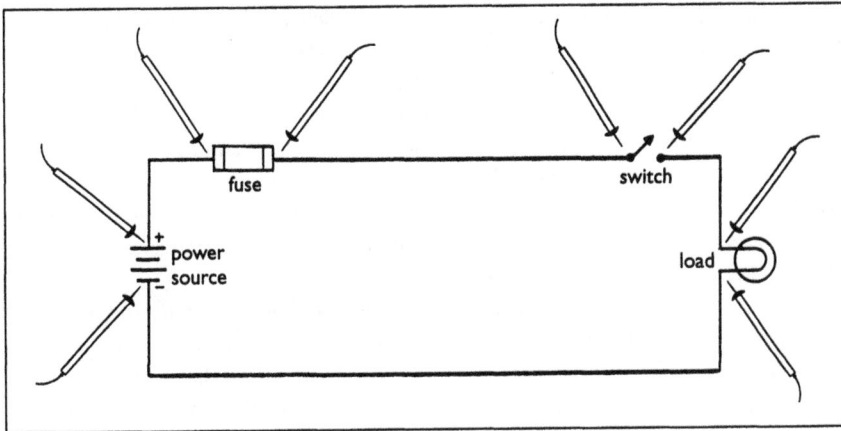

Figure 11-3. Probes indicate different locations in a typical circuit where voltage and resistance (continuity) readings can be taken.

happened to be a self-resetting circuit breaker; the test indicates whether or not the breaker is making contact.

Most troubleshooting involves simple voltage checking. Tests that show a difference in voltage may indicate a problem that can be tracked down by taking various readings along the circuit until the voltage drop is isolated. Multimeters are so sensitive to voltage that they may show a reading of full voltage even when there is enough resistance in the circuit to prevent the necessary amperage from doing its job. If the multimeter is showing full voltage when you know there is a problem, it can be confirmed by doing a resistance check of the circuit.

Another caution: Be extra careful when taking voltage readings in an AC system. Never touch any metal parts of the circuit, lead, or probe. Use only one hand to hold the probe or probes. If necessary, have someone else hold the meter to free up your hands while taking the readings.

Checking Battery Voltage

The measurement of DC voltage for checking batteries is the most frequent test made. Touching the red lead's probe to the positive post of the battery and the black lead's probe to the negative post provides the voltage reading.

The measurement of DC voltage for checking batteries is the most frequent test made.

Check the voltage of each battery in a bank. To compare the voltages against an overall voltage of the bank, read the voltage between the positive post of one battery

229

and the negative post of the other. In 12-volt, parallel-wired battery banks, often one battery has a slightly different voltage. This happens because of the way current flows between the two batteries. One battery can carry more of the load imposed, and either of the batteries can receive more of a charge, depending on how they are wired. (To work batteries equally, it's a good idea to rotate them in a bank often.)

Most of today's 12-volt batteries do not have exposed straps connecting the cells together as older-style batteries did, but, if they do, the straps can be used for measuring the voltage of individual cells. Six-volt and large 12-volt batteries may have these straps.

When checking battery banks wired in series—either 6-volt batteries in a 12-volt system or 12-volt batteries in a 24-volt system—use the same technique as for a parallel-wired bank. Measure each battery separately and then the entire battery bank. When there is a 2-volt drop in total voltage of a bank, there is a dead cell somewhere. To find the dead cell, measure the individual cells by using the exposed straps. If the battery doesn't have straps, use a hydrometer. If one cell is consistently low, the battery should be replaced.

When checking battery voltage, make two tests: First, touch the probes to the posts and read the voltage, then touch one probe to the clamp attached to the post and again read the voltage. A difference between the two readings means that the clamp is not making good contact with the post. A resistance reading taken with the multimeter probes between the clamp and post will confirm this. Check both clamps this way. Remove the clamps and clean them as described previously in this chapter.

Resistance and Continuity Checking

For resistance and continuity tests with an analog multimeter, after properly connecting the leads to the jack holes, select the resistance setting, short out the probes by touching their tips together, and turn the ohms-adjust wheel until the needle on the ohms scale is at the zero-resistance reading. Touch the probes to the two ends of the circuit or the wires or contacts on a device to be tested. When the needle deflects to the zero marking on the scale, it indicates that current (from the meter's internal battery) is passing through the circuit without resistance, making a continuous circuit; therefore, the continuity is okay. If the needle remains stationary, there is no current flow and no continuity.

The needle coming to rest at any point on the scale in between indicates resistance in the circuit. For example, on a multimeter with an RX1KΩ setting, when the needle is on 15, it means there is a resistance in the circuit of 15,000 ohms (15 multiplied by 1,000). If the setting were RX10Ω or RX100Ω, the same needle reading would indicate 150 or 1,500 ohms of resistance, respectively.

Analog multimeters are excellent for taking resistance or continuity readings because the needle reaction is so definite. Digital multimeters are not so positive; resistance appears on the readout as a steady number, but flashing zeros or numbers indicate continuity. This same flashing occurs when the meter is switched on, so there can be some ambiguity about what the meter is reading. Some digital multimeters have a special continuity setting on the rotary selector switch (indicated by either a diode symbol or a sound symbol—a drawing of sound waves). If continuity exists, these meters beep and/or the readouts display steady zeros.

Resistance or continuity tests should be made only when the main power to the circuit being tested is turned off. If it is not off, the normal current in the circuit may give faulty readings and, in the case of AC circuits, might damage the multimeter.

Resistance or continuity tests should be made only when the main power to the circuit being tested is turned off.

Resistance problems can often be traced to improper ground connections, especially in taillights, turn signals, and brakes, but also in other equipment. The practice of using the chassis of vehicles as the return negative conductor is particularly troublesome. Wires must be connected to the chassis in some way, generally by a lug fastened with a bolt or screw, which may be of a different metal than the chassis. Galvanic corrosion between the different metals causes the fastener to rust or corrode in short order, setting up resistance. To eliminate resistance, fasteners must be replaced on a regular basis. To avoid this maintenance job, we run ground wires instead of using a chassis ground whenever we install new equipment. When a problem occurs with a chassis ground connection, we replace the connection with a ground wire. Eventually, all our old chassis connections will be replaced. When a multimeter indicates that a problem exists, suspect a faulty ground connection first.

When a multimeter indicates that a problem exists, suspect a faulty ground connection first.

AC and DC Ammeter Readings

For checking amperage, the ammeter function of many analog multimeters provides a readout in milliampere measurements, which are too low to be of value to RVers. Most inexpensive digital multimeters have readings up to 200 milliamperes maximum—and many of both types of meters have only DC readings. Higher-priced digital multimeters provide ammeter readings of 10 to 20 amperes for both AC and DC. Usually this function is not fused, and since the full amperage load of the circuit goes through the meter, care must be taken to prevent damage by overloading.

To use any of the amperage settings, the probes must be placed in series with the circuit being tested. This can be a nuisance because the circuit must be broken where the probes are to be attached. Sometimes the break can be made on a light fix-

231

ture or a switch, where it is usually not too difficult to do. (Earlier in this chapter we described the accessory we made to avoid disconnecting wires for DC amperage readings.)

To make the check, first turn off the power to the circuit to be tested. Then, at the break in the circuit, attach the probes with alligator clips and take the reading. If spade-type, quick-disconnect, solderless connectors are used in the circuit, the circuit can be conveniently broken at the connectors. A special set of leads with the same type of connector can be made—a male connector on one lead and a female on the other—so the leads can be attached directly into the circuit. When checking DC amperage, if the probes are connected with reversed polarity, usually there is a minus reading.

Current Leakage

Current leakage can be detected by using DC voltage and current measurements. Leakage can slowly discharge batteries during periods when the RV is not in use. Leakage may occur when wiring has been subjected to wear from vibration. Water and moisture can then penetrate the insulation, and an unwanted pathway for the current back to ground becomes established.

Current leakage can be detected by using DC voltage and current measurements. Leakage can slowly discharge batteries during periods when the RV is not in use.

Before making the test, make sure all circuits are turned off at the switch of each piece of equipment and there are no known loads on the battery; don't forget to turn off any equipment with a phantom load. Do not pull fuses or turn off circuit breakers; all the circuits must be complete except for the open, or turned-off, equipment switches.

Remove the clamp from the positive battery post. Set the multimeter for measuring DC voltage. Place the probe of the red lead on the battery post and the probe of the black lead on the clamp. A no-voltage reading indicates that no current is leaking. A reading of 12 volts or more indicates that leakage is occurring or a circuit may still be on. After rechecking for active circuits, switch the meter to read DC amperage and take a reading, which will show the amount of current leaking—usually milliamperes. Some multimeters are so sensitive that they can measure current flow as tiny as one thousandth of an ampere.

If there is leakage, isolate it by continuing the test after pulling fuses or tripping circuit breakers, one at a time, until the offending circuit is found. This test shows any leaks present in the wiring from the positive post of the battery to the various pieces of equipment, but it does not show leaks in the wiring from the equipment back to the ground battery connection. This doesn't usually matter unless the problem has been traced to a circuit that is normally kept on all the time, in which case the test can be completed by performing it with the equipment switch of the suspect circuit on and all other switches off. This confirms or denies the existence of a leak on that circuit.

To avoid damaging the multimeter during amperage tests, keep its milliamperage rating in mind. It is best to do this test with a meter that reads to 500 milliamperes or more.

If there is leakage, isolate it by continuing the test after pulling fuses or tripping circuit breakers, one at a time, until the offending circuit is found.

Testing Electronic Components

It is possible to test many electronic components, from simple resistors to complex semiconductor devices, with even the simplest of multimeters. Replacing a faulty component in a piece of equipment is certainly less expensive than having it repaired or purchasing a new one.

Resistors

A resistor can be measured easily when out of a circuit, but when it is in an active circuit, all power must be removed before taking the measurement. Failure to do so results in a faulty reading and may damage the multimeter. The selector switch should be on the resistance setting.

To measure a resistor in a circuit, disconnect the power supply first. It's best to also unsolder one side of the resistor before taking the reading to ensure that only the resistance of the resistor is being measured. Attach a probe to each side of the resistor and take the reading. To measure a resistor out of a circuit, attach the probes to the two resistor wires and read the value.

Variable resistors, or potentiometers, are measured by reading first the full resistance across the device and then the resistance as it is varied by the wiper arm contact. Rheostats also may be checked in the same way by measuring across the two contacts. Analog multimeters do a better job of reading variable resistors than digital types because the smooth movement of the needle mirrors the movement of the resistor's adjustment.

A capacitor should always be removed from the circuit before testing and its two contacts shorted out to ensure that no residual charge remains. A shock can be received if the charge is not removed.

Capacitors

A capacitor should always be removed from the circuit before testing and its two contacts shorted out to ensure that no residual charge remains. IMPORTANT! A SHOCK CAN BE RECEIVED IF THE CHARGE IS NOT REMOVED, and the meter could also be damaged. Leaky or shorted capacitors can

233

be detected simply by measuring the resistance. A good capacitor shows high resistance, 20,000 ohms or more; a reading of no resistance indicates a shorted capacitor. A leaking capacitor shows considerably less resistance than the very high reading of a good one.

Inductors

Inductors, coils, chokes, and transformers all can be measured in one of two ways, depending on whether the device is a coil or a transformer. Most coils and chokes can be checked by testing the wiring for continuity with the power source disconnected.

Problems with coils and transformers are usually due to broken or shorted wires. The continuity test shows any broken wires or shorting between the wires and the core of the coil. Shorting between several adjacent wires is hard to detect. Transformers can be checked by applying power and checking the AC voltage across the primary coil and then the output voltage across the secondary coil. The values of the two voltages should show if the transformer is performing properly. Prevent shocks when working with AC by ensuring that the power is off when attaching the probes; then turn the power on to take the reading. Continuity checks on these devices can be made with the power disconnected to determine if any wiring breaks exist.

Semiconductor Devices

Diodes

Resistance readings can be taken on diodes to determine if the diode has shorted out. Placing the red positive lead's probe on the cathode end of the diode and the black negative lead's probe on the anode end should show a very high resistance—20,000 ohms or more; reversing the probes should show a low resistance—10 ohms or less. Low resistance readings made both ways indicate a shorted diode.

Large diodes are used in RV equipment such as alternators, isolators, converter/chargers, and inverters, and are available as either cathode or anode base. It is easy to tell one from the other by doing a resistance test; current will flow one way but not the other. The positive side of the diode in which the current flows is the cathode side. Remember that a voltage has to be developed across the diode equal to the forward-biased voltage drop in order for the diode to become conductive. The battery in the meter provides the necessary voltage for taking resistance readings.

Resistance readings can be taken on diodes to determine if the diode has shorted out.

234

Diode-type Isolators

The easiest way to test the diodes in an isolator is to use the multimeter's DC voltage setting. While a vehicle's engine is running, attach the negative lead to a suitable ground (such as the negative post of the battery), then measure the voltage by touching the positive probe in turn to each of the isolator's two battery posts and its alternator post. Readings should show a difference that equals the voltage drop. Differences can be from 0.2 to as high as 1.2 volts, depending on the type of diode and the amount of current flowing across it.

A voltage-drop test does not show a shorted-out diode; a continuity or resistance reading is needed. With the engine off, first disconnect the alternator wire from the isolator. Check for low resistance with the red lead's probe on the alternator post and the black lead's probe alternating between each of the two battery posts. Next check for high resistance between each of the two battery posts and the alternator post, when the probes are reversed. If resistance is low in both directions, the diode being tested is bad. Diodes in other devices can be checked the same way.

Transistors

Since a transistor is nothing more than two diodes butted together, with three leads instead of two, various types of transistors can be checked in the same way as diodes. Each side of a transistor has a forward bias with low resistance and reverse bias with high resistance, measuring from the base pin. As we discussed previously, polarity can be either way depending on whether the transistor is NPN or PNP. The NPN has high resistance with the base negative and the PNP with the base positive. Transistors should be tested out of the circuit.

Field-Effect Transistors and Silicon-controlled Rectifiers

FETs and SCRs can be tested with a multimeter, but the method for testing is complex and beyond the realm of troubleshooting covered in this book. The Radio Shack book entitled *Using Your Meter* describes in detail how to test these semiconductors.

Relays

Coil-operated switch relays can be checked in several ways. The operation of the magnetic coils can be either AC or DC. Two problems usually affect relay operation: burned and pitted contacts on the switches, and failure of the operating coil, probably due to a broken wire.

Two problems usually affect relay operation: burned and pitted contacts on the switches and failure of the operating coil, probably due to a broken wire.

Coil operation can be checked visually by turning the control current on and off to see if the coil is moving the arm of the relay toward the open side of the con-

235

tacts. Then check the spring to see if it moves the arm back toward the closed side when the current to the coil is off. If both are functioning, the coil is probably working properly; if not, replace the relay. A shock hazard exists if the coil operation is AC, so be careful when testing.

The next test requires that the power to the switches be disconnected and the power to the coil be operative. With the multimeter on the resistance setting, measure the resistance through the switch contacts of the normally closed side. Then activate the coil current and measure the resistance through the normally open side. In each case there should be no resistance when each side of the switch is closed. If there is, the contacts are either pitted or burned and the relay should be replaced. If the relay is a DPDT type, remember to check each set of switch contacts for resistance.

How to Troubleshoot Basic Circuits

Unless you know definitely where a problem lies, the first place to start troubleshooting a circuit is at the fuse or circuit breaker. It's amazing how often the problem is nothing more than a blown fuse. It's often assumed that if the fuse is blown, then something must have been wrong in the circuit or device to have caused it to blow. This is not necessarily the case; fuses often blow because of a voltage surge, and they sometimes fail on their own. Sometimes a glitch causes several fuses to blow when, in actuality, nothing is wrong with the circuit. Fuses used at a high amperage rate for a long period fail eventually. When several replacement fuses are tried and they all blow, the problem is not the fuse, but it still may be traced to something simple—a loose connection, perhaps—that can be easily remedied.

Before inserting a glass-cylinder fuse into the holder, wipe off fingerprints from the metal ends. Oiliness from skin can cause corrosion, setting up a resistance that causes the fuse to blow. To eliminate corrosion, wipe the ends of the fuse with a clean cloth sprayed with WD-40 or LPS before inserting it into the holder. Spade-type fuses arc if they are inserted into the block when a load is on the circuit, so everything on a circuit should be turned off before replacing a fuse. Such arcing eventually burns the spring clips enough to render them useless.

Most trouble spots are caused by poor electrical connections, either because of loose wires or corrosion.

To track down the problem, if it is not with the fuse, start with a visual check along the circuit. You can start at the power source and work along the circuit, but we have found it is sometimes easier to identify the problem by starting at the appliance and working backward.

Most trouble spots are caused by poor electrical connections, either because of loose wires or corrosion. The vibration an RV receives can loosen electrical connections and cause wires to break. Corrosion can occur if the RV is used or stored in a high-humidity atmosphere. With a visual inspection of the circuit, the problem may be obvious. In addition to loose or corroded connections and broken wires, look for burn marks or discolorations, especially on electronic parts such as diodes and transistors. Circuit boards often show burned areas around bad resistors, capacitors, and other components.

As an example of troubleshooting a simple circuit, let's say a reading light has stopped working. The light-bulb has been replaced and the fuse for the circuit is okay, but the light still will not work. What next? Remove the bulb and unscrew the fixture from the wall so it hangs by the wires. With the multimeter set to DC voltage, clip the negative probe to the ground wire of the fixture and touch the other probe to the center contact of the socket to see if a voltage is present (Figure 11-4). If so, then the new bulb is either bad or it is not making good contact in the socket. (Poor contact is a common occurrence in badly designed RV fixtures.) If the problem is poor contact, turn off power to the fixture, then bend the contacts to make better contact with the bulb.

Look for burn marks or discolorations, especially on electronic parts such as diodes and transistors. Circuit boards often show burned areas around bad resistors, capacitors, and other components.

For tracking down other problems, disconnect the fixture from the two circuit wires. Clip the negative lead of the multimeter to either wire on the fixture, and use the probe of the positive lead to check for continuity at the switch, on various parts of the socket, and even on the bulb. The continuity check should locate the problem spot; if the circuit and socket are okay, current flow should be continuous in all parts of the circuit and socket.

Other common trouble spots are cigarette-lighter sockets. Often the plug of the appliance used with this type of socket does not make good contact. If the appliance is not working, check for voltage at the socket. This is tricky because of the danger of shorting out

Figure 11-4. A multimeter being used to check a 12-volt light fixture. With the black lead attached to the ground conductor and the red lead affixed to the positive bulb contact in the fixture, the reading is the voltage present through the switch to the socket.

237

the two probes while trying to take the reading. The best method is to place the positive probe on the center contact deep in the socket and, while holding it in place, touch the negative probe to the side of the socket, making sure not to touch the metal of the positive probe. If this is done carefully there will be no sparking or shorting. Once voltage potential has been confirmed, try bending out the contacts on the lighter plug to see if that cures the problem. The only way to eliminate all problems with these miserable plugs is to replace them with other 12-volt connections (see Chapter 4).

Troubleshooting Trailer Brakes

Brake failure and poor braking performance with trailers usually can be traced to an electrical rather than mechanical problem. The entire braking system is unprotected from road debris, which can cause exposed wires to break, subjecting them to wetness when it rains, which creates corrosion. On most trailers, the wire for the brake system is strung between clips that hold it in place or, worse, taped to an axle in the routing from one side of the trailer to the other. There would be far fewer brake problems if the wiring were (1) put in some sort of conduit or tubing; (2) sufficiently supported so it cannot move; or (3) protected from chafe by rubber grommets where it passes through holes in the chassis.

Brake failure and poor braking performance with trailers usually can be traced to an electrical rather than mechanical problem.

When brakes don't operate properly, the first thing to check for is a broken or disconnected wire. Tall undergrowth once pulled a brake wire loose on our trailer; another time, the wire to one of the magnets chafed through from wear. Poor electrical connections at the TECC affect brake operation, and, since the brake system is essentially a one-wire system, faulty ground connections also can cause problems.

In the event of total brake failure, first check for voltage between the blue wire of the brake controller and any ground connection you can make (Figure 11-5). Refer to the instruction manual for your controller for detailed information. If there is voltage, next check the TECC's female connector for voltage between pin numbers 1 and 2 (Figure 11-6). If there is voltage, connect the TECC and check for voltage at each of the trailer's wheels as the brake pedal is depressed. (An assistant is needed to operate the brakes.) With the brake's single-wire system, the negative probe can be touched to any convenient ground (e.g., the chassis). When there is no voltage at all at the wheels, there may be a broken wire or a bad ground contact at the TECC between the trailer and the tow vehicle. If multimeter readings show a voltage drop between the brake controller and the rearmost wheel in the circuit, it may be that the wrong gauge wire has been used. All wiring in this circuit should be no smaller than 12 gauge. If a voltage drop exists, rewiring the system is in order. (When rewiring, putting the wires in conduit or tubing helps to prevent future problems.)

Because of the multimeter's sensitivity to voltage, sometimes the voltage appears to be correct but the brakes still don't function properly. In this case, the next step is to make a resistance check between the chassis of the tow vehicle and the trailer. Also check resistance between the ground pin of the TECC plug and the trailer chassis. Make another check between the female ground connection of the TECC socket on the tow vehicle and the chassis of the vehicle. If resistance is present, check for corrosion at the connections. An often overlooked connection is where the brake wire for each wheel is grounded to the chassis. All brake wiring has a parallel circuit that comes from the main circuit for each wheel's magnet, with all wires eventually going to a common ground—the chassis.

The efficiency of brake systems can be checked with a multimeter if it reads amperage up to 20 amperes. The job is easier if a special set of leads is made and the brake controller wires are modified. Coming from the back of the controller is a blue wire, which is the positive wire in the circuit going to the trailer's wheels. Make a cut in this wire and install a female, quick-disconnect, solderless connector on the con-

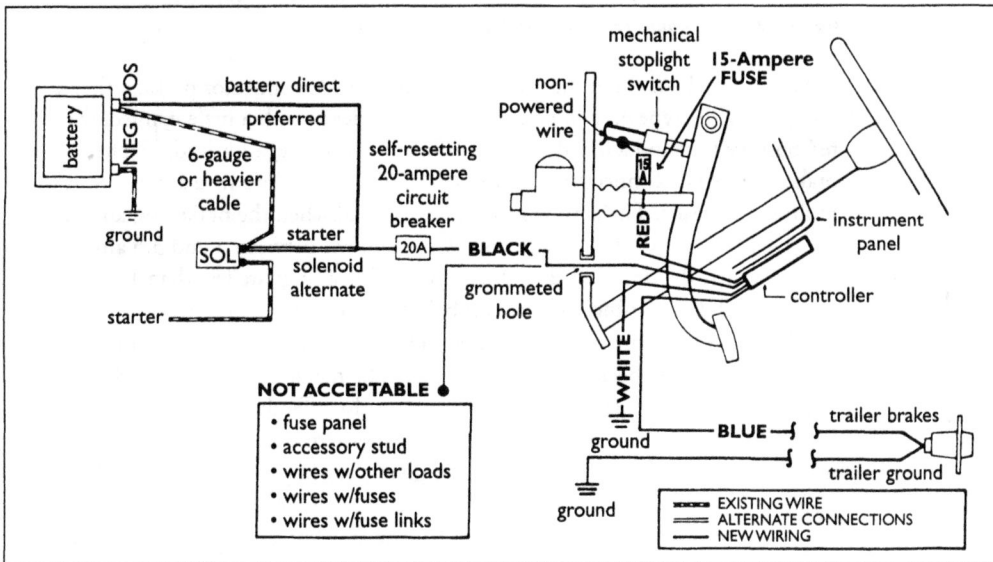

Figure 11-5. Diagram of brake controller wiring. The blue and ground connection of trailer wiring is in the lower right corner. (Illustration courtesy of Kelsey-Hayes)

Maintenance, Troubleshooting, and Repairs

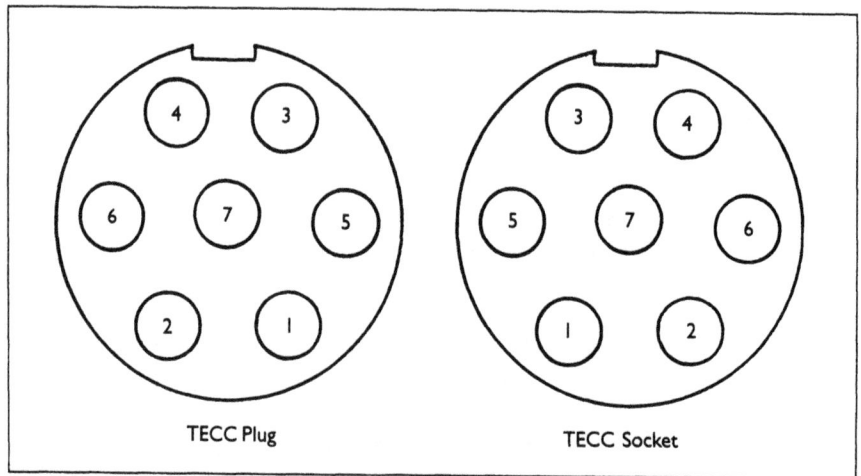

Figure 11-6. TECC pin configuration. Recommended pin connections are (1) White: common ground; (2) Blue: brake; (3) Green: tail, running, and license plate lights; (4) Black: battery charge; (5) Red: stop and left turn signal; (6) Brown: stop and right turn signal; (7) Yellow: auxiliary circuit. These are suggested wiring connections; no industry standards exist, however, so wiring harnesses may vary.

troller side of the cut and the counterpart male spade connector on the other side. Using the same type of connectors, make meter leads with a male connector on the red positive lead and a female connector on the black negative lead. To check the brakes, simply disconnect the connectors on the controller's wire and connect the multimeter's leads. The amperage load can be read when the brakes are applied.

Each magnet on 10- and 12-inch wheels draws between 3 and 3.5 amperes. On 7-inch wheels the draw is 1.2 to 2.2 amperes. If readings are less than 12 amperes for a trailer with four 10-inch wheels, probably one of the magnets is not working. Break the positive wire to each magnet and, using multimeter leads with clips, clip on the probes and check the amperage load. The magnet that does not draw 3 amperes (or 1.2 amperes for a 7-inch wheel) is the offender.

It's easier to check and monitor the brake system with a permanently installed automotive-type ammeter. The ammeter gives a reading whenever the brakes are applied. It is wired in series on the blue wire from the brake controller.

It is important to use a meter that has the smallest amperage range possible so readings of 1 ampere or less can be taken. The Dyer Company makes a meter that reads from zero to 15 amperes (Figure 11-7). Kelsey-Hayes also makes an induction ammeter that clips onto the wire. It doesn't have to be wired in series because it reads the amperage by the amount of the magnetic field around the wire. This ammeter reads from zero to 20 amperes and would be suitable for six-wheel trailers.

Troubleshooting Trailer Running Lights and Dinghy Towing Lights

Problems with trailer running lights or dinghy lights can be checked using the same methods. The easiest way to troubleshoot these lighting circuits is to first check for voltage at the problem lightbulb socket. Check between the center contact and the outside case of the socket, similar to the method used for cigarette-lighter sockets. If there is voltage, the problem is poor contact at the socket or a burned-out bulb. If there is no voltage, check the TECC socket on the tow vehicle for voltage. When no voltage is present there, the probable cause is a bad connection at the problem light's counterpart in the tow vehicle or motorhome that provides the power. Often when the dealer hooks up the wiring harness, a solderless wire tap-in connector is used to attach one wire to an existing wire. These clip-on tap-ins sometimes make poor contact and have to be replaced. They can be checked by using wire-piercing adapters on the ends of the meter's probes, attaching one to the main wire ahead of the tap-in and the other to the added-on wire. A continuity or resistance test shows whether there is a good connection. After making this check, use electrician's tape to cover the pierced holes to prevent moisture from entering through the insulation.

If these tests do not locate the problem, then the trouble lies in concealed wiring, such as in the circuit between the TECC and a trailer's taillight. Using a long length of wire that will reach between the TECC and the taillight, attach one end of the wire to the TECC and run it to the light; then check for continuity between the wire and the taillight

Figure 11-7. Dyer brake ammeter, which shows the efficiency of the braking system. The ammeter is wired in series in the blue brake wire from the controller. *(Photo courtesy of Dyer Company)*

Often when the dealer hooks up the wiring harness, a solderless wire tap-in connector is used to attach one wire to an existing wire. These clip-on tap-ins sometimes make poor contact and have to be replaced.

241

Maintenance, Troubleshooting, and Repairs

socket. With this method, each section of concealed wire in a circuit can be checked. If there is a problem, the only solution is to somehow replace the problem wire with a new one—not always an easy job.

Troubleshooting Furnaces, Refrigerators, and Converter/Chargers

The electrical tests and repairs that can be made on furnaces, refrigerators, and converter/chargers are limited. This equipment has complicated electronics, some with IC module boards, and may require special test equipment along with schematics to track down problems. Schematics are essential for the troubleshooting of many components because, without them, operating voltages and amperages cannot be known. Usually if a component on a module board is bad, the entire board has to be replaced.

The basic tests RVers can make may isolate the problem, but the actual repair may have to be done by a qualified repairperson. Isolating a problem is worthwhile because it could save you some money. Knowing where the problem lies and being able to discuss it intelligently may discourage repairpersons from trying to track down the problem themselves at your expense. Recently we had a refrigerator problem and, after making a few tests, we suspected the problem was in the module board. The company-authorized repairperson wanted to replace not only the board, but also the eyebrow module, and suggested replacing several other components "just to make sure we solve the problem." This repairperson may have known about refrigeration, but we could tell he was on shaky ground when it came to electronics because he was trying to cover all the bases. Only the module board was replaced and that solved the problem.

Knowing where the problem lies and being able to discuss it intelligently may discourage repairpersons from trying to track down the problem themselves at your expense.

Furnaces

Before trying to locate problems with a forced-air furnace, consult the troubleshooting section in the instruction manual. If the furnace fails to operate at all, first check the thermostat, because it is the most common cause of furnace failure. Remove the cover from the thermostat and move the temperature selection lever until the two contacts come together. When the contacts are touching and the blower does not start, remove the thermostat from the wall. Keep in mind the time delay of up to 60 seconds before the blower comes on.

Temporarily disconnect the two wires to the thermostat and fasten them together with an alligator clip. If the blower then starts and the burner ignites, the thermostat is the problem and needs to be replaced. If the thermostat proves to be working properly, reinstall it and set it to the maximum temperature position. Using the multimeter, see if there is at least 12 volts at the main circuit breaker on the furnace. Be sure the circuit breaker is closed. If the reading is lower than 12 volts, the batteries may need charging, or, if the RV is using 120-volt AC power, the converter/charger may be at fault.

Temporarily disconnect the two wires to the thermostat and fasten them together with an alligator clip. If the blower then starts and the burner ignites, the thermostat is the problem.

In most furnaces a relay, incorporating the time delay, is activated by the thermostat to turn on the blower. Check the relay, allowing for the 30- to 60-second delay to close the blower contact.

If the blower still does not start, try a continuity check to see if the *limit switch* is stuck in the open position. If it is closed, then power is available to the module board—the board is the problem and a repairperson is needed.

If the blower operates but the burner does not fire, the trouble may be in either the sail switch or the module board. The *sail switch* is a door-like flap that moves with the force of the air from the blower; it trips a switch that activates the burner ignition circuit. Sometimes the flap sticks, although it should move easily. If the switch is okay, then the problem is in the module board itself.

WARNING: The burner ignition circuit uses a very high voltage. To prevent a serious shock, it is best to leave it alone.

Refrigerators

RV refrigerators are the absorption type that use heat to create cooling. The heat comes from one of three power sources: propane from the RV's supply or built-in 120-volt AC or 12-volt DC heater coils. The refrigerator in many large motorhomes may be a three-way model that operates on all three power sources (the 12-volt mode for use only when the engine is running), but most others are two-way units that operate on propane and AC. Newer refrigerators have automatic switch-over between the different power sources. (Many refrigerator problems, which aren't covered here, can be other than electrical. Consult the instruction manual for troubleshooting suggestions.)

Often the unit runs on one source of heat when it won't run on the other, which helps to isolate the heat source causing the problem. First, switch to a heat source other than the one on which the refrigerator has been running. After a reasonable cycling period—as long as 8 to 10 hours—check to see if cooling has occurred. If the box has not cooled down, the best electrical procedure to follow is to first check for the presence of DC voltage, because the controls of almost all RV

243

refrigerators operate on 12-volt DC power. Next check for corroded or loose connectors in the back of the refrigerator. Pay particular attention to the connections on the main module board and the ignition module if the problem is gas operation. On the gas setting, you should be able to hear the solenoid of the gas valve click or see the main burner burning if everything is operating normally. If not, check for voltage at the solenoid terminals. There is no way to check the module boards on refrigerators, so a repairperson is needed when the basic checking doesn't identify the problem.

Faulty AC operation suggests checking first for AC power at the outlet receptacle in the refrigerator compartment. If voltage is present, disconnect the plug and test resistance on the heater element. Check with the manufacturer for the proper resistance value of the element. If the reading shows no resistance, the element is burned out and must be replaced. The same test applies to 12-volt heating elements.

Converter/Chargers

The only tests that can be done on a faulty converter/charger are the transformer, diode, and relay checks described previously in this chapter. Make sure the power has been disconnected from the converter/charger before making tests, except for those requiring that power be applied. Because of the shock hazard, be careful not to touch any capacitors that may be in a filter circuit.

The only tests that can be done on a faulty converter/charger are the transformer, diode, and relay checks described previously in this chapter.

Troubleshooting Air Conditioners with a Multimeter

If the air conditioner does not work, first check the campground voltage; it may be too low to start the compressor. If the voltage is okay, check the connector terminal under the ceiling shroud to make sure it is plugged in—it can vibrate loose. If the problem still exists, unplug the shore-power cable—this is very important; don't fail to do it—and check for continuity on the rotary switch to see if it is working.

Failure to find the cause of the problem with these tests requires a repairperson. A repairperson is also needed when the air conditioner runs but does not cool. In this case, usually a leak has developed causing the refrigerant to evaporate, and soldering and recharging are involved.

Water Pumps

Only two electrical tests can be performed on a water pump that does not run. Check for DC voltage at the two pump wires. After removing the pump section, which may be jammed, check whether the motor runs separately when voltage is applied to its wires.

Engine Starters

While this book is not intended to be an automotive repair manual, there are a couple of tests that can be done to uncover why an engine is balky in starting. The cause of starters that won't work or that turn the engine over too slowly to start may be either a discharged battery or poor battery connections. On all battery cables, perform the resistance and voltage tests. If the solenoid clicks but the starter does not turn the engine over, the problem is with the battery or the starter motor is bad.

If the starter turns over, the next test that should be performed requires the use of an *induction ammeter*, or as it is sometimes called, a *current-indicator meter*, which is available in auto supply stores for about $15 (Figure 11-8). The one we have measures to 600 amperes on the high scale and to 75 amperes on the low scale. Induction ammeters can be used for checking alternators and for making other amperage checks. In a wire with current flowing through it, an induction ammeter reads amperage by measuring the magnetic field present around the wire.

Before making this starter check, the starter amperage must be known. Call the dealer for this information; it probably ranges from 180 to 250 amperes. If the engine's ignition has a coil, disconnect the coil's high-tension wire and ground it so the engine can't start during the test. If it is not a coil-type ignition, disable the engine in some way other than disconnecting the batteries. With an assistant in the vehicle to turn the ignition key, place the ammeter's notches (on the back of the instrument) over the starter cable, turn on the ignition, and read the starter's amperage as the starter motor turns the engine over. If the reading shows an amperage higher than the starter amperage, there is a problem with the starter motor itself.

Figure 11-8. An induction meter, or an ammeter that measures magnetic induction around a wire. It has two ranges: zero to 75 and zero to 600 amperes. This type of meter is useful for checking alternators and starters.

If the starter motor spins but does not engage the flywheel and turn the engine over, the problem may be in the solenoid and is either electrical or mechanical. Have your assistant turn the ignition key to activate the starter circuit. Check the hot (positive) wire to the solenoid for voltage. Also do resistance checks on both the solenoid and starter grounding connections, which are usually made through the engine block. If there is resistance, tighten the bolts of the starter housing or clean the ground strap.

245

Alternators

Two types of electrical tests can be done on alternators: one when the alternator is on the engine, and the other when the alternator is off the engine and dismantled (this is not covered here because it requires special equipment and knowledge and is best left to a qualified repair facility). First, check the obvious problems for poor alternator performance; with high-output units, this is often a loose fanbelt. Then do a visual check of all electrical connections. With the engine not running, check voltage at the battery; it should be about 12.6 volts. Next, measure the voltage drop at the battery as the engine is started; it should drop to about 10 volts or so for a moment while the engine is cranking. When the engine is running and while continuing to measure the battery voltage, the voltage should slowly rise to 14 volts or higher if the alternator is charging properly (Figure 11-9).

For the next test, turn on the lights, have your assistant rev the engine to about 1,500 rpm, and place an induction ammeter over the alternator output wire. A reasonable amperage flow should show. It will not necessarily be high because the battery may have a good charge in it and the engine rpm may not be enough to produce a high-amperage alternator output, but the reading should be 10 amperes or more. This indicates that the alternator is producing current flow.

When the voltage at the battery is not the proper voltage, measure the voltage between the alternator output terminal and ground; it should be 14 volts or higher. If the batteries have not been charging and there is a satisfactory voltage at the output terminal, check the isolator (if there is one); it may be the problem.

If the voltage is low at the alternator terminal, do a quick magnetic check when the engine is running and when it is off. Hold a screwdriver blade to the back of the alternator to see if any magnetism is present. If there is more magnetism when the

Figure 11-9. For checking alternator voltage output, use a small extension wire with two alligator clips on each end. Attach one clip to the positive post of the alternator (not visible) and clip the other end to the red lead of the multimeter. Clip the black lead to the negative post of the battery. Output voltage is 13.97.

engine is running than when it is off, the field coil is working. If there is no magnetism present, the alternator's regulator may be the problem. If the alternator has an internal regulator, there is nothing further you can do and a qualified technician must make the repairs.

If the alternator has an external regulator, with the engine off, remove the field wire from the regulator. Using a small jumper wire with clips at both ends, connect the field tab on the regulator to any 12-volt source (such as the positive post of the SLI battery) if the alternator is a P-type, or to ground if it is an N-type. Start the engine and take an amperage reading; it should show the alternator charging at full rate. To avoid damage to the alternator, do not run it at full output too long. If the alternator is not charging at full rate, someone who has a test bench must repair it by dismantling it so resistance tests can be made on the stator, rotor, and diodes to determine if there are any shorts or breaks in the windings.

Troubleshooting Campground Outlets

Checking campground outlets with a circuit analyzer and checking outlet voltage with a multimeter have already been discussed; however, a multimeter can also be used to check an outlet for reversed polarity and other conditions. It is easier to use the circuit analyzer to determine the status of a campground outlet, but occasionally the multimeter might be needed as an additional check.

Keep uppermost in your mind that AC is the voltage being checked. Strictly observe the safety precautions outlined before: Plug the leads into the multimeter before making any tests; handle the probes with one hand only; don't touch any metal on the probes or the outlet box; be sure you are insulated from ground; and make no tests in wet conditions.

Check for voltage by placing a probe—for AC it doesn't matter which probe is used—in both the hot and neutral slots on a receptacle. The hot slot is shorter than the neutral slot. To get a reading, which should be 120 volts or close to it, it is sometimes necessary to wiggle the probes in the slots for the tips to make good contact with the clips inside.

A definite difference in the voltage between the hot and neutral and the hot and ground indicates a dangerous leakage of current to ground somewhere in the system. Do not use an outlet with this condition.

Checking for voltage between the hot and neutral slots will not show the existence of reversed polarity; doing a series of other readings will. Take another voltage reading by shifting the probe from the neutral slot to the grounded U-shaped hole; a reading should be obtained if the wiring is correct. If there is no reading, shift the probe from the hot slot to the neutral slot

247

Maintenance, Troubleshooting, and Repairs

to see if voltage exists between the neutral slot and the ground hole; if it does, reversed polarity is present.

A definite difference in the voltage between the hot and neutral and the hot and ground indicates a dangerous leakage of current to ground somewhere in the system. Do not use an outlet with this condition.

Neutral and Ground Conductor Reversal

A circuit analyzer does not normally indicate the condition of reversed neutral and ground wires or if the wires are shorted out together; however, this condition can be determined with a multimeter or a circuit analyzer, if certain techniques are used. If this condition exists in the campground outlet, it does not necessarily affect power to the RV or create an unsafe condition because the neutral and ground conductors are bonded together at the service panel.

If the neutral and ground conductors are reversed or shorted in the wiring of the RV, it is a dangerous condition, but one you probably will not be aware of until, after plugging in, you come into contact with a metal part of the RV and receive a shock. Since the current coming into the RV is still grounded through the plug, part of the current is going to ground, so the shock may not be lethal, but it will certainly get your attention.

If shocking occurs, immediately unplug the shore-power cable. Then, using a multimeter, do a continuity check on the cable plug between the neutral blade and the round grounding pin. If continuity exists, then somewhere in the RV's system the neutral wire has been grounded to the chassis of the RV. (If continuity doesn't exist, the system is okay.)

The reversal of the neutral and ground conductors or the grounding of the neutral conductor can also be confirmed by using a circuit analyzer. This test has been suggested by John Lerch of Power Alarm, Inc., manufacturer of the Line Alarm circuit analyzer described in Chapter 8. To make the test, in addition to the circuit analyzer, you need either a two-wire extension cord or the modified two-to-three-prong grounding adapter of the type we use to correct reversed polarity (see Chapter 8).

Plug either the extension cord or the grounding adapter into the campground outlet in the normal manner (using a 30-ampere male/15-ampere female adapter if necessary). Make doubly sure the adapter is not turned around as it would be for reversing polarity. The adapter is plugged in properly if its grounding pin hole is in line with the receptacle's grounding pin hole. Do not connect the ground wire. When plugged in, the circuit analyzer should show an open ground condition exists. This is exactly the condition needed for this test: no ground. (The circuit analyzer shows an open ground no matter how the adapter is plugged in, so make sure it is not turned around, creating reversed polarity.)

Remove the circuit analyzer and have your assistant plug it into a receptacle inside the RV. Have the assistant open a window to communicate easily with the person outside. Be sure this is done while the shore-power cable is still unplugged; the metal window frame may carry current when the cable is connected to the outlet. The person inside should be careful not to touch any metal parts of the RV when the shore-power cable is plugged in during the test.

Next, using the 15-ampere male/30-ampere female adapter, plug the shore-power cable into the extension cord or the grounding adapter so current again flows to the RV. The circuit analyzer inside probably shows that the wiring is correct, but this is a false reading. It really means that the neutral and ground conductors are reversed, or that the neutral is shorted to ground, so the RV's AC wiring has to be thoroughly investigated. (If the RV's wiring is correct, the circuit analyzer shows an open-ground condition, the same condition shown when the test was done on the campground outlet; however, the chance of getting this indication is remote because you wouldn't be making these tests if you hadn't received a shock.)

A confirming test can be done at the same time with the multimeter. Check for voltage potential between the hot and ground contacts of the interior receptacle. If a voltage is read, then neutral and ground reversal or shorting exists. If there is no voltage reading, the wiring is correct. Any further tests must be made with the shore-power cable unplugged.

When a neutral-grounding condition exists, it is remotely possible that a new RV was wired incorrectly at the factory—a condition that would be discovered the first time the unit was hooked up to AC power and someone touched the doorknob or another metal part of the RV and got a shock. Although some manufacturers have strange wiring practices, it is highly unlikely that reversing or grounding the wires would be one of them.

The neutral-grounding condition is commonly caused by shorting out of the wires in the windings of generators, converter/chargers, or inverters, so check this equipment first.

In a new RV, the condition most likely would occur if the dealer made alterations in the AC wiring while making after-market installations. In older RVs the problem can be created either by a short in equipment or by repair or modification work.

The neutral-grounding condition is commonly caused by shorting out of the wires in the windings of generators, converter/chargers, or inverters, so check this equipment first when trying to track down the problem. Improper wiring of newly installed relays can also cause the condition; perhaps the problem stems from a new outlet installed in the RV. Maybe putting a replacement plug on an appliance that is normally left plugged in—a coffeemaker, for instance—has caused the trouble. To

249

find the problem, retest the shore-power cable for continuity, but remove appliances one at a time by switching them off or unplugging them from the system to isolate which one has been improperly wired.

If the problem isn't solved with any of these tests, then look for grounding of wires or cords within the system. Check for grounding at the distribution panel between the neutral bus bar and ground. Begin disconnecting various circuits from the main distribution panel until the troublesome circuit is found; continuity checks made along that circuit will eventually pinpoint the problem.

* * * * * * *

So much of what contributes to the comfort and convenience of RVing depends on an RV's 12-volt DC and 120-volt AC electrical systems. Electricity is needed for heat, cooling, light, and water, and for operating equipment for our enjoyment: stereos, TVs, and personal and galley appliances. RVing wouldn't be nearly so pleasurable without electricity. A little knowledge of what electricity is, how it works, and how to track down problems when it doesn't—which we hope has been imparted in this book—enables you to enjoy RVing, or at least the electrical aspect of it, to the fullest.

Recommended Reading

For more information about RV electrical systems, we recommend the following books. Although some deal with boat electrical systems, they are applicable since electrical systems in boats and RVs are basically the same.

Solar Living Sourcebook, edited by John Schaeffer, Real Goods Trading Corporation, Ukiah, California, 1992. May be ordered for $25 plus postage from Real Goods Trading Corporation, 966 Mazzoni Street, Ukiah, California 95482, 800-762-7325.

The Bullet Proof Electrical System, Cruising Equipment Company, 1986. May be ordered by mail for $6.95 plus postage from Cruising Equipment Company, 6315 Seaview Avenue NW, Seattle, Washington 98107, 206-782-8100.

Getting Started in Electronics, by Forrest Mims, III, 1983. Available from Radio Shack stores; Catalog No. 276-5003.

Living on 12 Volts with Ample Power, by David Smead and Ruth Ishihara, Rides Publishing Company, Seattle, Washington, 1987. May be ordered by mail for $25 plus postage from Ample Power Company, 1150 NW 52nd Street, Seattle, Washington 98107, 800-541-7789.

RVers' Guide to Solar Battery Charging, by Noel and Barbara Kirkby, Aatec Publications, Ann Arbor, Michigan, 1987, revised 1993. May be ordered by mail for $12 postpaid from RV Solar Electric, 14415 North 73rd Street, Scottsdale, Arizona 85260, 602-443-8520 or 800-999-8520.

The 12-Volt Bible for Boats, by Miner Brotherton, Seven Seas Press, Camden, Maine, 1985. May be ordered from International Marine, P.O. Box 220, Camden, Maine 04843, 207-236-4837.

The 12-Volt Doctor's Alternator Book, by Edgar J. Beyn, C. Plath North American Division, 1986. May be ordered for $20.50 plus postage from Weems & Plath, 222 Severn Avenue, Annapolis, Maryland 21403-2569, 410-263-6700.

Using Your Meter, VOM, and DVM Multitesters, by Alvis J. Evans, Master Publishing, Inc., 1985. Available from Radio Shack stores; Catalog No. 62-2039.

Wiring 12 Volts for Ample Power, by David Smead and Ruth Ishihara, Rides Publishing Company, Seattle, Washington, 1989. May be ordered by mail for $18.50 plus postage from Ample Power Company, 1150 NW 52nd Street, Seattle, Washington 98107, 800-541-7789.

Directory of Suppliers

This directory lists the addresses of all manufacturers and retailers mentioned in the text, tables, and figures of this book. Some of the RV-related products they manufacture are also listed.

American Honda Motor Company
    4475 River Green Parkway
    Duluth, Georgia 30136
    404-497-6000
Portable generators.

Ample Technology Products
    Power Tap, Inc.
    1513 NW 46th Street
    Seattle, Washington 98107
    206-789-4743, 800-541-7789
Alternators, ammeters, ampere-hour meters, battery cables, diesel generators, monitor panels, multistage chargers, multistage regulators.

Amprobe Instrument Company,
    Division of Core Industries, Inc.
    P.O. Box 329
    Lynnbrook, New York 11563
    516-593-5600
AC ammeters.

Astro Power, Inc.
    Solar Park

Newark, Delaware 19716
    302-366-0400
Solor panels.

Automated Engineering Company
    10209 Gibsonton Drive
    Riverview, Florida 33569
    813-671-1581
Ammeters, circuit analyzer/voltage monitors, voltmeters.

Automatic Equipment Manufacturing
    Company
    One Mill Road
    Industrial Park
    Pender, Nebraska 68047
    402-385-3051
Auxiliary-vehicle towing equipment.

Balmar Power Systems
    1537 NW Ballard Way
    Seattle, Washington 98107
    206-789-4970
Alternators, generators, inverters, monitor panels, regulators.

Carson Manufacturing Company, Inc.
5451 North Rural Street
Indianapolis, Indiana 46220
317-257-3191
Distribution panels/converters.

Cole Hersee Company
20 Old Colony Avenue
So. Boston, Massachusetts 02127
617-268-2100
Trailer connectors.

Coleman Powermate, Inc.
125 Airport Road
Kearney, Nebraska 68848
308-237-2181, 800-445-1805
Portable generators.

Cooper Bussmann Industries
P.O. Box 14460
St. Louis, Missouri 63178
314-394-2877
Buss fuses.

Country Coach, Inc.
P.O. Box 400
Junction City, Oregon 97448
503-998-3720, 800-547-8015
Class A motorhomes and bus conversions.

Cruising Equipment Company
(CECO) Sales Distribution:
Cruising Systems
5245 Shilshole Avenue, NW
Seattle, Washington 98107
206-782-8100
*Alternators, ampere-hour meters,
batteries, inverters, monitor panels,
regulators.*

Dayton Electric Manufacturing Co.
5959 West Howard Street

Niles, Illinois 60714
708-647-8900
Relays.

Dyer Company
Box 3405
Central Point, Oregon 97502
800-643-8297
Brake ammeters.

Epower
1346W-400S
Albion, Indiana 46701
219-636-2099
Portable generators.

Equus Products, Inc.
17291 Mt. Herrmann Street
Fountain Valley, California 92708
714-432-1184, 800-544-4124
Ammeters, analog and digital voltmeters.

Exeltech, Inc.
7018 Baker Boulevard
Fort Worth, Texas 76118
817-595-4969, 800-886-4683
True sine-wave inverters.

John Fluke
P.O. Box C9090
Everett, Washington 98206
206-356-5500, 800-443-5853
Multimeters.

Fortron International Corporation
46714 Fremont Boulevard
Fremont, California 94538
510-490-9474, 800-388-0099
Pocket inverters.

Generac Corporation
P.O. Box 8

Waukesha, Wisconsin 53187
414-544-4811
Gensets.

GR Battery Systems, Inc.
7730 185th Avenue NE S-2
Redmond, Washington 98852
206-885-4344
Distributor of Prevailer batteries.

Guest Company, Inc.
48 Elm Street
Meriden, Connecticut 06450
203-238-0550
Battery selector switches.

Heart Interface Corporation
21440 68th Avenue South
Kent, Washington 98032
206-872-7225, 800-446-6180
Inverters.

Hubbell, Inc.
1613 State Street
Bridgeport, Connecticut 06605
203-337-3100
Electrical connectors, adapters, cables.

Industrial Commercial Electronics, Inc.
2421 Harlem Road
Buffalo, New York 14225
716-892-1111
Circuit/voltage analyzers.

Innovative Marketing, Inc.
4575 South 119th Circle
Omaha, Nebraska 68137
402-330-8193
Power Maximiser.

Interstate Batteries
12770 Merit Drive, Suite 400

Dallas, Texas 75251
214-991-1444
Batteries.

JEMTECH Enterprises, Inc.
2519 McMullen Booth Road
Suite 510-241
Clearwater, Florida 34621
813-725-2087
Voltmeters.

Kawasaki Motors Corporation
9950 Jeronimo Road
Irvine, California 92718
714-770-0400
Portable generators.

Kelsey-Hayes
38481 Huron River Drive
Romulus, Michigan 48174
313-941-2000
Brake equipment.

Kohler Company
Generator Division
N. 7650 County Trunk L.S.
Sheboygan, Wisconsin 53083
414-565-3381
Gensets.

Kwyatt Generators
Distibutor: Schwalm & Associates
460 County Road 15
Elkhart, Indiana 46156
219-293-8680
Gensets.

Kyocera Solar Systems Division
8611 Balboa Avenue
San Diego, California 92123
619-576-2600
Solar panels.

Lestek Manufacturing, Inc.
   6542 Baker Boulevard
   Fort Worth, Texas 76118
   817-284-0821, 800-433-7628
Alternators.

MagneTek
   305 N. Briant Street
   Huntington, Indiana 46750
   219-356-7100
*Converters, converter/chargers, transfer
   switches, distribution panels.*

Mercantile Manufacturing Company
   Auto-Gen Electric Division
   P.O. Box 895
   Minden, Louisiana 71058
   318-377-0844
*Portable generators, propulsion-engine
   generators.*

Modutec, Inc./Emico
   920 Candia Road
   Manchester
   New Hampshire 03109
   603-669-5121
*AC and DC ammeters and
   voltmeters.*

Newmark Products, Inc.
   10648 South Painter Avenue
   Santa Fe Springs, California 90670
   213-941-0295, 714-521-8210
*Converters, converter/chargers,
   distribution panels.*

Onan Corporation
   P.O. Box 32925
   Minneapolis, Minnesota 55432
   612-574-5000
Gensets.

Opti-Chip Technologies, Inc.
   53224 Marina Drive
   Elkhart, Indiana 46514
   219-264-3812, 800-522-2447
Opti-Charge charger controller.

Perko, Inc.
   16490 NW 13th Avenue
   Miami, Florida 33169
   305-621-7525
Battery selector switches.

Photocomm, Inc.
   930 Idaho-Maryland Road
   Grass Valley, California 95946
   800-544-6466
*Monitor panels, solar panel systems, solar
   regulators.*

Power Alarm, Inc.
   462 Rusty Drive
   Santa Rosa, California 95401
   707-579-8084, 800-786-6610
Circuit analyzers.

Powerline Division, Hehr International
   4616 Fairlane Avenue
   Fort Worth, Texas 76119
   817-535-0284
Alternators.

PowerStar Products
   10011 North Foothill Boulevard
   Cupertino, California 95014
   408-973-8502
Inverters.

Power Technology, Inc.
   10385 Brockwood Road
   Dallas, Texas 75238
   214-348-9191, 800-732-7693
Propulsion-engine generators.

Power Technology Southeast, Inc.
  635 State Road 44 West
  Leesburg, Florida 34748
  904-365-2777
Diesel gensets.

Real Goods Trading Corporation
  966 Mazzoni Street
  Ukiah, California 95482
  1-800-762-7325
*Voltmeters, ammeters, monitoring panels,
  solar panels, chargers, inverters.*

Remco
  4138 South 89th Street
  Omaha, Nebraska 68127
  402-339-3398, 800-228-2481
Auxiliary-vehicle towing equipment.

Roadmaster, Inc.
  5602 NE Skyport Way
  Portland, Oregon 97218
  800-669-9690
*Auxiliary-vehicle wiring harnesses, tow
  bars.*

RV Solar Electric
  14415 North 73rd Street
  Scottsdale, Arizona 85260
  602-443-8520, 800-999-8520
*Solar panel kits, solar panels, regulators,
  inverters, fuses, gelled-cell batteries.*

Schauer Manufacturing Corporation
  4500 Alpine Avenue
  Cincinnati, Ohio 45242
  513-791-3030, 800-877-2786
Portable battery chargers.

Schumacher Electric Corporation
  7474 North Rogers Avenue
  Chicago, Illinois 60626

312-973-1600
Portable battery chargers.

Siemens Solar Industries
  P.O. Box 6032
  Camarillo, California 930ll
  805-482-6800
Solar panels.

Simpson Electric Company
  853 Dundee Avenue
  Elgin, Illinois 60120
  708-697-2260
Multitesters.

Solar Bill/Solar River RV
  95 E. Ironwood Street
  South Highway 95
  P.O. Box 2588
  Quartzite, Arizona 85346
  520-927-7256, 800-74-SOLAR
  (summer 619-588-9852)
Solar.

Solar Electric Specialties Company
  P.O. Box 609
  Elk Grove, California 95759
  916-686-4898
*Solar systems and monitoring
  panels.*

Solarex Corporation
  630 Solarex Court
  Frederick, Maryland 21701
  301-698-4200
Solar panels.

Specialty Concepts, Inc.
  9025 Eton Avenue
  Canoga Park, California 91304
  818-998-5238
Monitor panels.

257

Statpower Technologies
  Corporation
  7012 Lougheed Highway
  Burnaby, British Columbia,
  Canada V5A 1W2
  604-420-1585
Inverters, multistage battery chargers.

Sunlight Energy Systems
  2225 Mayflower NW
  Massillon, Ohio 44646
  216-832-3114
Solar panel regulators.

Sure Power Industries, Inc.
  10189 SW Avery
  Tualatin, Oregon 97062
  503-692-5360
Isolators.

Todd Engineering Sales, Inc.
  28706 Holiday Place
  Elkhart, Indiana 46517
  219-293-8633
Converter/chargers.

Trace Engineering Corporation
  5916 195th Northeast
  Arlington, Washington 98223
  206-435-8826
Inverters.

Tripp Lite
  500 North Orleans
  Chicago, Illinois 60610
  312-329-1777
Inverters.

Vanner, Inc.
  4282 Reynolds Drive
  Hilliard, Ohio 43026
  614-771-2718
*Battery chargers, battery equalizers, DC
  to DC converters, inverters, isolators.*

Watermaker RV Specialties
  319 Camelia Street
  New Iberia, Louisiana 70560
  318-367-2890
Noise-deadening kit for generators.

Weems & Plath
  222 Severn Avenue
  Annapolis, Maryland 21403-2569
  410-263-6700
*Alternator regulator controls, ammeters,
  distribution panels, isolators, monitor panels, percent-of-charge meters,
  voltmeters.*

Wrangler Power Products
  P.O. 12109
  Prescott, Arizona 86304
  520-776-7840, 800-962-2616
*Alternators, batteries, connectors, isola-
  tors, meters, regulators, wire.*

Yamaha Outdoor Power Equipment
  Division
  P.O. Box 6555
  Cypress, California 90630
  213-962-5522
Portable generators.

Index

engine-starting, 18–22; gelled electrolyte, 19–20; golf-cart, 22–24; house, 18; immobilized-electrolyte, 19; installation of, 35–36; location in motorhomes, 28, 72–74; location in trailers, 27–28, 72–73; maintenance of, 219–224; monitoring, 199–202; multistage charging of, 31–35; no-maintenance, 18–20; in parallel, 35–36; primary cell, 14; problems with location of, 72–74; recharging rates of, 29–35; rotating, 230; sealed-type, 18–20; secondary cell, 14; selector switch for, 57–59; in series, 35–36; 6-volt, 22–24; SLI, 18–22, 24, 25, 27; theory of, 12–14; wet-cell, 14, 18; wiring of, 35–36. *See also* Battery

Battery: capacity, 20–27; cells, 14–16; cell voltage, 14; charging harness, 76–81; discharge rate of, 25–26; equalization, 34–35, 105; equalizers, 104; gassing of, 16, 20, 33–34; isolators and, 56–62; life cycles of, 28; maintenance, 219–224; recharging rate, 29–31; reserve capacity, 21–22; safety, 219–223; self-discharge, 16; sense lines, 60–62; sulfation, 28, 34, 220; symbol for, 82; temperature, 29, 33–34; ventilation, 27, 224. *See also* Batteries

Battery cable corrosion, 223–224,

Battery chargers: constant current, 104–110; constant voltage, 99–102; equalization with, 105; hum in, 98; linear-unregulated, 104–106; multistage regulation of, 103–104; phase-controlled, 105; portable, 104–109;

types of, 28; voltage regulator, 105–106. *See also* Converter/chargers

Battery charging: the perfect system, 129–130

Battery charging lines, 76–81, 86, 204

Battery condition meters, 199–201

Battery Council International (BCI), 21–24

Battery equalizers, 104

Battery sensing lines, 60–62, 80–81

Battery tools and accessories, 219–224, 226–227

BB analogy, 4

BCI: *See* Battery Council International

BCI Group size, 21–24

Block diagrams, 81–83

Boat cable, 137–138

Brakes, trailer: problems with, 238–241

C

CCA: *See* Cold-cranking amperes

Cables. *See* Electrical cable

Campground hookups: problems with, 149–156; troubleshooting, 150–156, 247–250

Capacitors, 84–85; charge and discharge of, 84–85; fixed, 84; shock hazard of, 85; short-circuit of, 234; testing of, 233–234; variable, 85

Charge-efficiency factor, 31

Charging devices. *See* Battery chargers

Charging lines, 72–74, 76–81, 86, 158

Charging process, 28–35; absorption stage of, 33–34; acceptance stage of, 33–34; bulk stage of, 31–33; conditioning stage of, 34–35; equalization stage of, 34–35; float stage of, 34; initial stage

of, 31–33

Chassis ground, 78, 79, 91–92, 136, 191, 192, 231, 238–239, 248–250

Cigarette-lighter plugs and sockets, 92–93

Circuit analyzers, 150–154; authors' use of, 151–155; importance of, 150–54; use of, 150–152, 155, 247–250

Circuit breaker panel. *See* Distribution panel

Circuit breakers, 75, 132–134; in battery charge line, 62, 77; testing of, 228–229. *See also* Ground fault circuit interrupters

Circuits: alternating current, 132–135; bonding, 135; improperly wired, 150–154; labeling of, 75–76; load calculations of, 153; over-fused, 149–150; troubleshooting, 236–238, 247–250; voltage drop in, 76–78

Coils, 8, 37; magnetic field of, 8. *See* Transformers

Cold-cranking amperes, 20–21

Cole Hersee Company, 57

Conductance, 4

Conductors, 4; ampacity of, 66–69, 74, current-carrying, 134; floating neutral, 134–135; grounding, 134–135, 248–250; neutral, 134, 248–250; resistance of, 4; voltage drop in, 66–74, 76–80

Connections: in schematics, 82–83; in wiring, 82–83

Continuity testing with multimeters, 230–231

Converters, DC-to-DC, 104

Converter/chargers, 66–67, 72, 73–74, 96–103; charger part of, 96–97; ferroresonant, 99–100; high-frequency switching, 101–102, 103; linear-unregulated, 97–98; location of, 66, 73–74; multistage

196; plug-in AC, 195; volt, 195, 199–202

MicroLite and Marquis gensets, 168

Micronta multimeters, 216

Modified sine wave vs. true sine wave, 175

Monitoring: AC system, 195; authors' systems, 204, 207–213; batteries, 74; combination panels, 206–207; DC system, 64, 195; LED vs. LCD readouts, 206–207

MOSFET. *See* Transistors

Motors: automotive starter, 245; comparison to alternators, 39; induction, 170, 180

MOVs. *See* Varistors, metal oxide

Multimeters: accessories for, 225–226; description of, 213–215, 224–225; selecting, 215–216; troubleshooting with, 228–250; use of, 195, 214–215, 224–225

Multistage charging, 31–35, 53–56, 63–64, 103–104, 106

Multitesters. *See* Multimeters

N

National Electric Code (NEC), 67–68, 134, 137

NEC: *See* National Electric Code

Neutral conductor, 134

Nightlights, 179, 198

Noise suppression, 168–169

No-maintenance battery, 18–20

Non-metallic sheathed wire (NM), 135, 137

NotePower pocket inverter, 181

O

Ohms, 4; measuring, 215. *See* Resistors

Ohm's law, 4, 25, 35, 69; definition of, 4; and voltage drop, 69

Onan Corporation. *See* MicroLite and Marquis gensets

120-volt AC electrical system, 2, 132–133

Open ground condition, correcting of, 155–156

Opti-Chip Technologies (Opti-Charge controller), 102–103

P

Parallel wiring: of batteries, 35–36; in circuits, 75–76

Perko, Inc., 57

Phantom loads: DC, 26–27; AC, 146–148

Phase-controlled converter/chargers, 100–101

Phase, out-of, 169

Photocomm, Inc. *See* SCI Mark III Battery Monitor

Plugs, blade crystallization of, 148–149; 12-volt, 92–93; 120-volt, 150

Polarity: alternating current circuits, 90–91, 150, 247–248; circuit analyzers, 150–154; direct current circuits, 82, 90–91, 228; importance of, 150; reversed, 150, 154–155; testing for, 151–155, 247–248; test light for, 227

Polyvinylchloride (PVC), 137

Potential difference, 3

Power Alarm, Inc. *See* Line Alarm circuit analyzer

Power: apparent, 5; consumption of, 5; true, 175

Power converters. *See* Converter/chargers

Power factor: with chargers, 107–109; with generators, 169–170; with induction-type motors, 170, 179–180

Power Maximiser adapter, 143, 149, 187

Power relays. *See* Relays

Power Technology, Inc. *See* Roadmaster, Inc.

Power tools, 228

Power transformers. *See* Transformers

Propane gas generators. *See* Liquefied petroleum gas generators

Pulsating current, 39, 41–42, 100

Pulse-width modulated converter/chargers (PWM). *See* High-frequency switching converter/chargers

Pure DC converter/chargers. *See* High-frequency switching converter/chargers

PVC. *See* Polyvinylchloride

Q

Quartz crystals, 114–115

R

Radio frequency interference (RFI), 98, 100–101, 129, 158, 159, 187; suppression, 98, 187

Radio Shack, 93, 195, 215, 216, 227, 228

Receptacles: 15 amperes duplex fused for 30 amperes, 149–150; 12-volt, 92–93

Rectification, 37, 39, 97; definition of, 37–39; pulsating in, 39, 41–42, 100

Refrigerators, troubleshooting of, 48, 242, 243–244

Regulation: voltage, 50–52; of voltage for lights, 52, 63

Regulators, automotive-type, 50–52, 63–64; for alternators, 51–56, 63–64; battery sense line, 60–62; for chargers, 96–97; for converters, 96–97, 100–101; external, 52, 53; internal, 52; multistage, 53–56, 63–64, 103–104; series-pass, 123–125;

www.ingramcontent.com/pod-product-compliance
Lightning Source LLC
Chambersburg PA
CBHW050358110426
42812CB00006BA/1733